Landlording on Auto-Pilot

LANDLORDING ON AUTO-PILOT

A Simple, No-Brainer System for Higher Profits and Fewer Headaches

MIKE BUTLER

John Wiley & Sons, Inc.

Published by John Wiley & Sons, Inc., Hoboken, New Jersey.
Published simultaneously in Canada.

Library of Congress Cataloging-in-Publication Data:

Butler, Mike, 1959–

      Landlording on auto-pilot : a simple, no-brainer system for higher profits
and fewer headaches / Mike Butler.
        p.   cm.
      Includes bibliographical references and index.
      ISBN-13: 978-0-471-78978-9 (pbk.)
      ISBN-10: 0-471-78978-X (pbk.)
      1. Real estate management.   2. Landlord and tenant.   I. Title.
HD1394.B88   2006
333.5′4068—dc22

                                   2006005815

CONTENTS

SECTION II

PROVEN WAYS TO CAPTURE HIGH-QUALITY LIFETIME TENANTS

How I Operated 75 Rental Properties While Working My Full-Time Job as a Cop

F ellow landlord investors, my goal in this book is to share my successful investing programs with you. Not all of it has been pretty: I have an honorary PhD from the School of Hard Knocks. I developed the auto-pilot system of holding and managing solid rental properties to help me to manage dozens of rental properties while holding down a full-time job as a police officer. First, I want to share with you a little bit about where I've been, what I've done, and how I've ended up.

My mom and dad raised seven kids (including me) in a two-bedroom home in Kentucky (see top of p. xii).

I grew up just a few blocks from the world-famous Churchill Downs, site of the Kentucky Derby. Most of our neighbors were blue-collar workers, whose definition of *successful* was to land a good job, at a good company, buy a home and get it paid off, buy a riding mower, and retire. In our neighborhood and church, I don't recall any doctors, attorneys, or certified public accountants (CPAs). Those folks lived on the other side of town.

Being the oldest of seven kids, I grew up with a strong work ethic. Pop worked at a slaughterhouse and proudly identified his occupation as a *meat cutter*. He would quickly let people know that anybody could be a butcher. Mom stayed at home and did a great job of keeping everybody fed, healthy, and in clean clothes. We had no clue that times were tough. We knew Dad worked hard; I admired him and wanted to be just like him. I got a paper route delivering daily morning and afternoon papers the summer after I finished eighth grade. This paper route was passed on to my brothers and sisters for almost a decade, and the money we earned allowed us to attend a private high school.

I did a short stint at a Winn-Dixie supermarket. I started as a bag boy and worked my way up to store manager. In November 1982, I had the wonderful

opportunity to get robbed at gunpoint, with a revolver nervously shaking inches from my nose.

This event, along with my experiences catching shoplifters (some violent), sparked my interest in law enforcement. I had never been satisfied with punching a time clock and relying on a single full-time job to take care of my family and me. While in high school, I took on odd jobs such as painting houses. In fact, for the first house I painted, I gave the elderly owner a quote of $60, which included painting the exterior from the foundation to the roof, all the windows, and all the doors. What a huge mistake that was, but I learned that lesson very quickly! For the next house I painted, I charged $400. At this time, I hauled all my supplies, ladders, bucket, and brushes on my Western Auto 10-speed bicycle with no brakes. I roofed garages and houses and took on small remodeling projects before I started driving. So, I guess I've always been a worker. You will need to be one, too, if you want to be a successful landlord, but it has sure paid off handsomely for me and for thousands of other landlords that I have trained or mentored.

I got married and when my second child was born, I pulled the plug on Winn-Dixie and changed careers, becoming a Louisville, Kentucky, police officer. I took a sizable cut in pay to become a cop: My starting salary was $17,000. I worked all the overtime I could get and worked off-duty jobs for extra income.

I also looked for something to supplement my police pension down the road. I read the classified ads daily, especially the "Business Opportunity" sections. Like many people, I was searching for a "magic pill." I thought it might be found in vending machines or coin-operated car washes and laundromats. There had to be a simple, easy way to financial success.

My goal was to spend my time and energy (because I had no money) on something that would grow in value and income. I wanted to find a way to make money as an *absent owner,* a hands-off system. My gut instinct kept directing me to real estate and rental properties, but I didn't have a clue how to get started and had no money.

In those days, the Department of Housing and Urban Development (HUD) advertised properties for sale in the classified ads of Sunday newspapers. I would drive by these properties in our 1986 Ford Ranger because I thought I could learn my market by seeing how much HUD was asking for the property. Then I would try to catch how much they sold for in just a few days or weeks. One Sunday in December 1990, a two-bedroom house on my old paper route showed up on the HUD list. I made an all-cash offer below the asking price although I had no cash. I just wanted the experience of going through the bidding process.

Low and behold, my bid was accepted!

Now what? We had about $1,000 in our bank account, and I got pretty nervous. I went to the Louisville Police Officers Credit Union and got a loan on my 1986

Ford Ranger, our old Monte Carlo, and an unsecured signature loan with automatic payments to be deducted directly from my paycheck. This still wasn't enough to pull it off and do the rehabilitation needed. I resorted to my last resource—cash advances on several credit cards.

We bought the house for $17,000, spent $2,000 on needed repairs, and completed it all in 13 days. I hauled trash and debris to my police station dumpster at night. After renovating this little house, I went to Office Depot and purchased a generic rental application and lease agreement and put a tenant in the property. (I was lucky. This tenant is still with me today in his third home with us.)

I quickly refinanced this house, paying off the truck, car, signature loans, and credit card advances and ended up with $5,000 cash in my pocket plus almost $200 per month in positive cash flow.

Another pretty house, ready to go, went up for sale across the street, and I repeated the process without having to do any repairs except for changing the locks. Wow! This was awesome. At this point, my wife, Tammy, jerked my chain and said whoa! Being wise and conservative, she ordered me to ride it out for 12 months to see if there would be any "too good to be true" jinxes.

After a year, we had over $6,000 in our real estate savings account, and she allowed me off my chain. I continued buying rental houses. In the beginning, it was simply a lot easier to buy stinky, broken, ugly houses in need of repair than to pay for more desirable real estate. I would fix up my houses and rent them out. People thought I was nuts. I was buying properties at a good price; but I was *not* selling them. The rest of the world seemed to want *fast cash now*. I was just trying to build something that would double or triple my police pension in about 15 years.

I accomplished several interesting achievements by accident.

- I *never* went to a bank to buy an investment property. I always bought the property first.
- I *never* used a "hard money" lender or a private lender for financing.

We started our first year with two properties, then added two more the following year, and I set a 1 year goal of one house per month resulting in eighteen properties purchased. After this, I planned to set an annual goal of two houses per month (twenty-four for the year). My good friend, local competition, and real estate education partner Jay Long and I had the opportunity to see Brian Tracy, the noted self-help speaker and author, in Florida during an annual real estate investor conference. Brian Tracy did a presentation on setting goals and challenged the listeners to "shoot for the moon! If you fall short and miss your goal," he asked, "Are you a loser?" His answer: "*No*, you're not a loser, you're just a *star!*" Because of Brian Tracy, I adjusted my goal from twenty-four houses for the year to ninety-six houses—and rounded it up to one hundred.

Thanks to Brian Tracy, we did 85 deals that year and purchased over 50 rental properties. Absolutely incredible! It sure blew the doors off my original aggressive goal. Getting this buying machine cranked up was a huge challenge that involved getting past many train wrecks and potholes. I share many of those stories in later chapters in this book.

One of the keys that made this plan work was my knowledge that I absolutely had to develop efficient systems, tools, and resources. There was no other way to have a realistic shot at achieving my goals. Keep in mind that I had to attain huge goals with part-time effort while working my full-time job. I hired my first part-time handyperson for my fifth rental house and have never swung a hammer from that point forward.

I was buying property, managing rentals, and keeping it all together from a small office in the corner of our basement. My communication tools were a pager and a cell phone. My real office was on wheels, my police truck.

As a cop and an undercover detective, I developed effective people skills. I had a special knack for getting bad guys to tell me their side of their story, either in a tape-recorded or a written statement. An admission of the criminal offense, taken properly and legally from a suspect, is one of the best pieces of evidence in a criminal case. What is weird is that the offenders usually thanked me as they were led away in handcuffs. I retired from the police force in March 2000 and still get pleasant calls from bad guys in prison and on parole. (Their girlfriends and family members have quite a different attitude about me.)

Although I knew I needed to have systems for our little empire to grow safely and quickly, I had no mentors or a proven system to follow. We were on our own, blazing a new trail. This was a blessing in disguise because it allowed me to create and develop an auto-pilot landlording system without any baggage or critiques from experts and professional naysayers. I simply focused on results and objectives when developing this system and procedures.

Once I realized that real estate could be more than a painful hobby, I chose to kick it into high gear and achieve financial independence. Tammy and I lived off our police officer and nurse wages. We chose to let our real estate grow itself.

I had a "Failure Is Not an Option" attitude. I researched and looked for answers and solutions without much luck. Knowing I could only spend a few hours a week on real estate, we developed a lean, trim, efficient system in our investing business. Many folks in my town thought our business was a full-time operation. I am confident that if we had a way to compare the results, we would find that our part-time effort surpassed the gains of many full-time investors in my town.

One beautiful Saturday morning, I checked the voice mail messages on my pager and found it was full, with 30 messages. I retrieved all the messages and began returning phone calls at 8:30 A.M. while sitting downstairs in our lower level kitchen. From our oak table, I could see the pond and swimming pool out back, the ducks and geese, and it was a gorgeous spring morning. I returned those 30 calls while watching my pager dance on the table with more messages. Tammy brought me a tuna salad sandwich at lunchtime, and I continued returning phone calls, retrieving and deleting messages from the pager, and calling more folks. At 8:30 P.M.,

I still had a list of 30 people to call, and I finally realized that I had blown an entire beautiful Saturday because of our real estate.

This was not what I wanted from our real estate investments.

I wanted our real estate to give us a higher quality of life, not a noose around my neck.

Tammy and I decided to hire a part-time office person to help manage our properties. Kim worked about five hours weekly from our basement home office. What a relief! She pitched vacancies and did a lot of clerical work in her five hours. If she got behind on something, she would work longer.

Our records showed we operated 75 rental properties, plus the rehabs and the buying machine, before hiring a part-time office person.

This book shows you exactly how to achieve the same success.

In Section I, I introduce beginner basics to show you the fundamentals, attitudes, and some pitfalls and lessons I learned from the School of Hard Knocks. But I also explain the rewards that come with auto-pilot landlording to give you the motivation and patience to stick with it. I compare it with learning to ride a bike. You will get banged up and dinged up a bit, but if you keep working at it, you'll soon be speeding along for the rest of your real estate career.

In Section II, we move to key steps in auto-pilot landlording with detailed and thorough coverage of the rental application and the procedure for screening tenants. Just imagine what your landlording life would be like if all your tenants were perfect tenants. That is my goal; I haven't achieved it yet, but I've gotten close a few times. When you have great tenants, almost all the headaches and nightmares associated with landlording seem to evaporate. Your life can be awesome.

Next, I discuss how to polish your system and crank it up to the next level where you can actually begin to get more than 100 percent of your rents. This sounds impossible, but I explain how I did it with my properties.

And finally, you can get the set of forms for the landlording on auto-pilot system in PDF and Microsoft Word format. These forms are immediately available by downloading them from a web site.

Real estate has rewarded me in so many ways. Money or cash in your bank account is not the only measure of success. Success or reward is not at the END of the road. Success *is* the road; it is the journey. With success (and money) we have helped more people than I ever dreamed possible with my job as a cop. I have met great generous people from all over this wonderful country of ours.

We are blessed to have all these opportunities in our world. It is up to us to take action and make it happen for ourselves and for our families.

Good luck, happy investing, and congratulations on getting your hands on a copy of *Landlording on Auto-Pilot*.

ACKNOWLEDGMENTS

I am not a genius. I have been blessed with a wonderful supportive family and circle of friends. I have learned a boatload of powerful life-changing information from many experts in life and in real estate. I have taken these techniques and strategies from these folks and have tweaked and twisted them to fit into my program of investing and landlording.

Thanks to my dad, mom, brothers, and sisters who lit my fuse and started me on my journey to achieve more in life. Again thanks to my wife Tammy and our daughters, who kept this fuse lit and fired me up to be the best I could be for us.

Also, thanks to my mentor and friend John Schaub who introduced me to wild man "Fixer Jay" P. Decima of Redding, California, who recommended me to Richard Narramore, my editor at John Wiley & Sons. Richard encouraged me to write this book.

I want to thank Ed Melton; Jay Long; Rue McFarland; Layne Smith; Chris McCarty; my CPA, Mike Grinnan; my attorney, Harry Borders; Henry Schildknecht; Mark Lechner; Chris Dischinger; Nick Sidoti; Pete Fortunato; Ron Legrand; Brian Tracy; Jimmy Napier; Jeff Taylor; Albert Aiello; Jack Miller; Paul Bauer, Dave Halpern, and our local Kentuckiana Real Estate Investors Association (KREIA) and Kentucky Real Estate Exchangors (KREE) groups, along with all those from whom I begged, borrowed, and stole ideas that allowed Tammy and me to keep "Cranking It 24-7."

BEGINNER BASICS OF AUTO-PILOT LANDLORDING

This section explains how to keep the big picture in perspective. If you can keep the big picture in perspective, it will give you the patience and motivation to implement your systems and put your landlording on autopilot. Attitude, philosophy, and an understanding of what you really want from your real estate investments are critical parts of this process.

I screwed up often during the first half of my investing career because I didn't have a clue about my final objective. Sure, I realized owning real estate was good, but I operated with that Nike attitude: "Just Do It." Too many times, I bought property and did things that did not move me toward my ultimate objective. Call it busy work, or a waste of time. I may have made some immediate money or profit, but such activities stole my time from the quick pursuit and achievement of my investment goals.

These beginner basics are the culmination of the many lessons I have learned from speakers from all over the country, along with some tweaking of my own.

One of my instructors made the following comment I've never forgotten: Are you stepping over dollars to pick up nickels?

CHAPTER 1

My Amazing Discovery: A No-Nonsense Plan for Getting Rich in Real Estate

In my town in Kentucky, house values do not go up in double digits the way they do in Florida, California, New York, or Las Vegas. A good solid rental house averages 7.25 percent appreciation annually in my area. I like to be conservative in my real estate investment planning, so let's say that a property I am considering investing in would only appreciate 5 percent a year over time. With an average annual appreciation of 5 percent:

$100,000 in property value = $5,000 increase in market value *each year*
$1,000,000 in property value = $50,000 increase in market value *each year*
$10,000,000 in property = $500,000 increase in market value *each year*

I'll be the first to admit and agree that this is only on paper. You won't find it in any bank account and you cannot buy groceries with it. But, if you can hang on to your investments, just like the beer cans on the rear bumper of the limousine at a wedding, you can crank some phenomenal numbers and grow your wealth unbelievably fast.

Let me immediately remove the "Pie in the Sky" aspects here, and start with the end in mind. Ask yourself, "Where do I want to land?" What is your objective of investing? I never thought about this when I got started, and it caused me a lot of grief. I was buying properties left and right because I believed they were good deals. But I neglected being clear about my goals.

Here's what you need to know: "$_____ in my pocket monthly would make me a happy camper!" Go ahead, fill in the blank. What is your answer? After working with investors all over the country, I can tell you that most investors are not like me. They are not greedy and have absolutely no desire to compete with Donald Trump. To my amazement, the number one answer here is $10,000. That's right, over 90 percent of investors say, "$10,000 in my pocket monthly would make me a happy camper."

The next part is a bit more challenging. How many of these properties would it take to dump your dollar amount into your pocket monthly? You also have to consider what kind of properties you would like to hold long term. Do you want a low-income area with high management and low appreciation, but excellent cash flow; or do you want nicer neighborhoods, less management, and less cash flow with wonderful appreciation and depreciation? This is your choice, not mine.

Let's keep this idea going. Assume that you filled in the blank with $10,000 and you want the nicer properties in a nice neighborhood. Using the market in my town would mean that about 20 solid $100,000 rental houses paid for would dump $10,000 into your pocket monthly. Using "real world cash flow" and not the dangerous definition used by many real estate agents, each one of these properties will give you about $500 monthly.

Real world cash flow on a $100,000 rental house in my town:

$$
\begin{array}{rl}
\text{Monthly rent income} = & +\$800.00 \\
\text{Minus Property tax} = & (\$91.66) \\
\text{Minus Insurance} = & (\$25.00) \\
\text{Minus Management fee} = & (\$80.00) \\
\text{Minus Repairs} = & \underline{(\$50.00)} \\
\text{Total} = & \$553.34
\end{array}
$$

These are the numbers used for single-family houses in my town. Your town might have a different property tax rate or insurance rate and may have homeowner association dues. You must factor in all these ongoing expenses associated with owning the property. If you are investing in multifamily housing, apartment complexes, or commercial properties, you should include a vacancy factor for your market. With single-family houses, I don't include a vacancy factor because I want my tenants to stay forever. Many of my single-family properties still have the original tenants today, years later. I'm not in the hotel business, and you shouldn't be either.

Using the preceding example, you can see that 20 of these rental houses (if paid for) would put $10,000 in your pocket every month from now on. Plus, there is a built-in hedge against inflation because you can raise the rent as the market value and market rents increase. This means you can always give yourself a raise. There is still another extra bonus behind the scene: You will have 20 houses paid for, resulting in your ownership of $2 million in real estate. At 5 percent annual appreciation, this results in an additional $100,000 increase in market value each year that you own the properties. Later in this book, I explain some tax benefits including depreciation.

So this fairly simple example of having a goal of 20 houses paid for will bring in $10,000 monthly into your pocket and your real estate will increase $100,000 in value every year.

Now, the hard part. How do you get there? How long will it take? Here is how I did it. I realized the preceding magic early on. I discovered that *time* was my biggest and scarcest resource. The sooner I got X number of properties under my belt, the sooner and faster and bigger the wealth would grow. I didn't want my real estate investing to be a painful hobby. Just like you, I wanted true financial independence for my family. I wanted to do it safely and efficiently. My wife and I were sticking our necks out, taking all the risk, with no one to turn to should our investing go belly up.

Here is my answer and battle plan. If I captured 100 of these houses *now*, I could "ride the bull" (dealing with tenants and rental property) for four years cranking over $500,000 each year. After four years, I would have picked up another $2 million in market value. If I had the discipline to sell off 80 of the houses and keep the best 20 for rentals, I could end up with 20 free-and-clear houses on this aggressive four-year plan. It was my original battle plan.

If it ain't broke, don't fix it might be an appropriate description of where I'm at today. With our investments cranking some phenomenal numbers in appreciation, even with just 5 percent annually, the big picture results are overwhelming and it's all on autopilot!

There is a common denominator for all the preceding results. Every single bit of it involves owning real estate. That means dealing with tenants as well as with the ugly word and world of being a *landlord*. The word sounds bad, doesn't it? It sounds evil—something ugly, not fun, not good. In fact, I prefer the word *investor*.

Definition of Investor

An investor is "[a] person who purchases income-producing assets . . . considers safety of principal to be of primary importance. In addition, investors frequently purchase assets with the expectation of holding them for a longer period of time." (David L. Scott, *Wall Street Words: An A to Z Guide to Investment Terms for Today's Investor*, Boston, MA: Houghton Mifflin, 2003).

What about those folks who buy, fix up, and sell? Are they really investors? I don't think so. They are in the same category as a builder, plumber, or electrician. They are getting paid for what they do, not what they own. When these people stop buying, fixing up, and selling, their income stops, too.

What about those who *wholesale* or quick-turn properties. These people also try to label their activity as investing. Far from the truth! Once again, when they stop wholesaling, it's over. Stick a fork in them, they're done!

I'm not against these two activities. It just burns me when some people try to say these two methods are the safest and easiest methods of investing. These activities by themselves are not investing; however, they can be an integral part of your investment battle plan. When I got started, I wanted to have a handyperson whose hours I could control so I wouldn't have to wait for a part-time worker to take care of my problem on one of his off-days from a regular job. I learned I could buy an ugly house, fix it up, sell it at retail, and make about $35,000 in a couple of months. This would pay a whole year's salary for a full-time handyperson and part of the wages for his helper.

I used the wholesaling and the buy, fix up, and sell activities to "feed the machine." By this, I mean that owning real estate is like owning a cash-eating monster business—especially when you are getting started with next to no cash and your investments are pretty much 100 percent financed with no money out of your pocket. These two noninvesting activities definitely kept me afloat while I was building my business.

I came to realize that the true path to financial independence involves *ownership* of real estate. This meant that it looked like I was going to be a landlord. Nobody seems to be happy about this line of investing. There are so many negative attitudes about it, toward it, and all around it. But I knew one thing. The successful investors I admired all owned real estate.

A good landlording system is the secret cornerstone of my wealth-building program. Putting my landlording on auto-pilot became my ultimate objective in achieving financial independence.

CHAPTER 2

The Hidden Tax Benefits, Especially if You Have a Job

This topic blindsided me. As a good cop raised in an old-fashioned traditional family in a blue-collar neighborhood, I didn't have a clue about how my investment activity would affect me in the income tax arena. Big words like *depreciation, tax shelters, business expense,* and *write-offs* might as well have been in a foreign language, I was totally in the dark. Looking back today, what really scares me is that not knowing any of this didn't bother me.

I honestly believed that good old simple math was how the whole investing thing worked. Buy an ugly, broken-down house at a bargain price, fix it up, and rent it. I thought as long as my rent was more than my house payment, I was doing pretty good and this relationship of money was called "cash flow." *Wrong.*

Back in the early 1990s, I realized I wasn't making or saving any money by swinging a hammer or a paintbrush. I needed a part-time handyperson. How did I pay for that helper? Aha—I did the buy, fix-up, and sell activity to feed the machine. I thought that was the solution. Little did I know the profit from buy, fix up, and sell was slamming me in the income tax arena. Doing a few of these properties a year and adding the profit to my wages as a cop and my wife's as a nurse put us over $100,000 for a couple of years.

A little powwow with my CPA at the time resulted in the creation of a *C corporation* (C-Corp). This would allow $50,000 of my real estate income from the buy-and-sell activity to be taxed at 15 percent. At the time, I thought this was a smart move.

Here comes my *tsunami!* (This is a good thing.)

Jump into my shoes for a moment. You are the long-haired, bearded, undercover cop who piddles part-time in real estate and never works any overtime as a police officer. The other dozen or so detectives in your unit work all the overtime they can get, along with off-duty jobs, and look forward to tax time every year. They anxiously await their tax refund for their yearlong effort. Many of these guys would get anywhere from $1,500 to as much as $4,000 back from Uncle Sam. What is sad is they didn't realize the IRS was holding their money all year without paying them any interest.

Here's the frustrating part. I was buying rental property like it was going out of style. I watched my numbers, watched my cash flow, and tried to operate efficiently. To my surprise, I also started getting tax refund checks from Uncle Sam. But they didn't come in at $1,500 or even $4,000. I was getting huge refund checks. I'm talking $15,000 and more. How? Why? I didn't understand it. What did my fellow detectives who worked with me think? Here I was, the guy who never worked any overtime and I was getting 10 times more in refunds than they were.

They looked at me as if they believed I was doing something illegal. Honestly, I felt I must have done something wrong. I wondered how my CPA could have maneuvered this. It just didn't seem right. It didn't make a lick of sense to this kid who grew up by Churchill Downs.

Depreciation: This is the five-syllable word that works magic on your taxes.

Let me share with you what I didn't know. Pretend for a moment that you are a self-employed painter. You buy your tools, equipment, and supplies such as a 50-foot extension ladder for $1,000. You write a check from your bank account to pay for it and you use this ladder in your painting business.

Although you spent $1,000 of your hard-earned, after-tax dollars on a new ladder for your painting business, the Internal Revenue Service (IRS) will not let you write off $1,000 as a business expense this year. The IRS has a schedule, or report, stating that the life of your ladder is 10 years and you can only write off $100 a year for the next 10 years to cover the cost of this piece of equipment. They might use the term *capitalized expense,* meaning that the taxpayer writes off the cost over the life of the item.

If you are a painter, what is interesting about this is considering the likely value of the ladder after 10 years (if you can find it). Odds are, if your ladder still exists, its value has dropped to next to nothing. This same idea holds for plumbers, printers, and other folks who have business expenses and investments associated with earning their taxable income.

Here's the beauty of real estate: It is really dirt and those things attached to it—houses, buildings, and so on. Uncle Sam will not allow us to depreciate dirt because dirt will always be here; however, Uncle Sam does allow us to say the improvements or buildings on the land have their own life. You might describe it as "How long will the building last or stand up?" For whatever reason, Uncle Sam has come up with two schedules for real estate:

1. Residential Improvements have a depreciation schedule (life) of 27.5 years.
2. Commercial Improvements have a depreciation schedule (life) of 39 years.

So how does depreciation affect me as an investor?

Pretend you have purchased a single-family rental house for $100,000. Please understand that you did not *spend* money here, you *invested* money. At tax time, you will ask yourself, "What's the value of the lot the house is sitting on?" Pretend the lot value is $15,000. Here is what should happen:

Purchase price:	$100,000.00	
	+ $1,200.00	(closing costs, title insurance, fees to buy)
	$101,200.00	Your total investment
Lot value:	($15,000.00)	(Subtract from your total investment)
	$86,200.00	Depreciated over 27.5 years
	$86,200.00	Divided by 27.5 years = $3,134.54

This means you get a *phantom expense* of $3,134.54 for owning this investment property. The IRS rationalizes this by saying the life of residential property is 27.5 years and theoretically, at the end of the 27.5 year period, the building(s) on the lot is worn out and worth *zero*; all you have left is your vacant lot. There is still more.

Let's say you make $50,000 year as *earned income,* whether from your job or as a self-employed worker. The simple version here gives you the following benefit *now:*

Your earned income:	$50,000.00
Minus Depreciation:	($3,134.54)
Your taxable income:	$46,865.46

If you are in the 33 percent tax bracket, one-third of $3,000 is $1,000 savings right now in your income taxes. Let's bump it up a bit. Suppose you have 10 of these rental houses.

With 10 of the same rental houses:

Your income:	$50,000.00
Minus Depreciation: $3,134.54 × 10 houses =	($31,345.40)
Your taxable income:	$18,654.60

In this tax situation, the IRS allows you to pay income tax as if you only made $18,654.60 instead of the $50,000 you made during the tax year. Wow! This can be a huge tax savings. Let's try one more simple scenario:

With 20 of these same rental houses:

Your income:	$50,000.00
Minus Depreciation: $3,134.54 × 20 houses =	($62,690.80)
Your taxable income:	($12,690.80)

You lost money!

If the IRS says you lost $12,690.80 for the year, this means *you pay no income tax!* In fact, if you have a job and have had money withheld from your paycheck for income taxes, odds are that you will get all your withholdings refunded to you. This is exactly what happened to me. I didn't understand this depreciation thing. So all my police officer wages and my wife's salary from working as a nurse were completely wiped out by depreciation. Some folks talk about a limit of $125,000 and I still don't really understand it, but I trust my CPA to handle this for me. He can cite all the pertinent sections of the U.S. Tax Code. He is the tax expert, I am the investor, and he is on my team.

Here is some icing for your cake while we are focusing on this depreciation thing. I might be using the wrong official term here, but in investor language, let's call it a combination of *income averaging* both forward and in reverse. Because I began acquiring assets fast and aggressively, my depreciation skyrocketed in a very short period. In just two years, we were showing huge losses in income for tax purposes. This is where my CPA stepped in with his knowledge and expertise. He took our tax returns for the past several years and somehow took this year's losses and amended previous years' returns. Then he did something else to carry some losses forward, which resulted in more tax refunds from previous years.

About a year ago, my CPA contacted me to sign another tax return, but it seemed to me that I had just been in his office about a month earlier completing a tax return. I asked him what this new return was about, and he proceeded to rattle off some stuff about some kind of new tax law changes. I said okay, but why me? He told me I might want to sign this return because I would be getting another $15,000 in tax refunds. My CPA, without any direction from me, took the changes from this new tax law and amended more of my previous years' returns, even going back to when I had my job as a cop.

This is mind-boggling to me. I didn't understand the magic of depreciation when I started investing. My unit involved detectives who targeted people who commit crimes for profit. My excitement about the huge dollar amounts of my tax refunds leaked out. The other guys worked their butts off with all the overtime they could get their hands on and took off-duty jobs at drugstores, apartments, banks, church picnics, and so on. They all suspected that I was doing something illegal instead of just renting houses.

In fact, this was so amazing to the guys I worked with that my boss began taking a serious interest in real estate. He, too, then bought rental properties and retired; and now my former boss, Sgt. Ron Cooper, works for me at Vista Realtors. He specializes in foreclosures and bank-owned properties in our town.

What's the catch with depreciation?

Here is the ugly part, but it, too, can have a happy ending. Go back to the $100,000 rental house you bought in the earlier example. Suppose you operate it as a rental property for 10 years and then decide to sell it for $200,000. Take a look at what might happen:

Selling Your 100K Rental House after 10 Years

Sale price:	$200,000
Minus Your investment:	($101,200)
Capital gain (Your profit)	$98,800

(True for real cash numbers, but false for tax purposes.)

Add depreciation back in:

$$\$3,134.54 \times 10 \text{ years} = \$31,345.40$$
$$\text{Real } \textit{taxable} \text{ capital gain (Your profit)} = \$130,145.40$$

You will be subject to capital gain tax or income tax on your profit from selling this rental house. Don't run yet. There are still several alternatives:

- *Plan A:* Remember depreciation in the big picture. If you have enough depreciation annually already going on, it may very well totally wipe out all your capital gain or profit from selling this rental property.

- *Plan B:* The IRS has another alternative for investors using IRS Section 1031 involving a "tax deferred exchange." The simple basic version of this exchange involves selling this rental property to upgrade into another investment property. Using this procedure properly allows an investor to defer the capital gain until the new property is sold.

- *Plan C:* As an investor and not as a dealer, you will have the additional alternative to use the *installment sale* method of selling your rental property. This simply means seller financing or owner financing. You will play the role of lender for your buyer. This sets the stage for investors to have the majority of the payment received monthly as *interest income* instead of capital gain income.

What happens here is that each year you own and operate this rental house, the IRS says the investment value of your asset drops by $3,134.54. For tax purposes, what began as a $101,200.00 investment has decreased to $69,854.60.

There are many courses, books, and experts on tax strategies. These sources often encourage investors to accelerate their depreciation and *componentize* their investment, by chopping up parts of the property. Using the example of the $100,000 rental house, you might elect to componentize your investment by breaking it down:

Purchase price: $100,000.00
                + $1,200.00 (closing costs, title insurance, fees to buy)
                $101,200.00 Total Investment
Lot value: ($15,000.00)
                $86,200.00   in improvements to be depreciated
Cabinets $7,000.00   depreciates on IRS schedule for cabinets
Carpet $3,000.00   depreciates on IRS schedule for carpet
Roof $5,000.00   depreciates on IRS schedule for roofs
Plus more stuff

The result using the componentizing method drastically increases the depreciation phantom expense annually. Using the first example in this chapter, as an investor, you would get $3,134.54 annually to write off for depreciation by simply depreciating $86,200 over 27.5 years. Using this componentizing method may allow you to write off as much as $10,000 for far fewer years. You are simply burning it up quicker.

Caution: There is an aspect of the big picture that involves accelerating your depreciation using this componentizing strategy.

Scenario 1

- Suppose you have a high-income job or business. Perhaps as a successful attorney, doctor, or business owner, your taxable income is $500,000 or more annually.
- You don't have very much rental property.
- You are getting spanked in a huge way on paying income taxes.
- You will benefit greatly from componentizing.

Scenario 2

- Suppose you are investing already.
- You've got a healthy chunk of depreciation annually that pretty much erases all your earned income and passive income.
- You cannot benefit any more from componentizing.
- In fact, you are simply burning it up quicker and you might jackpot yourself down the road in just a few years.

Suppose you have $150,000 in depreciation annually and you make $100,000 in the same year. The IRS views you as having lost $50,000 for the tax year. In short, you have literally wasted $50,000 in depreciation. So why would you use the componentizing method to write off as much as $250,000 right now causing you to show a loss of $150,000 instead of $50,000?

Here's the method to this madness. I have made it a point to pay attention to the veteran supersuccessful investors in my town and across the United States. It is the common denominator for all the old-timers: *They complain about how much they pay in income taxes.* Large dollar amounts. Obscene dollar amounts. Why?

- Their properties are usually paid off.
- They are fresh out of depreciation. They have no depreciation left!

So picture yourself a few years down the road—all or most of your properties are paid off and you have zero dollars phantom depreciation expense because you componentized your investments and wrote them off quicker. *Ouch!*

Because I have so much depreciation today, my strategy is to keep piling on capitalized expenses and improvements to d-r-a-g out my depreciation for years to come. I don't want to end up like the old-timers who have no depreciation to reduce their staggering income taxes. This idea pretty much contradicts what many advisors encourage investors to do. Review your personal situation before taking action. Don't shoot yourself in the foot because other investors insist it works great for them.

When I discovered the magic of depreciation, I was excited. As far as my bookkeeping goes, I was the Depreciation King. I set up schedules for all the real estate that I owned and for all my capital improvements and expenses.

This was one of my biggest mistakes as an investor. It made me feel good having all of this depreciation documented, and my CPA was proud of me. But there was something totally wrong with this picture. Remember, I had a family and a full-time job as a cop. Something had to give here timewise. I was not doing any deals. My real estate investing business came to a grinding halt—zero activity—but I sure was proud of my depreciation stuff. I soon realized that I had simply transitioned from being an *investor* into being a *bean counter,* and this never would put a nickel in my bank account. Today, I think of depreciation in simple terms. In the big picture, I am concerned about depreciation at two specific times or activities involving my real estate investing:

1. When selling a property, I want to know my *cost basis* of the property I am considering selling. (Cost basis is simply the dollar amount invested after writing off depreciation for X number of years operating it as a rental property.)
2. When preparing tax strategies for each year, I want to know how much depreciation I have for the year. My simple strategy is to get that information from my CPA. Then for the most part, I know I can make X amount of money before paying income taxes.

Suppose that 10 years ago you purchased a rental house for $80,000. A buyer has just offered you $150,000 cash for this rental house. As an investor, you would be concerned about your *capital gain* on this property. Let's run the numbers:

- Ten years ago, you bought a rental house for $80,000.
- You cannot depreciate dirt. It lasts forever.
- Suppose your land value is $5,000 allowing you to depreciate $75,000 over 27.5 years. Without using a calculator, I can simply take $75,000 and divide it by 27.5 years, rounding it off to 25 years. I ballparked this figure at about $3,000 annually.
- 10 years × $3,000 per year = $30,000
- 20-Second Cipherin' Session results in learning:

$80,000 Investment 10 years ago
Minus Depreciation ($30,000)
$50,000 Adjusted cost basis

$150,000 Sale price
Minus Cost basis ($50,000)
$100,000 Capital gain

Earned Income versus Passive Income

For investors thinking about taxes, the two terms earned income and passive income are crucial. For the first few years, I didn't understand the difference nor did anyone encourage me to find out the difference. Many CPAs, accountants, tax attorneys, and experts assume that you and I know these terms and understand how these two types of income affect us for tax purposes. Here's my version of it from an investor's perspective.

Earned income: is getting paid for something you do. Buy, fix up, and sell are things you do and may be flagged as earned income. Your job, my job as a cop, my wife's job as a nurse, real estate agents' commissions, and so on, all are earned income, as described in the following definition:

The term earned income *means wages, salaries or professional fees, and other amounts received as compensation for personal services actually rendered, but does not include that part of the compensation the taxpayer derived for personal services he or she rendered to a corporation that represents a distribution of earnings or profits rather than a reasonable allowance as compensation for the personal services.* (September 2004 Tax Brief by American Institute of Certified Public Accountants)

The major difference involves your payroll withholding taxes. If you have a job, on each paycheck you receive as an employee, you pay 6.2 percent of your earned income for Social Security and 1.45 percent for Medicare. The two combined equal a deduction of 7.65 percent. (Your employer also pays the employer's portion, exactly the same, over and above what you pay as an employee.) In real numbers, folks, if you have a job and earn $100,000 annually on your job, you're paying $7,650 for Social Security and Medicare.

It's not over. If you are self-employed and you are your own employer, it gets uglier. Now you must pay both the employee and employer portions on these taxes. Being self-employed, you must pay 15.3 percent of your earned income for Social Security and Medicare. Hold on to your bank account. If you are self-employed with $100,000 in earned income for the tax year, you must pay $15,300 for Social Security and Medicare. *Ouch!*

As an investor, your rental income (income from assets, . . . stuff you own) is considered *passive income* and not earned income. This simply means you won't have to pay the huge 15.3 percent in additional income tax on this amount.

Tax-Free Profit in Real Estate

Did you know *tax-free* profits are available to you today? This is not a misprint. You really can have tax-free profit in your real estate investing by using the Self-Directed ROTH Individual Retirement Account (IRA). Tax-deferred profits can also be achieved using a Self-Directed Traditional IRA.

This can be frustrating and challenging because the majority of so-called financial investment advisors and experts vehemently state you cannot use your Roth IRA or Traditional IRA to invest in real estate. Many of them will boldly announce that it is illegal. Often they are only knowledgeable about the "in-house" products offered by their firm. *Be cautious* about getting advice from wanna-be experts.

You should have a Self-Directed ROTH IRA set up for yourself, your spouse, your kids, and your family members. Do it now. Time is your biggest and best resource as an investor. Check out my "Jump Start Your Roth IRA in 14 Days" home study course at www.wealthbuilding247.com for more information.

The Big Picture: The Simple "Cut to the Chase"

All the items mentioned in this chapter are the tip of the iceberg for investors. They can affect your investing and tax situation in a major way. Common sense doesn't always apply. Old-fashioned horse trading math doesn't always apply.

Here are some simple guidelines. First, develop a good bookkeeping system now.* Second, keep in mind that your tax strategies have to factor in asset protection and estate planning. When I got started, I didn't have anything to lose, so I wasn't concerned about asset protection and estate planning. As I grew our little empire, these two concerns became critical factors.

If you are just getting started, your biggest challenge might be to "just do it." Move forward. As you grow, you may seriously consider establishing a tax entity (LLC, or corporation) for doing buy, fix up, and sell along with any wholesaling of properties. My C corporation, Vista Properties, Inc., is my property management company; it is my *dealer* for tax purposes to do "buy and sell," along with wholesaling, and my brokerage for handling all our real estate agents. I discuss this in Chapter 8.

Once again, if you are just getting started and have zero properties, don't worry about having all your entities laid out properly. After you get a dozen or so properties under your belt, you may do some research into establishing an entity to operate as your property management company and to handle all your dealer activity. Keep in mind that this entity's profit will be flagged as earned income, not passive income.

My objective in this chapter was to introduce you to the major tax concerns involving investors that no one explained to me when I was getting started. You can help yourself best by taking these few topics and discussing them with your CPA, who is an expert in real estate investing.

---

*I created my own software called *Tenant Tracking*, which uses Intuit's Quickbooks Pro. It does your books behind the scenes as you pay bills and make deposits; I use it every day in my business. Check it out at www.TenantTracking.com.

CHAPTER 3

What Is Best? Houses, Apartments, Commercial Property, or Dirt?

I'm asked this question frequently. The real answer depends on you. Gather as much information as possible on each kind of property and pile all the data on *your* scales to see which one gives you the most benefits and the least amount of headaches. For me the answer is a no-brainer: single-family houses.

You will get the good, the bad, and the ugly with each choice. The ultimate decision is yours. Each will provide benefits and challenges, along with problems.

Single-Family Houses

This is, by far, the number one simple, solid investment. For beginners to the old pros, it is a hard one to beat. Let's begin with the benefits.

Easiest to Acquire

Single-family houses, as a rule of thumb, are the easiest investment to grow your wealth with the least amount of risk. Houses can be bought at wholesale prices. You will usually be dealing with owner occupants or just plain ordinary consumers.

Because most house sellers aren't investors, you are at a tremendous advantage as a smart investor. *You can buy wholesale* and *sell retail* and sometimes more than retail if you're really sharp.

Years ago, I asked John Schaub, my good friend, successful, experienced investor, and mentor from Sarasota, Florida, why he likes single-family houses. The following paragraph summarizes his simple answer:

With single-family houses, I get to deal with everyday people—homeowners. I feel pretty knowledgeable, competent, and the odds are probably more in my favor of creating a good deal for me. I can use my knowledge and experience to create a win-win situation for both the seller and myself. In the commercial arena, you're usually not dealing with everyday homeowners. You're dealing with high-dollar specialized attorneys who are probably sharper and more ruthless than you.

Buy wholesale, sell retail is a sound business plan. You can do this pretty easily with houses. I am *not* promoting buy-and-sell as an investment strategy. My point is, with single-family houses, you can buy at wholesale prices, and if the opportunity arises as part of your big investment picture or battle plan, you can sell these houses at retail prices and sometimes a little more. If you handle the transactions properly, you can avoid commissions, defer capital gains taxes and most expenses involved with selling houses the traditional way.

You can buy wholesale, rent it for a while, and then sell it at full retail price with a tenant buyer. You may also choose to rent your house to a tenant with an option to buy. They can get their own financing somewhere down the road while renting from you and then buy the property. You may choose to help finance part or all of their purchase using the *installment sale* benefit for investors.

With the sale of any investment property, a Section 1031 tax-deferred exchange allows you to transfer your profit, or gain, into another investment property. This means you can defer the payment of capital gains tax while letting your deferred capital gain earn appreciation on your new property.

Another benefit is that the tenants live in the home they are renting. With single-family houses, the tenants usually are responsible for all lawn care, trash removal, and utilities. Although not always required by your local or landlord tenant laws, many tenants will do minor maintenance and repairs at their own expense.

Investing in single-family houses spreads your risk. If you own several houses in the same town, you wouldn't be shut down if one were to burn or get smashed by a tree from a storm. If tragedy strikes an apartment building, you might lose all your tenants until the property is livable again. Suppose you own an 18-unit building and you have a tenant who can't cook. This person starts a nasty grease fire on the stove. Wait till you see your local fire department in action. They ought to be in the crash demolition business. They will chop holes in your roof, knock out windows and doors, even if they are unlocked, and will make the utility company disconnect service to your building.

Now what? What about your other 17 tenants? It looks like they, too, might be homeless for at least a short period.

Flying below the radar is another benefit with single-family houses. You can maintain a low profile in your town. You can acquire a boatload of houses and wealth without attracting attention. Start acquiring a bunch of apartments and commercial property and you will be flying loud and proud on your local "who's who" radar screen.

Duplexes and Houses Chopped into Units

This one gets my goat. I've heard these called *flats, doubles,* or *triples.* It doesn't matter; there are different names and terms for your region and town. It still boils down to a free-standing house with two or three units. These are misery magnets. Most towns allow regular maintenance of single-family houses such as lawn care and pest control to be a tenant responsibility. Many communities, however, make the landlord responsible for the common area maintenance of duplexes and triplexes. You will have the responsibility of lawn care, trash removal, water, perhaps utilities, and more.

If a tenant visits Kentucky Fried Chicken and tosses the chicken bones and soft drink cups into the yard, you may get cited by your city because you are responsible for maintaining the grounds. Municipal governments usually don't cite tenants living in a multifamily dwelling. They cite the owner.

You can argue your skills as a great landlord in assigning these responsibilities and tasks to tenants; however, you are still responsible. It sets the stage for you to become a referee. Unit 1 tenant complains that Unit 2 plays music too loud, parks crooked in the driveway, or commits any other offense you could imagine.

Bizarre situations involving utilities, heating, and trash may develop. Are your units separately metered for utilities? Will you have to prorate utilities between tenants; or will you include utilities in the rent and cringe when you see tenants washing cars or keeping windows open in the winter because it gets too hot inside? Some communities require separate meters for each unit if the landlord wants tenants to pay utilities. Some towns make it illegal for landlords to charge tenants for utilities unless there is a meter on the unit. All these things can become time-eating tasks or cash-eating monsters. Strive for an auto-pilot investment system. It is a whole lot easier.

If you want to argue "but the cash flow blah, blah, blah . . ." take a moment to measure your time-eating tasks of babysitting these high hands-on management units versus the same number of houses. You will quickly see that single-family houses will give you more free time. I was doing an all-day Saturday workshop in Tampa and was challenged about the wonderful cash flow on a huge two-story house in an older section of town. I allowed this person to ramble on about how she could "chop this house up" into seven efficiencies or studios and perhaps restructure the rent period from monthly to twice a month, or even weekly.

I cringed at the thought. This woman honestly believed her challenge was awesome, great and good, and profitable. *Wrong!* I'll bet you I can operate as many as 75 single-family rental houses with about the same level of hands-on management. I know, because I operated 75 rental properties and a full-time job before I hired a five-hour per week part-time office person. The other eye-opening discovery for her involved my statement: "I'm not in the hotel business. How long do you want your tenants to stay in your rental property?" The whole class almost unanimously replied, "Forever." This is the correct attitude. Many of my rental properties still have had only one tenant. This is pretty darn good for the long term.

Tenants living in a house call your house their *home*. Tenants living in an apartment usually call it their *apartment*. I want my tenants to call their unit home, get attached to it, and stay a long time. Apartments, efficiencies, and studios are designed for short-term or temporary housing.

Trailers, Mobile Homes, Modular Homes, Trailers with Wheels, Trailers without Wheels, . . . You Got the Idea

Without a doubt, these can be cash cows, but trailers should not be viewed as an investment. You buy investments for long-term growth. Trailers are like cars and go down in value with time. Many trailer owner investors are proud and protective of their trailers. These golden cash cows really crank in the cash flow department. The only problem is that they are not investments. Perhaps you could think of them as vending machines (probably cost about the same as well). You can purchase a vending machine and crank some pretty good cash flow if you place it in a high-traffic location.

Insurance can be a bear with trailers, especially those with fireplaces. Before my wife became a registered nurse, she worked in insurance. At that time, trailer insurance was approximately three times the cost of a good homeowner's insurance policy on a house. If the trailer had a fireplace, the owner would really get spanked.

You must find a location to park your trailer(s). A trailer park will charge rent. You could buy your own trailer park and charge lot rent yourself. Keep in mind, it is like owning a vending machine park or mall.

You could buy dirt, pour a concrete pad, and park your trailer, or you could capture a modular home, set it on a foundation, and tie it down.

Most of the time, a taboo label is attached to trailers and modular homes. Modular homeowners will vehemently deny their home is a trailer; however, when their guests leave, everybody still seems to call it a "trailer" or "mobile home."

There are exceptions to every rule. In my town, I'll stick to my guns on my opinion of mobile homes and trailers. I have made many trips into them as a cop. In my travels around the country, I've seen some nice trailer parks. In Florida, there are gated community retirement trailer parks. They have all kinds of amenities— tennis courts, a clubhouse, swimming pools, and a golf course with membership privileges. But, we still call them trailer parks.

You could view trailers in the same arena, or category, as low-income neighborhood houses, which I think of as "disposable houses." Perhaps we should look at trailers in that light. Buy them for cash flow and not necessarily for appreciation or tax benefits. I have met some supersharp and lucky investors who buy beat-up, ugly trailer parks full of Jerry Springer's guests; these investors demolish the trailer parks and convert them into valuable commercial properties. Doing so takes time, effort, and money, but many folks have done this profitably.

Apartments

There are basically three grades—A, B, C—just like school grades:

1. A is high quality, nice.
2. B is a cut above average, but not much.
3. C is not very desirable. Although a school grade of C is considered average, many investors view a C-quality apartment community as "bottom of the barrel." Owners usually have trouble getting adequate insurance.

When attending my local Kentucky Real Estate Exchangors meetings, I have observed that many investors and agents tag an apartment community or even a commercial property with these same letters. For example, an agent may say he has a B+ apartment community for sale.

Apartments are those structures built for this purpose. Don't try to take a single-family house, chop it up, and call it an apartment building. Those things belong up there with the duplexes and triplexes, even if they have 10 units.

Apartments can range from a simple stand-alone fourplex (a building designed with four units, usually two units on each floor with a common entrance) all the way up to an apartment community with several hundred units, pools, clubhouse, and many other amenities.

From my perspective, most successful apartment owner investors are stuck on their investments and seldom cross over to equal numbers of apartments and houses. That is simply their preference and comfort zone, but let's look at apartments as investments.

Apartment owners like the following benefits only because they are wearing blinders that prevent them from openly entertaining new ideas:

- Having everything in one place is efficient.
- On-site help is easier to control and manage.
- There is no need for transportation for help.
- Having many units in one location involves less risk because the occupied units will cover the mortgage payment with several units vacant. Owners will argue that you can't do this with houses. (The very same thing can be achieved. Suppose you have a 60-unit complex and another investor has 60 single-family houses. With an efficient management program, the investor

with 60 single-family houses is more profitable across the board, including the time required to manage them.)

Here is an eye-opener. Experienced apartment community owner/investors will admit this staggering rule of thumb with apartments:

- Their *operating expenses are 50 percent of their gross rents.*

This does not include any mortgage payment. In most cases, the debt service (mortgage payment) is at least 50 percent of the gross rents. This means that if you own an apartment community and have it paid for (you own it free and clear and have no mortgage payment), approximately 50 percent of your rental income goes toward the costs of operating the apartment community.

What happened to your so-called efficiency?

Let's compare *50 apartments* to *50 houses* with a monthly rent of $600 per unit or house. Both have gross rents of $30,000 ($600 × 50) Keeping it simple, the apartments will have a higher vacancy rate due to the frequent tenant turnover associated with apartments. Single-family houses, operated properly, have such a low vacancy rate that I do not factor them into any of my formulas for buying rental houses.

Apartment Owner with 50 Units

The owner is free and clear with $600 monthly rent per unit.

Monthly gross rent = $30,000
Operating costs of 50 percent = ($15,000) includes:

- Electric house meter
- Water
- Grounds upkeep
- Trash and dumpsters
- Property tax
- Insurance
- Management
  —Office
  —Phone
  —Fax
  —Copier
  —Supplies
- Repairs
- Vacancy

Net to owner = $15,000.

Owner of 50 Single-Family Houses

Owned free and clear with $600 monthly rent.

$$\begin{aligned}
\text{Monthly gross rent} &= \$30{,}000 \\
\text{Operating costs} &= (\$4{,}500)
\end{aligned}$$

- Repairs as needed
- Taxes and insurance
- Owner manages

$$\text{Monthly net to owner} = \$25{,}500$$

or

Operating cost with property manager + 10 percent = 25 percent or ($7,500)

$$\text{Net to owner} = \$22{,}500$$

So even investors who pay a property manager 10 percent of the rent to manage their 50 single-family houses will still make more money than the owner of the apartment community. It is plain to see how the owner of 50 houses, even when using a property manager *smokes* the apartment owner. The 50 paid-for apartment units earn $15,000 profit, whereas 50 houses paid for with the same monthly rent will earn $25,000 if the owner takes care of maintenance, or $22,500 if the owner uses a property manager with a 10 percent management fee.

Here are more factors to consider: If you captured some apartments for a heck of price, who can you sell them to? How long will it take (probably longer than selling a single-family house).

Who buys apartments? Investors buy apartments. Like you, investors are looking for a deal to steal. From a simple fourplex to a community with several hundred units, your buyer/investor, just like you, wants a steal. With a house, you can buy at wholesale and sell at retail.

If you ever needed to have a fire sale, you would have to take a huge hit on an apartment community, whereas you could quickly sell off one or two single-family houses to meet your fire sale need.

How will you handle stigmas? Suppose a violent criminal act occurs at your apartment complex. A buddy of mine had this happen at one of his large apartment communities. He pretty much went into panic mode. He hired extra off-duty police to patrol the parking and was terrified that the existing tenants might choose to move, while new prospective tenants would avoid the highly publicized dangerous apartment complex that he chanced to own. You need to have cash reserves to weather hurdles and storms like these.

What about tragedies? A storm, a tree crashing into a building, or worst yet, an environmental danger from asbestos, lead, mold, and so on. Imagine the panic cancer spreading throughout your units. Tenants may jump on the bandwagon to get out of your unhealthy units.

How about lawsuits? The "help us find somebody to sue" attorneys will follow up if a tragedy strikes you. They already know where to find your tenants . . . in the apartments that were displayed on TV. If you had houses scattered around town, it might take a little more effort.

Many apartment buildings have central heating and air systems. Simply put, this means *not if it goes out, but when it goes out,* it's out for everybody. Then what? So your boiler dies in the cold of winter. Are you going to put all your tenants up in a hotel? What and how will you pay to rent a temporary boiler while your cash evaporates from the cost of repairing or replacing the boiler? A single-family house has its own system, which can be easily serviced or replaced by any competent licensed heating, ventilation, air-conditioning (HVAC) technician.

And finally, apartments for the most part fit the bill as "long-term temporary housing," just a notch above a hotel or motel. Yes, we can find folks who live in an apartment for years, but most tenants are short-term occupants and move more frequently than those who reside in a house.

Finally, it is challenging to maintain a high-quality ranking for apartments. It takes some serious effort and money to keep everything in order. You absolutely must screen your rental applications closely. Many times as a cop, I saw investors get lazy and greedy, trying to cut expenses and plug vacancies. They would put just about anybody into an empty unit. *Wrong!* This is one of the worst things you can do.

Picture this. You have excellent tenants in your building. You screw up one time and without realizing it, you put a dirtbag tenant into your building. It will not take long for you to discover this. Your responsible tenants will let you know by making complaints and demanding you fix this problem. Your good tenants will threaten to move if you don't take immediate action. Most states' landlord/tenant laws require the landlord to follow a specific process to evict a tenant. It may take anywhere from one to three months to get the bad tenant out, even without any challenges from the tenant. What will your good tenants do before you get the bad tenant out? Yup, they'll move! Now you've started growing a cancer and your building will probably get labeled as the bad building.

One last important issue with apartments. Suppose you operate in a market with too many units and not enough tenants. In my town, this is happening now and it leaves us with the painful process of selecting "cream of the crap." How do you combat this market condition?

I have no intention of lowering the quality of my tenants; however, I can lower my rent to drive good responsible tenants to my properties for a wonderful below-market rent. (Keep in mind, with my tenant tracking system, I get more than 110 percent of my rents where most investor/landlords get only 85 percent of their rents.) For example, if market rent on a single-family house is $900, I might advertise the rent on this home at $799 coming in at least $100 cheaper than my competition. I'll get more applicants and will not have to resort to lowering our qualifying standards to fill the vacancy.

But, what about apartments? Can you take a building with, let's say, 24 two-bedroom units with a market rent of $700 and lower the rent to $599 for your next tenant to help fill your vacant unit(s)? No way! Regardless of what others tell you, *tenants talk*. If you do something like this, be prepared to lower everybody's rent to $599 across the board. With single-family houses where the tenants do not know each other, I can lower rents as needed on individual houses to fill vacancies in a brutal market while maintaining standards of a high-quality tenant.

Commercial Property

Just like some of the games in a casino, commercial property might be viewed as a game for the big players. Many owners can say they have phenomenal returns on their investment; however, I've seen many (including me) almost cry like a baby when their commercial property is sitting vacant without a tenant. These properties don't sit empty for a day or two. They don't sit empty for a month or two. I've seen some commercial properties sit empty for years. The big dilemma with commercial property is the relationship of its value to its income. Your property's value is generally determined by the income it produces. Therefore, if you discount the rent on your commercial property, you have just shot yourself in the foot big time because you have lowered the property's value.

Suppose I had a fast-food building paid for, and a national fast-food chain leased the property for $5,000 per month. This would mean approximately $60,000 in annual rent and no mortgage payment. Investors like to consider the capitalization rate (cap rate) of the property when handicapping the property for investment. If this property could crank $60,000 to the investor annually, along with annual increases in rent, and there was a long-term (perhaps a 20-year lease) in place, the investor's desired cap rate would determine the value of this property to the investor when paying all cash, with no loan on the property. The cap rate is the annual return the cash investment is making for the owner:

> With a 12 percent cap rate, the property would be worth $500,000.
>
> With an 8 percent cap rate, the property would be worth $750,000.
>
> With a 6 percent cap rate, the property would be worth $1,000,000.

The great advantages with commercial property involve what is called *triple net* (NNN), meaning there are absolutely no expenses for the owner other than debt service or their mortgage payment. The tenant pays for all property repairs and maintenance, all property taxes, and all property insurance including naming the owner as an additional insured on the tenant's insurance policy. This is beautiful when it works.

When this same property is vacant, things quickly get ugly. The owner must pay the commercial rate property taxes, insurance, debt service, utilities, ground maintenance, and advertising to capture a new tenant. When a commercial unit is vacant, it can sit and sit and sit and sit for a long, long, time. These properties just don't move as fast as a house can.

Imagine putting a commercial lease together. It is not as simple as your standard rental agreement with a house or an apartment. A competent commercial tenant will want to lock in as much as possible to control expenses and will try to beat up on you in devious ways. Large national anchor tenants have leasing departments with full-time attorneys whose specific task is negotiating lease agreements with owners.

John Schaub tells a story of an investor friend who owned a nice retail strip center. A national chain drugstore negotiated a detailed lease for the property. When his buddy pursued leasing the other vacant units located behind the drugstore, he had a bomb dropped on him. He rented one of the units to a business that happened to sell an item that was the same as a product carried by the chain drugstore.

There's a lesson here. His buddy did not rent to another drugstore behind the national tenant drugstore. It could have been a retailer as unrelated as a hobby store. The national drugstore chain attorneys (or their reps) watched closely as new retail tenants began to set up shop in the strip center. They found one item sold by the new tenant that competed with products sold by them. This allowed the national anchor tenant to pull the trigger on a clause in their lease stating that if the owner rented space to another tenant carrying any item that competed with merchandise sold by the national anchor tenant, the anchor tenant would not have to pay any rent during the tenancy of the competing tenant. Long story short, his buddy took a bath on this one and the national drugstore chain did not have to pay rent during the tenancy of the small retailer in the strip center. Ouch!

The stakes are high for commercial property, but if it is managed properly, the payday can be phenomenal.

Dirt

Unimproved plain old dirt. No buildings, no structures, just dirt. For starters, I don't know many investors who actually get a check in the mail each month because they own dirt. Years ago, my uncle, who owned hundreds of acres, would rent X number of acres to a farmer who would grow crops and pay my uncle a percentage of the monies received from the sale of those crops. He also leased ground to hunters on a yearly basis to hunt deer, squirrels, and rabbits.

One of the best investment strategies involving dirt is purchasing an *option to buy* to gain control of the real estate. In a desirable area, a dirt owner strapped for cash, who is struggling to pay property taxes, might present an opportunity for you to step in with your Roth IRA and purchase an option to buy that would lock in your purchase price for x number of years in exchange for paying the property taxes every year.

Your Roth IRA gets to capture all the appreciation of the property without the risk of ownership allowing you to shop at your leisure for a qualified buyer using the new appreciated value.

Some sharp investors use this same idea to gain control of several parcels of dirt located next to each other and when all parcels are combined, their combined value is double or triple the value of the individual smaller parcels. It has been used over and over in my town, especially in the high growth and expansion areas for shopping centers and apartment complexes.

Dirt is tough as far as providing monthly cash flow now, but used properly it can have a place in your long-term strategic investment battle plan.

So what's best for me? Hands down, my choice is single-family houses, especially for those getting started with little or next to no cash. What's your choice?

CHAPTER 4

Never Call Yourself a Landlord

This chapter is likely to ruffle some feathers. I'm gonna chop up some sacred ground in the area of operating rental property; however, hang in there until the end to see the big picture and where you fit in. It's your choice.

Landlord: A Challenging Issue

Just say the word out loud to yourself. Seriously, just do it. Just say "Landlord."

Is this a friendly word?

Is it a positive word?

What feelings or opinions are associated with this word?

What do other people think about this word?

What does it imply?

My gut feeling tells me the word *landlord* is totally negative. The word simply sounds bad. It sounds evil, doesn't it? Eddie Murphy on *Saturday Night Live* did a skit similar to *Mr. Rogers' Neighborhood* with the slogan, or catch phrase, "Kill My Landlord! Kill My Landlord!" Many totally negative and evil characteristics are associated with this word.

Landlords have deep pockets is another misconception that is almost impossible to shake. It doesn't matter a hill of beans whether this landlord is an aggressive, honest, entrepreneur trying to do something good and positive in his neighborhood or town. This title can touch sensitive personal issues. I know, it did with me, too.

Several years ago, my local investor group, the Kentuckiana Real Estate Investors Association (KREIA), invited an attorney who represented tenants in court to speak at our monthly meeting. The purpose of the lecture was to educate our members about tenants' rights and landlords' responsibilities from a legal perspective.

Rob Smith worked at the Legal Aid office, which provides legal counsel for people who can't afford representation. Housing is a hot button with these folks. Rob had been employed by this agency for a long time, perhaps since its creation, years ago. He proceeded to give real-life examples of how landlords who don't know the local landlord/tenant laws (although they are readily available to the public) can screw up and get their clocks cleaned by attorneys. The speaker definitely put a twist on everything in our local laws that would benefit the tenant and attack the landlord.

This was an eye-opener for all of us in the room that night. Some members became absolutely furious. They would have thrown tomatoes had they been available. Rob Smith, the *free* attorney who received a paycheck every week from taxpayers to represent tenants who wouldn't pay their rent, made the following comment to a room full of more than 200 investors. I am paraphrasing his statement, but it went something like this:

> *I get a paycheck from you guys [taxpayers] every week. I don't care who I offend. I love my job. I feel like my objective and goal is to cause as much grief to landlords and to get into their pockets as deep as I can because they are the ones who made the decision and chose to become a landlord.*

You could hear the rumbling grow in the room, like the wave at a football stadium. But the point is, Rob Smith is right! For the most part, we can't even acknowledge his perspective because we don't hang out with that kind of tenant. We don't associate with them. He does. This guy was as serious as a heart attack. His passion and conviction for what he believed in was 100 percent sincere. This was a superb eye-opening experience for the members of our group.

Go back in time with me for a moment. Perhaps this will ring a bell with you as well. As mentioned, my first house was a HUD house—a foreclosure listed in the Sunday paper. Ugly, stinky, and in need of a lot of help. But it was located in a great area for me. In fact, it had been on my paper route when I delivered papers to earn money when I was in high school.

Some of the neighbors still lived in the area. They had been there since 1973 when I delivered papers to them. It made me feel comfortable to buy my first investment property on this street. After buying it and hocking everything we owned, including my Ford Ranger pickup, I rehabbed this two-bedroom house in 13 days. A long 13 days. (At the time, I was a Louisville police officer and was assigned to the substation about two miles from this house. My pickup carried loads of trash, debris, and garbage to the police station dumpster after dark.)

After rehabbing this house and getting rid of the smell, I decided to make it a rental property. It would be an investment for the long haul to supplement my police pension when I retired.

Now, picture this. I am searching for a good tenant. Who am I? What role or position did I have? Remember, I was a smart police officer who assumed that I was immediately a smart investor/landlord. *Wrong!* I went to the nearby office supply store and purchased a generic rental application and lease agreement (another stupid mistake).

After putting a "For Rent" sign in the yard, I met every prospect at the property (40-minute drive) and identified myself as the "Owner" or "Investor" and soon graduated to that proud-feeling word: "Landlord."

For a kid who grew up in a blue-collar neighborhood, becoming an investor/landlord put me leagues above my local peers. On that little street with just one small rental house, I felt as smart as Donald Trump. It made me *proud*. It made my wife proud, and my parents were proud. Pretty good feeling isn't it?

Well, this was all totally wrong on my part. I was setting myself up for one heck of an expensive lesson in the School of Hard Knocks:

Problem 1: About 6:00 P.M. on a Friday evening, I had the opportunity to take my wife and kids out to dinner together. This was a precious moment because we both were working full-time jobs and a chance to eat out together was rare. As we were exiting our home and getting the kids in the car, a "crop duster" land barge came clunking down our street and pulled into our driveway. Yup, our tenant, who said he was out this way after dropping off his "old lady" at his outlaws. He didn't want to stay there, so he decided to come over and visit me, along with dropping off the rent to save 29 cents on a postage stamp. I was guilty of being a nice guy. Tammy, my wife, had smoke coming out of her ears while I was being friendly and polite to our tenant.

Solution to Problem 1: Rent a Post Office box and never disclose your home address.

The next problem is related to ego, personal pride, and the faint odor of real estate investing success. This happened to me after I acquired the first rental house. One rental house had graduated me to a higher level of success in the United States. It moved me to the arena and the special insider club called *real estate investor.*

After acquiring our second rental house within 60 days of the first one, it was a pretty darn good feeling for this police officer to be called a landlord. *(That's the special smart person who has all the money, is knowledgeable in real estate, and has deep pockets, . . right?)*

This was a very long painful learning experience in the School of Hard Knocks. No one told me not to do this. Plus, if they had done so, I probably wouldn't have been receptive to their comments.

It was kinda neat. Tenants were contacting me for repairs and help in finding a home to rent. Power and respect as a businessperson was still new to me, and it felt pretty good to be treated this way. Never mind the baggage, the good feeling this stuff gave me far outweighed the bad . . . at the time. Keep in mind that this was the kid from the blue-collar neighborhood with a huge, over-the-moon work ethic. There is always a little work with success.

After getting a few properties under my belt, working a full-time job, driving a buying machine, and rehabbing as many as four to six houses at a time, the fun wore off. Because I took pride in being a hands-on investor, everybody had my phone number and my pager number. Looking back, they seemed to ring nonstop with calls from tenants, local inspectors, people answering ads for vacant rental units, contractors with questions and bills, and real estate agents or sellers calling with deals.

Unknowingly, I jackpotted myself as the landlord. By answering my phone, I put myself immediately in a situation of having to deal with tenants and make a decision on the spot because I was the authority. I had to deal with such things as a tenant calling and whining about her grandma who had just passed away (for the fourteenth time), and could I please make the late charges go away this month? As a nice guy, with a big heart, it sure was hard to say *no* when I was put in this situation and had to confront it head-on.

Go ahead and say you're tough enough to handle that. Baloney! I thought I was, too. Be honest with yourself. Most investors I know are good people with big hearts. Sure, there are a couple of investors in every town who would enforce late charges on their mother, but most investors are really nice people.

If you're an old seasoned pro trying to be tough and cold, think back to when you got started. There you go; now, you must admit this has happened to you as well.

Problem 2: Here is where I screwed up big time. I took pride in identifying myself as the boss, owner, and landlord. I was the guy with the authority to make the decisions and call the shots. This belief also came pretty darn easy and naturally to me because, as a cop, I was already sort of groomed for it.

Solution to Problem 2: This answer is amazingly simple. *Never* identify yourself as the owner, real estate investor, or worse, . . . landlord.

Always identify yourself as the *property manager.* This powerful, stuck-in-the-middle position allows you a boatload of flexibility to dodge bullets. These two words give you an easy out to avoid making rash "shoot from the hip" decisions that may be emotionally charged or that you may regret later.

Don't freak out. In public, you can be the property manager; while behind the scenes, you are still the owner. In fact, you can also state: "I know the owner."

Here are two powerful examples to save you money and grief.

The Late Charge Story

Your phone rings and when you answer a tenant says, "Hello, this is Sally at 123 Main Street. I know I'm late with this month's rent and I know it was due last Tuesday. My rent is $900, but Bill fell down while walking home from the bar last week and busted his head and hasn't been working since. I've got $900 now, but not enough for the late charge. It's okay if you'll let us pay $900 to get caught up, right?" *Your new answer:* "Wow, I'm sure sorry about Bill and your situation, Sally; however, I'm just the property manager. There are rules and policies I've got to follow or I'll get in trouble. Only the owner can make exceptions to the rules. The owner is not available now, but I'll be in touch with him sometime next week."

The Local Inspector Example

This scenario is just as valuable as the previous one, perhaps maybe more. It doesn't matter if it involves a Section 8 (HUD subsidized housing program for low income families) tenant or a straight rental unit with a tenant.

Suppose you receive a notice or citation for a violation involving one of your properties. In dealing with local government agencies, the easiest way to handle problems is to let employees at the government agency believe they have the authority. They are all-knowledgeable, they are the wizards, and they have the power (sounds pretty good, doesn't it?).

So, you have received your notice, and you telephone the inspector or contact person listed on the notice or violation. Explain that you received this notice from them and you would like or appreciate any assistance or help they may be able to give you because you are only the property manager.

(Some of our local inspectors, especially in the Section 8 arena have a poor attitude toward investors and have commented that they've made certain investor(s) wealthy because of their lenient inspections. Perhaps they're jealous or envious of investors because they don't have the desire or motivation to get off their butt and become an investor, too.)

When you present yourself as the poor ol' property manager stuck in the middle between the tenants and those greedy old tightwad owner/investor/landlords, the inspector generally opens up and offers a helping hand, or at minimum a helping attitude.

Here comes the great part: Having a conversation with you as the property manager gives you the insulation and space to avoid having to answer or make an on-the-spot decision. As a property manager, you have the luxury and benefit of deferring all questions and all situations to the owner. The owner can be yourself, or it can be your spouse. As a property manager, you have the golden opportunity to pass the buck when placed in a tight spot unexpectedly. It also allows you to avoid being the bad guy by making the owner the bad guy.

Many times over the years, this position of property manager has saved the day and saved money. When my office manager, Shirley, stumbles into a hairy situation, she knows she can always dodge the bullet by saying she'll have to "check with the owner first and get back with you."

When this occurs, Shirley can research any information needed and consult with me for a plan or plans of action. Sometimes Shirley hits a bull's-eye and has the answer; and sometimes we rediscover the old saying, "two heads are better than one" and develop a battle plan or solution that is less devastating than a quick knee-jerk answer from a landlord on the phone.

As a member of our local investment group and a charter member of our chapter of the National Association of Residential Property Managers, I have had the opportunity (or curse) to be a participant in meetings involving representatives and leaders of local government agencies that deal with housing. This is how they play the game: *Never* will they commit to any plan of action while sitting at the table during the meeting. Their knee-jerk answer to everything *always* is to get with the director, the boss, or even the mayor to make sure a suggestion or plan can be put into action.

They will always get back to us, but they never position themselves as having the authority to make a decision on the spot. We should learn to do the same. As property managers, we can submit a proposal to the owner for approval. This permits us, the owners, to chew on it, brainstorm, and run all the "what if" scenarios out to the fullest.

Always a Property Manager, Never a Landlord

But, but, but . . . my tenants already know me as their landlord!

Been there, done that, too. It's tough. The transition is the hardest part. In fact, I still have many tenants today who knew I was the boss man or the "rent man" as some would say.

The easiest path of transition, without lying, would be to say from now on, you are only the property manager. If you are involved in any kind of asset protection program, you should be using land trusts or limited liability companies (LLCs) as owners. The title may feel a bit uncomfortable at first, but it will gradually become reassuring to know that this layer of protection and insulation means you do not have to resolve delicate issues on the spot.

Keep in mind that this chapter is *not* about how to operate as a property manager. I am simply explaining how to present yourself as one and how to be perceived by others as a property manager. We have two ears and one mouth for a reason. Use it to your advantage.

The small exception to using this strategy involves your local landlord/tenant laws. If they are similar to ours, you cannot dodge the label "landlord" or "tenant" on legal documents. You must address these titles properly in your forms, especially when taking legal action, such as an eviction action.

The property manager title is simply a way to identify yourself, set the stage to pass the buck, and avoid the challenge of making a decision right now because you have the authority to do so. There are many benefits for you if you call yourself a property manager instead of a landlord.

Avoid Any Misunderstanding of the Title "Property Manager"

First of all, this is simply a word—a title that identifies you for your tenants and others involved in your landlording business. In no way am I encouraging you to market yourself as a professional property manager or anything close to it.

In general, *property manager* means someone who manages property for others for a fee. Most states require property managers to be a licensed real estate broker or an agent, at minimum. Don't freak out over this requirement if you are not licensed. Just understand and accept that calling yourself a property manager does not mean you are in a legal position to manage properties for others for a fee.

There is absolutely no problem if you manage properties you own. You could identify yourself as landlord, boss, rent man, rent lady, landlady, hey you, Mr. Smith," or anything you choose, including and preferably *property manager.* Use the KISS (Keep It Simple, Stupid) Method and don't make it complicated for yourself.

With all the information today encouraging investors to protect their little empires, most of us implement some kind of asset protection program to protect and help with taxes as well. I have a C corporation that is my property management company and my dealer. My property management company manages property owned by several of my limited liability companies. These are all still mine. Therefore, I would not need to be licensed.

If I wanted to manage property for other investors and their entities of ownership, I would have to be a licensed real estate broker in my state to charge a fee for this service.

The point is, it is safe to call yourself a property manager if you manage properties you own and control.

Never call yourself a landlord again. Now you are a property manager.

CHAPTER 5

Your Tenants Are Not Your Customers

Recently, I was a speaker at a national conference for landlords. During my presentation, I asked: "How many landlords think your tenants are your customers?" The majority of the audience raised their hands. Then I dropped a mental bomb by stating, "Your tenants are *not* your customers!" After making this statement, I intentionally paused for a few seconds to observe the reactions in the room.

It was amazing. The expressions on the faces in this room full of landlords ranged from mostly confusion to one fella who refused to have an open mind even after paying a registration fee to attend a learning environment focused specifically on benefiting landlords. His behavior reminded me of a selfish greedy child who has to win at all costs or pick up his ball and go home. He decided not to play and left, making a scene, slamming a chair, and stomping his feet. What a display of temper by a self-proclaimed 30-year landlord. (This kind of outburst might be more likely from some folks who have applied to become one of our tenants.) This was unexpected entertainment for attendees as well.

That's why we have two ears and one mouth. We learn by absorbing information and new ideas.

What is a definition of insanity? Doing the same thing over and over, but expecting different results. I have been guilty of this at times during my investing career.

We should understand the legal role of tenants and the legal position of our role as investors, property managers, and landlords. In addition to the legal definition, we are running a business. Our objective with our investment properties is to increase our wealth, cash flow, and our quality of life for ourselves and our families. It doesn't matter if your business is small or large, it is still a business.

Business Relationship

Here is your challenge. From the standpoint of a business relationship, are your tenants customers? Think about it for a moment.

Most retail establishments have a slogan, "The customer is always right." Do you really want to adopt a slogan—tenants are *always* right? Hmm . . . did you hesitate a minute here on this one? Can you etch this in stone or train your staff to think and believe tenants are always right?

Don't pull the trigger yet on your mental knee-jerk reaction to these comments.

If you operated a retail store, you would be at the mercy of your customers, and the customer-is-always-right slogan could apply. You would have to get them in the door to buy.

If you operated a flower shop, would each customer have to fill out an application and sign an agreement? If you operated a stop-and-shop food mart, would your customers have to fill out an application and sign an agreement to buy beer, cigarettes, or lottery tickets?

Don't get me wrong, some businesses, such as rental car companies, loan companies, and credit cards, require customers to fill out applications and agreements. The word *customer* covers a wide range of circumstances. There are cash-paying, no agreement, always right customers at one extreme and then, all the way at the other extreme, customers who must be qualified by an application process.

As far as the business relationship definition, try this on for size: *Tenants are not your customers.* Try this mind-set: *Tenants are your employees!*

Think of them and treat them as highly valued employees. This should be a good thing. It is an attitude.

At the national conference mentioned earlier, the landlord who couldn't accept this idea of tenants being employees vividly displayed his attitude that customers are more valuable than employees. Wow! What a horrible boss and leader.

Thinking of your tenants as your employees may generate intense emotional opinions. Your range of reaction to this comment is based on your experiences with the word *employee.* It is great! Use it to your benefit. A similar concept might be Stephen Covey's paradigm shift of the position or role of boss versus leader. If you are a boss and follow the stereotypical role of boss as a dictator and the person who simply announces things to do, we can all grasp the tremendous negative vibes associated with this behavior.

If instead, the boss has behavior more in line with that of a leader, the boss becomes a role model, a positive, respected, and friendly person. I am not an expert on all this stuff, but I have attended several courses on this subject and have learned how to put these ideas and concepts into my real estate business. We can apply many of the same ideas in our world of real estate investing and dealing with tenants.

Keep an open mind here. Don't fight or challenge this thought-provoking brainstorming session. On the surface, I'll admit tenants are customers because we provide a product or service for a fee and they pay for it; however, how can you make it better, more profitable, more efficient?

Here is your education challenge. Instead of the typical landlord/tenant relationship, let's make a relationship change to employer and employee.

When your tenants become your employees, you become their leader. Interesting? Employees should be viewed as a great asset. Good employees enable your business to be profitable and should make your life easier, not harder.

Try this exercise. Read the following statements and see if you can substitute the word tenant for the word employee:

- You should have a good relationship with good employees.

- Good employees are valuable.

- Exceptional employees should be rewarded for outstanding performance.

- Employees have responsibilities.

- Employees are expected to perform satisfactorily or suffer the consequences for poor performance.

- An employee who is a bad apple can ruin the good apples.

- Allowing one employee to remain with poor performance can bring down the performance and attitudes of good employees.

- Not treating all employees the same is not fair.

- Employee appreciation programs promote good performance, loyalty, productivity, and profit.

- Length of service should be a guideline for additional benefits to employees and will promote employee retention.

- Outstanding or exceptional community service or personal achievements by employees or their immediate family members should be recognized.

- Employees with poor performance should be dealt with in a fair, consistent manner, including termination.

In the following list, substitute the word property manager for the word employer and tenant for employee.

- Employer should be responsive to employees' concerns.

- Employer should be a leader, not a boss.

- Employer has responsibilities along with consequences.

Got the idea? This new attitude changes your dealings with tenants. Effective communication among responsible parties sets the stage for great results. I assume you want to have the lifestyle of the successful real estate investor as played out in the infomercials on late night TV. It doesn't matter whether you have one or two investment properties or hundreds, this paradigm shift of thinking of tenants as highly prized valuable employees should get you some long overdue results, as seen on those infomercials.

Your Rental Application Becomes a Job Application!

Try this attitude. The next time you give a prospective tenant your rental application, change your mind-set and try to view this applicant as a prospective employee. Imagine that you own a manufacturing plant and it takes 43 people, trained properly, to operate the line. For whatever reason, a position is vacant and you need to fill it quickly.

You hand out your job (rental) application, review it quickly, call the applicant with the good news, and instruct the person to meet you at the plant (rental house). You sign the papers quickly, perhaps on the kitchen counter or worse yet, on the hood of your truck, and point the new employee (tenant) to the vacant station (your rental unit).

How will this new employee respond? What will he do? He will bring all his past experiences and knowledge from previous job(s) (rental units) and might try to do the best he can, giving him the benefit of our doubt.

If he fails and performs poorly, whose fault is it? Perhaps the person worked in below-average jobs (rented from low-quality landlords).

While in high school, I got a part-time job as a bag boy at a Winn-Dixie supermarket. You might think that sacking groceries is a simple no-brainer job. Absolutely not. The store manager treated it as if it was a level or two below brain surgery. I had to watch training videos, go through manuals, exercises, and practice, practice, practice in the back, out of view of customers before I graduated to performing the real job at the front of the store. I don't recall exactly, but I'm guessing I had at least six hours of training before I was cut loose to bag groceries.

How many hours do you spend with your qualified applicants, reviewing paperwork and discussing your policies and the responsibilities of both you and the tenants before you give them the key to your investment property? You may have invested $50,000 or $100,000 or more in your rental property, but we (I've been guilty of this, too; you're not alone here) meet them in a McDonald's parking lot or at the vacant unit with an attitude of hurry up, sign here, give me the money, and here's your keys.

I can't tell you how many times when I got started I did stupid things like that. Perhaps I was in a hurry to meet Momma and my kids for supper, or I thought by doing this real quickly on the way home from work, I'd get an extra day's rent. I don't have any legitimate excuses for operating in this manner other than thinking and believing I didn't have time.

I was stupid. If I'm giving the keys to tenants who are gonna live in my investment, I ought to spend at least six hours with them beforehand so we all start off on the same page. We all should know what to do, and what the consequences are for failing to perform properly. This has made a huge difference in our operation.

Before handing over the keys, we have a meeting in the office for paper sign-ing and discussion of procedures; we refer to it as the *Rent Talk*. (I discuss this in de-tail in Chapter 16.) We allow a minimum of two hours to do the paperwork before a tenant receives keys to their home. In fact, about six months ago, while Shirley was doing a Rent Talk with approved applicants, the tenants politely told her that this was simply too much for them and they made the decision, on the spot, to back out and not rent our unit. What a blessing! Wouldn't you rather have this happen now than discover that you've rented to dirtbags after they're already in your property?

Having a mind-set of tenants as your "employees" allows you to have tenant reward programs. Tenants can earn discounted or free rent with long-term, consis-tent performance on their part. This incentive is called our *All-Star Program* and is described in detail later in this book.

Don't keep this focus on tenants only. Spread it around. How about your own help? Office staff and maintenance staff should be treated as highly valuable em-ployees. These include your furnace person, electrician, plumber, roofer, lawn serv-ice provider, painter, carpet installer, and carpenter.

The Holiday Season Is Your Opportunity to Shine as a Leader

Here is a powerful and inexpensive way to reward your employees. Most investors I know have had a job or still have a job today. For those of you who are not em-ployed, go back with me for a moment to the days of punching the clock.

Think about the holiday season. From Thanksgiving to the end of the year, those folks (including me) who had jobs in government or the corporate world went to holiday parties and more holiday parties. There were bashes for the unit I worked for, along with invitations to parties for all the other districts. It was almost a competitive atmosphere: Who could throw the most extravagant holiday party? The bragging rights for the best holiday bash usually went to the police district that had live entertainment, a dance floor, a huge hall, plenty of food, booze, beer, and even limousines. Sounds great doesn't it?

Switch gears with me for a moment. While I worked my full-time job as a po-lice officer and observed all the free holiday events for me and my wife, I happened to reflect on the holiday happenings of those who are valuable to me in my real es-tate investments.

Remember my furnace person, electrician, plumber, garage killer (the amaz-ing little 72-year-old man who can attack and kill an old dilapidated garage, tearing it down and making it disappear by hauling it off someway, somehow like magic for only $200 cash). Most of these folks have mom-and-pop operations (we use them because they are usually cheaper than the ones who have the full-page ads in the Yellow Pages). What are they doing during the holidays and where are they going?

Do they get invitations to any holiday bashes? I guess some do if their spouse has a job somewhere.

Here's what I do every year for my vendors, contractors, banker, attorney, insurance agent, resident managers, electricians, HVAC technicians, plumbers, tree and lawn service people, window and door specialists, roofer, pest control person, concrete paver, my in-house real estate agents, and the sheriff's deputies who serve the Set Out Warrants, and all those who are an integral part of my real estate business. For the past several years, I have reserved the private lower level banquet room at a nice local Mexican restaurant for the Saturday before Christmas. We mail homemade full-page simple invitations to the Annual Vista Holiday Bash from 6:00 P.M. to 10:00 P.M. They can bring their spouse or significant other of the month. This banquet room has a small bar, and we include an open bar as part of this annual holiday event. We have never had any issues of someone abusing the open bar. In fact, my experience is just the opposite. These folks are not used to extravagant holiday bashes in their honor and are very appreciative of this event. In fact, every year they try to pay the bartender for their drink and are amazed when the bartender waves his hand and says "no charge."

The restaurant presents the food buffet style in raised foil pans with candles underneath to keep the food hot. Nothing fancy—pick and choose what you want and how much. The menu includes tortilla chips and hot cheese dip; beans, chicken, beef, and soft flour tortillas, along with several vegetables and sauces. This covers almost every food taste including vegetarians, making me politically correct. Good music, fun, food, and drink set the stage for these folks to network and have a good time. I usually take the floor around 7:00 P.M. or so and introduce each vendor by name along with the person's product or service and tell a little light-hearted humorous story about that guest. This is powerful. It allows every person, especially the guys, to feel proud and to be a hero. It also makes their spouses grin from ear to ear when they hear their man or woman being recognized as an expert in his field. I'm fortunate to have a garage killer who has outrageous stories, and he usually becomes the center of attention before the evening is over.

As a bonus, my daughter has a friend who has a passion for magic and is obsessed with Houdini. In fact, this kid changed his name to Aaron Houdini. I hire him for a small fee and he puts on a terrific interactive magic show.

I also pretty much force my office manager, Shirley Hamilton, and my technical services supervisor, Dan Gibbs, to take the floor and make some comments. Nothing scripted, just take the floor, wing it, and say some good things. Usually, it is just an old-fashioned thank you for all the vendors' help and patience throughout the year. My intention is to make Shirley and Dan feel that they are hosting this event, because they pretty much drive the entire operation on a day-to-day basis. As they take the floor and make their comments with a little stage fright, they are proud and honored (it shows) and their spouses also smile with pride. You can't measure personal rewards and benefits like this in any bank account.

These folks come from all backgrounds and dress accordingly. My electrician starts talking about this annual event in June of each year and has said his wife really looks forward to it, even though she's not much fun (his words, not mine).

Okay, now the bad news. This annual event costs approximately *$800 total*. That's right, room, food, booze, and tip for the waiters and bartender. Believe it or not, this is a nice restaurant just two blocks from my office. The paybacks can't be measured.

Benefits from the Annual Holiday Bash

Guess where I am on the vendors' lists of valued customers? I'm willing to bet Vista (my company) is probably at or near the top of each list. I might not be the biggest account, but I'm probably one of the best.

We've had a rash of horrible storms and tornadoes recently and guess where my tree guy put me on his priority list? I didn't even have to call him. He called me asking where to go first! In addition to the great business relationship this kind of event promotes, it makes me feel like a million bucks to see the wonderful feeling of appreciation and value of the skills, trades, and workmanship of these folks. Several vendors told me no one has ever done this for them and their spouses before. This is a great way to let those who make your business successful know that you really appreciate them, their work, and relationship. Not only are they doing a good job for you, they are a walking, talking billboard for your business by referring tenants, sellers, and loan customers.

Work on this one now and start planning for your own event for the coming holiday season. I'd like to hear how your party works for you. Here are some vendors and service people to consider: your banker(s), furnace person, electrician, plumber, carpenter, lawn service, resident manager(s), office manager, bookkeeper, CPA, attorney(s), siding and gutter person, tree service, pest control, roofer, insurance agent, highly valued real estate agent, auto mechanic, Section 8 inspector(s), helpful service clerk(s) at local hardware store, paint store, supply house, newspaper for your classified ads, your painter, garage killer, trash/junk hauler, and the person who lets you place your dumpster in their rear parking lot for free, and those law enforcement folks who help you out throughout the year. The invitation to your party creates goodwill even for people who cannot attend.

This is just a small list to assist you in identifying those who might be important links in your strong real estate chain. Good employees make your life easier and more profitable.

CHAPTER 6

The Many Hats You Wear as an Investor

As an investor and landlord, you wear many hats (see Figure 6.1). In the following list, check off the hats you wear:

✔ Spouse
✔ Parent
✔ Son or daughter
✔ Brother or sister
✔ Aunt or Uncle
✔ Grandparent
✔ Neighbor
✔ Church member
✔ Hobbies and other interests
✔ Employee? (if you have a job)
✔ Investor
✔ Property owner
✔ Buyer
✔ Property manager (landlord)
✔ Seller
✔ Asset protector
✔ Taxpayer
✔ Business owner
✔ Insurance guardian
✔ Legal decision maker @ investing
✔ Estate planner
✔ Rehabber
✔ People manager
✔ Marketer

FIGURE 6.1   It's Gotta Roll and Can't Be Lopsided

✔ Student
✔ Mentor
✔ Plus many more

The bottom line with all of this has an absolute *must* factor. Your *life wheel* *must* be able to roll. It won't roll if it is square. It can be a bit lopsided, but it still must roll. If you allow any of your hats to eat up part of your other hats, you will create a monster or, at best, a time-eating, cash-eating, painful hobby. Knowing this up front will make your investing path much smoother and less chaotic.

Let's go through some of your hats:

Investor: This is a huge hat. Do you have goals? Objectives? What do you want from investing? Do you want a painful hobby or financial independence?

Buyer: This is a major stumbling block for investors, including me. I got caught up in setting aggressive goals of buying and acquiring rental property with a straightforward mind-set:

✔ Buy an ugly, broken house.
✔ Fix it up, make it pretty.
✔ Put a tenant in it.
✔ Do it again, and do it again.

This lesson from the School of Hard Knocks might look simple to many folks, but it sure blindsided me. Since I made my mistakes, I have seen many other investors head down the same road and fall victim to the same hidden pothole of misery. Here is the short version of the journey.

Somewhere, somehow, I discovered a wonderful magic pill called real estate investing: I can buy property with no money out of my pocket and let somebody else pay for it. It also puts money in my pocket monthly, gives me tax benefits, and goes up in value! *Where can I sign up!*

Once I convinced myself and Tammy that this was really true, I launched my aggressive buying machine. I bought houses simply to put another notch in my belt. Plugging tenants in them was pretty easy, too. Move on to the next one.

Well, much to my surprise my property manager hat (landlord) began to appear like one of those mirages seen in the movies when folks travel across the desert. I had to deal with tenant problems: not paying rent, making late payments, tearing up stuff I had just rehabbed, not cutting the grass, not properly handling trash, keeping animals without permission, having unauthorized occupants, filing evictions, signing work orders, and more and more and more.

Nobody Told Me about This Part!

It was an almost unbelievable discovery. I couldn't imagine anyone not being responsible like me. Oh, yeah, I had seen plenty of the Jerry Springer types when making police runs to houses in run-down neighborhoods and could accept that not everybody lived in a clean home like mine; however, I just assumed everybody pretty much paid their bills. *False!*

This rude awakening is not something you can play ostrich with and bury your head hoping it will go away. Just the opposite will happen. Ignore the problems and they will get worse. Many investors have tried that approach only to end up with a train wreck. When their tenants stopped paying rent, the result was a cash-eating monster. Investors who could not make their mortgage payments ruined their credit, and their properties ended up in foreclosure because it was impossible to pay off the deficit. They had traveled too far down the path of no return.

Some investors get a huge buying machine cranked up with radio ads, billboards, bus benches, and TV ads. Meanwhile, the other hats associated with being an investor can really eat up those investors' time if they don't plan properly. Many investors almost shut down every year at tax time while they are getting stuff together for taxes, going over the numbers, and completing Form 1099s. Their mammoth advertising bill keeps cranking, and they can't respond to any leads from their advertising because they are buried in tax stuff. Their advertising meter and other expenses don't turn off when this happens.

As a buyer, raise your head up and look down the road. What is going to happen? Owning and operating rental property is not like owning stock. There's a little more to it.

In operating rental properties, *the quality of your property parallels the quality of your tenant.* That is the real magic pill.

After realizing this, I focused tremendous effort and emphasis on tenant screening. Putting the right tenants in my properties sure makes landlording much easier.

Property Manager (Landlord)

This one hat will grow your wealth while you sleep, eat, think, shower, vacation, and live and love life. It allows you to crank it 24-7 every day of the year, including holidays. Heck, it even cranks while you are working at your job! Learn to love it!

All the Other Hats

The other hats you wear as an investor have specific concerns and *consequences.* When I went to my first monthly meeting for investors in my town, some estate-planning expert from another state was giving a presentation on how to chop up your assets into blocks of $600,000; this would save your estate gobs and gobs of money in inheritance taxes or some kind of tax. I wasn't the least bit interested in anything he had to say or offer because I didn't have any estate. My net worth wasn't looking too good at the time. A whole lot of debt and a lot of real estate. I convinced myself that I would worry about estate planning years later when I had something to protect.

Those few years clicked by pretty quickly. A buddy of mine passed away as well as one of my mentors, Ed Melton Sr. It was time to do the estate planning thing. Tammy and I hired the best estate-planning attorney we could find. He led us blindly down the road of building a wonderful estate plan for our two young daughters. It covered such things as their living expenses, a legal guardian, and educational expenses, and provided for graduated or incremental disbursements with the last and biggest disbursement occurring for each daughter on her 45th birthday.

Many entities were needed to pull off this grand master estate plan. They included *revocable* and *irrevocable* trusts, multimember limited liability companies with minority interests, living wills, health care directives, last will and testament, charitable remainder trusts (CRTs), and family limited partnerships (this is just the stuff I'm rattlin' off the top of my head).

Here's where I sort of shot myself in the foot again. A huge legal bill for preparing all this stuff accompanied the process. It came to several thousand dollars, besides the filing fees, all for about a 6-inch-high stack of documents that we had to sign.

FIGURE 6.2 Interlocking Rings

The ugly surfaced at tax time, every year. This wonderful grand master estate plan was crucifying Tammy and me. It seemed as if we had more tax returns to file than we had deeds to properties. Tax returns were not prepared for free. We paid our CPA to do our tax returns because we liked his name and "CPA" signed on our tax returns right next to our signatures.

Each one of those trusts, entities, and CRTs had a tax identification (ID) number, and almost all of them required filing a separate annual tax return. Blah!

Lesson learned. A Grand Master Plan involving any one hat might crucify you in another arena. Just like those interlocking rings, what might be good and wonderful in one arena might cause chaos and more expenses in another circle (see Figure 6.2).

You must look at the cost benefit for you in the big picture. Keeping that in mind, as well as keeping yourself aware of all the hats you wear, will make the road much smoother for you and your family.

CHAPTER 7

Laws—Common Sense
Is Not Allowed

In this chapter, I discuss forms, laws, and the hats investors wear. I tackle the painful, hidden confusion and frustration that investors can experience when they are simply trying to do the right thing.

When I got started as a real estate investor, I had a job as a plain clothes detective in my town. I'd like to think I was promoted from uniform patrolman because I did a good job. Some of the baggage associated with being a good cop involves your knowledge of the laws, your people skills, and a good work ethic, along with an acceptable and not too offensive level of confidence and authority when needed.

With all this cop stuff already in my noggin, I had a serious handicap that I failed to see or grasp. I was totally in the dark on this one. I thought or assumed I had the legal side all figured out. I was the guy who was going to court every day, dealing with the "criminal side only" of the courthouse, and slamming defense attorneys at every opportunity when they represented or tried to help "dirtbags and tax-eaters" who took pride in ripping off taxpayers and honest people. It drives attorneys bonkers when police think they know all the laws.

So, I captured a little two-bedroom HUD house, renovated it using my hands and elbow grease (to save money . . . big mistake) and then plugged in an ex-con who had gone to prison for writing bad checks. At that time, I had no clue how to process a rental application or where to even get one.

Here's what I did. I ran up to my local office supply store and started browsing through the forms section. Aha—I found it! A rental application and a lease! I was in business! Here comes the story of my dangerous behavior. Having never taken the most basic class or even read a book about investing or landlording, I simply chose to do what I thought I knew. What I'm about to tell you is absolutely wrong and illegal. Ignorance of the law is not an excuse; however, I was dumber than a brick in this situation.

My applicant filled out the application, and I made a beeline for my police station office and did a little local check to see if the applicant had been arrested on any criminal charges. Sure enough, not only had he been arrested, but he had a history of writing bad checks and had even been sent to prison for "hanging paper." Now, I thought I was a sharp cookie for this neat little discovery, and I met with my applicant again.

Once again, my confidence level combined with a little authority sort of put me in a unique situation. I simply confronted "Jim" about his little financial habit of writing bad checks and proceeded to let him know he would have to be a *cash only* tenant. Jim agreed, and I immediately pulled out my lease agreement like an expert investor, did the paperwork, and gave him the keys.

I was lucky. Jim turned out to be a great guy with an ugly past. I could write a whole chapter on just our relationship over the years. We made a win-win relationship for both of our families. Jim and his family are still with us today in their third Vista home. His two oldest kids are grown and married with kids of their own, and Jim's youngest is in high school.

After having done this first rental house slick as a whistle, I repeated the same process on our second rental property. Here's where my term in the School of Hard Knocks really began. The house across the street from the first rental house went up for sale. It was identical to the first one—same floor plan and square footage. I used the same rental application and the same lease agreement.

About three or four months down the road, Jim kept paying on time like clockwork. The second rental house tenant was another story. I heard so many excuses that I probably went through all the grandmothers dying, aunts and uncles getting sick, paychecks getting lost in the mail, and more. I fell for the alibis and allowed the tenant to make measly little payments that didn't put a dent in the total amount owed.

Then my wife, Tammy, jerked my chain. I think she might have even called me stupid for putting up with these folks. The big E word was lurking around the next corner for me. Here I was, the all-knowing cop about the courthouse and legal system and I was totally in the dark about this thing called an *eviction*. I didn't have a clue where to go or how to get started.

After realizing these tenants weren't going to pay, I had to take some legal action. I traveled to the courthouse and found the department for starting the eviction process. I filled out the paperwork the clerk handed to me, and then she told me I had to pay about $50 or so to file the papers that would start the eviction process. The court system calls this a *forcible detainer action*. I assumed that not paying rent was a crime and I was a victim. *Wrong!* That was a shock to me because I usually got paid to go to court and I had never seen a victim charged a fee to go to court. (Attorneys are grinning big time on this one.)

The Court Date

After paying my $50 or so to the clerk, she gave me a court date. I asked, "Why am I getting a court date? These folks have not paid their rent for almost three months and I want them out now!" (I was about to get my wings clipped again.) I was informed that the tenants have the opportunity to appear in court and present their side of the story to a judge. I was beginning to boil now. I was totally shocked that these dirtbags got to stay in my house while this whole process was going on. To really tick me off, my court date was about three weeks away . . . another month with no rent. I was getting my clock cleaned on both ends now. The tenants were laughing at the stupid cop landlord, and Tammy was on my butt something fierce. Plus, now I had to make the mortgage payment for this rental house from our grocery money (not really, but that's the way it felt).

It Gets Worser! (Kentucky Word)

I was foaming at the mouth and waiting for my court date. I was used to going to court and flat-out slamming criminals. I always had all my i's dotted and my t's crossed. One of my favorite sayings to defense attorneys was "let's tee it up" (meaning, I'm not afraid to go to trial because I've got my whole case in order with absolutely no loose ends).

Off to Eviction Court I went. I had my files—my great logbook of chronological activity in dealing with this tenant—and I was just so looking forward to slamming them and getting them thrown out of our rental house. My tenants showed up in court with a free legal aid attorney. The judge called our case, and I proceeded up to the bench in front of the judge, and my tenants with their attorney did the same. I even knew the judge sitting on the bench. Detective Mike Butler [me] had a reputation in this courthouse as an excellent, thorough police officer and detective (I thought I might have an edge with this judge knowing me . . . *false*).

The judge asked me about their nonpayment of rent. I informed the judge they had not paid rent for over three months. Then the judge asked the attorney for my tenants to respond. Their attorney immediately took off on a tangent about not having received proper notice from the landlord. I responded by pulling out my little chronological record of correspondence with the tenant, and I told the judge on these specific dates I informed the tenants that I would evict them if they didn't pay. Plus I had the signed lease agreement with me, where it spelled out in Paragraph 7 that they would be evicted if they did not pay rent.

Kaboom! . . . I'm thinking no-brainer. I win. Tenant loses. *False*. Landlord loses! What in the world was going on? I was about to explode! What part of this story did the judge miss? They did not pay their rent. I'm a victim!

Here's the real deal. I had just graduated from the School of Hard Knocks without ever knowing I had entered the classroom. Like most American towns today, my town has local and state landlord/tenant laws. In my town, landlords must give a tenant who does not pay rent a seven-day notice to pay their rent in full or return possession of the rental unit to the landlord.

In most states, specific language or words must be included in this Pay or Quit Possession Notice. Many states spell out in detail how this notice is to be given to your tenant. Some states say certified mail or registered mail. The bottom line is I did not follow our landlord/tenant law and my case was dismissed. I had to start over!

I was madder than a mashed duck! I was furious! This was not fair. Plus, when I told Tammy what happened, I think she called me stupid again. Unbelievably, I discovered I could not just return to the little room in the courthouse to file for another court date. I would only be repeating the same process I had just finished. Here's what I later learned the hard way: *If a Tenant doesn't pay rent in my town, I must:*

- Send the tenant a seven-day notice to pay or quit possession. It must include the proper language and some more stuff specific to my state and county.
- I have to be able to prove the tenant received the notice.
- If I accept any partial payments of rent from the tenant during this seven-day period, my eviction process will be thrown out and dismissed. I know this because I did it and received another big diploma from the School of Hard Knocks.
- Only after giving the tenant seven days to make the rent current, could I file for and start the eviction process in the court system.
- In my town, I would get a court date about three weeks down the road. If things went my way, the judge would give the tenant seven more days to get out, and then I would have to file for what is called a *writ for possession* or a court order to be executed by the sheriff's office. The sheriff's deputies physically remove the tenants from the property and return possession to the landlord. I thought the deputies removed the tenants' personal property in an action known as the *set-out.* Wrong! They enter the property, secure and remove any persons, and then supervise the set-out. The landlord must provide five people at the property, ready to go, before the deputies will execute the set-out warrant. (Your town will have different policies, too.)

Wow! So brutal! There's a whole lot more to it than this little bit.

Here's another frustration from the School of Hard Knocks. Several years ago (before I figured out the right way to screen applicants), I had another tenant who chose not to pay rent. Aha! I was all over this one! Got my seven-day letter out the right way and dotted my i's and crossed my t's. Tee it up!

Yup, I hit a home run. Tenant found guilty. I won and we moved forward in the court system to finally reach the physical set-out of this tenant from our property.

The sheriff's deputies showed up along with our five guys to forcibly remove the tenant and all his personal property. It was all placed carefully at the street on the curbside. I had brushed up on my landlord/tenant law after being burned in previous situations. I instructed my guys not to touch the tenant's property sitting at the curbside for at least 48 hours. Our landlord/tenant law states the landlord shall leave the tenant's property on the street for at least 48 hours to allow the tenants to gather his belongings and move on his way.

Another kaboom! Mike lost again. The local city inspector happened to ride down the street and saw all the junk set out at curbside. Guess what the city inspector did? The property owner (me) got a citation and a $100 per day fine for having all this junk improperly set out at the curb.

Once again, I was furious! How could this be? Make up your dang-gone mind! This landlord/tenant law says I must give the tenant 48 hours before cleaning up his mess and disposing of his junk. Now the city was citing me for trying to do the right thing!

What's the Method to the Madness?

Here's the point I'm trying to get across. There are many different forms, rules, regulations, and laws. You can't become an expert on one particular set and assume you've got all of your bases covered.

Many laws contradict each other. You will find local, state, and federal laws with different rules and regulations for the same topic or situation. This is our wonderful legal system. Get used to it. It will not change. The long and short of the frustration about the tenant's property being placed at curbside from an eviction:

- My landlord/tenant law says it must sit there 48 hours.
- My local city ordinance issues a $100 per day fine.

What's the answer? As an investor, I was in a catch-22 position. I was backed in a corner either way. But I knew one thing for sure—I was not touching that personal property for 48 hours. I could appeal to some boss about the $100 daily fine, but if I violated the landlord/tenant law, the tenant might be in a position to take me to court to replace all his valuable personal property (junk to you and me).

In the preceding situation, I was wearing the hat of a property owner in one position and the hat of a landlord in the other. And I still had all the other hats involving my job, family, investor, and more.

This is not information about the eviction process but it shows you how frustrating it can be to operate legally and successfully in our world of real estate investing.

Here's another example. Odds are you have probably heard of the Federal Housing Administration (FHA) and the Section 8 Program operated by the U.S.

Department of Housing and Urban Development (HUD). Both are federal government agencies involved in residential housing across the United States.

These two government agencies made me pull my hair out the first time I had to deal with their regulations. The Section 8 program requires the housing unit to pass the HQS (Housing Qualification Standards) of the Section 8 program before a family can be placed in your unit and receive subsidized rent payments from HUD. Being a good and responsible investor, I got my own copy of the Housing Qualification Standards (HQS) for Section 8. Here are a couple of things I recall. To qualify as a bedroom, the room had to have a minimum of 70 square feet, a ceiling height of no less than 84 inches (7 feet) and a window with a minimum of 5 square feet for exit in case of a fire. Sounds pretty reasonable doesn't it? I thought so except for the 7-foot ceilings. (As a kid, I stayed in an upstairs room with a ceiling height of about 5.5 ft.)

During part of my early investing career, I bought broken houses, rehabbed them, and sold them at retail prices usually to a first-time home buyer. Almost always, the first-time home buyer would use some kind of FHA guaranteed loan resulting in a home inspection to meet FHA housing guidelines.

I dropped my teeth again. I took an ugly house, made it real pretty and nice—a super renovation! New cabinets, wiring, roof, kitchen, bathroom, and all the bells and whistles. This beautifully renovated home failed the FHA inspection because a bedroom did not have a closet. This house happened to be a shotgun style house (one-story home built similar in same to a mobile home, except the front door and back door on the ends allowing a person to see clean through the entire house from the front to the rear . . . thus a person standing at the front door could shoot a person standing outside the back door) and never had closets in any bedroom.

I made a huge mistake assuming the HUD Section 8 Program housing guidelines were used by all federally funded agencies. Wrong!

The FHA has its own housing qualifications and many items are completely different from the rules of other federal agencies.

The Ultimate Icing on the Cake!

In the late 1990s, Dick and Sandy Vreeland, along with Rob Massey, encouraged me and several other investor/brokers in our town to create a local chapter of National Association of Residential Property Managers (NARPM). I signed on as one of the local charter members.

We met once a month at a nice country club and the leadership of our group would have a speaker at our luncheon to keep us up to date in our field of investing and managing property. One of the early meetings featured an enforcement officer from the federal fair housing agency. This was an eye-opening experience for me both as an investor and as a landlord.

This well-educated officer represented her agency very professionally and offered a question-and-answer session following her presentation. This was the same era when the Americans with Disabilities Act (ADA) rules and regulations were coming out of Washington.

Here's the eye-opener: There were many questions about rental applications especially since this new ADA law was out in our world. This enforcement officer after being asked a question, rattled off a small list of things you can ask and not ask on a rental application.

I can't tell you how many real estate investor seminars and conferences I've attended where I was blasted for having certain questions on my rental application, especially one that asked an applicant's date of birth.

About a dozen sharp veteran investors, including me, about fell out of our chairs when the enforcement officer told us: *"It's okay to ask for a* date of birth *for identification purposes on your rental application. . . . You cannot ask applicants for housing how old they are!"*

Talk about our tax dollars at waste! We could not believe what she just said. Here is what was amazing—this woman was dead serious. She was not laughing!

What can you do? Here are some tips to minimize your forced placement into the School of Hard Knocks:

- Get your own hard copy of your state's and your town's landlord/tenant laws and become familiar with the basic do's and don'ts.
- Find a *competent local real estate attorney* who is knowledgeable about real estate laws in your town. Avoid family members and friends at work or church.
- Join a group in your town allowing you to network and stay abreast of local laws involving investors.

Be especially cautious with forms. Run them by your competent real estate attorney or take the ideas and concepts from my forms and work them into your forms by adding another paragraph or section. As an active police officer in my town, I thought I had a grip on the legal system and our court system. Although I was greener than Shrek when it came to real estate investing and landlording, I honestly believed I had the upper hand or a trump card because I was a police officer. Wrong! Here are just a few of the School of Hard Knocks real-life seminars I attended and graduated from with honors.

School of Hard Knocks

Lesson 1: Forms—Rental Agreement or Lease

Now remember, folks, I had access to absolutely no one who could act as a mentor or provide basic advice about landlording and investing. As a cop, I thought I knew all this stuff. I resorted to asking criminal defense attorneys or our prosecutors.

They don't have a clue about landlording laws other than what they recall from law school.

Make it part of your investing program to have an excellent, knowledgeable real estate attorney on your team. Have your attorney review your rental agreement for several reasons:

- Fair housing
- Lead-based paint laws
- Mold, mildew, and environmental hazards such as asbestos
- Compliance with your landlord/tenant laws in your town and state (Some states such as Pennsylvania almost require lease agreements to be approved by the state's attorney general because of a consumer protection concern that the form should be easy for the tenant to understand.)
- Forms such as late notices and "pay or quit possession notices"
  —Make sure they are legal and proper.
  —Learn how to properly word them.
  —Include as many safeguards as possible to protect yourself (consult your attorney).
  —Ask about the most common mistakes made by landlords so you won't fall victim to the same errors.
- Follow the same process for all your important legal processes and forms, such as:
  —Rental Application
  —Rental Agreement, Lease Agreement
  —Lease/Options
  —Option to Buy Agreement
  —Move-In Inspection Form
  —Late Notices (for nonpayment of rent)
  —Rental Agreement Violation Notice (for things other than nonpayment of rent—grass too tall, music too loud, and so on)
  —Property Inspection Notices (48 hours, 72 hours, and so on)
  —Proper handling of tenant's security or damage deposit
  —Fair housing laws (both federal and local)
  —Do's and don'ts for collections
  —Tenant chargeable repairs (during tenancy and after moving out)
  —Unauthorized occupants
  —Locks (some states do not allow dead bolts)
  —Smoke alarms
  —Additional issues with multiunit buildings
- If central heat and air, the seasonal change dates
- Common area housekeeping responsibilities

- Utilities
  —Renter's insurance
  —Catch-up payment plans (are they allowed; do they kill your eviction process? Most states stipulate that if a landlord accepts any kind of partial payment of rent after the eviction process has been started, the eviction action will be dismissed.)
  —Fees and forms associated with tenant chargeable fees

Lesson 2: Written Correspondence Is Evidence or Proof

Judge Wapner, on the *People's Court,* began a case by allowing each party to make a short statement. After that, he wanted proof. It didn't really matter what it was, as long as it wasn't noise coming out of their head. It could be a phone log, a note with a date stamp on it, a chronological record, a notepad, or receipts. The point is that you need something other than "he said, she said" to make your case.

Although this may sound like overkill to some, document messages you receive from your tenants. I don't care if they leave a message on your answering machine or voice mail, if they mail in a note with their rent payment, fax you something, or send you an e-mail (I'm reluctant to encourage e-mails from tenants). Document it somehow and put it in your tenant's file folder. I strongly recommend one of those phone message pads from Office Depot or Staples with the carbonless copy that remains in the spiral-bound book. Take the original and place it in your tenant's file folder. Save these and write the dates on the front cover of the book. I can't tell you how many times I have used these messages to research phone numbers, dates, and things other than dealings with tenants.

Lesson 3: Learn the Differences in All the Rules, Laws, Regulations, and Ordinances in Your Town

You will be amazed at the number of laws that conflict. In my town, we have a local ordinance requiring property owners to be given a 10-day notice to cut their grass if an inspector sees grass 10 inches or higher, or the property owner will get a $100 per day fine for each day in violation of the local code.

Get ready to pull your hair out. My landlord/tenant law says I must give the tenant a 14-day notice to correct the rental agreement violation of the grass being too tall and unkempt. How can this be? This happens in many towns across the United States, not just mine.

You need to become aware of these conflicting laws and figure out how to operate as best you can in this challenging arena of being a real estate investor and landlord. You are not the first landlord to discover this. Many have gone before you and survived and many are doing it today and still survive.

Many of these issues are preventable by doing your homework on the front end and selecting only quality tenants.

Lesson 4: Fair Housing Laws

This is sacred territory. It goes hand in hand with the American Dream. The federal government and local governments across our country bend over backward to protect people and their homes. There are seven protected classes within the Federal Fair Housing Act (taken from HUD's web site):

> *In General—It shall be unlawful for any person or other entity whose business includes engaging in residential real estate-related transactions to discriminate against any person in making available such a transaction, or in the terms or conditions of such a transaction, because of*

1. *Race*
2. *Color*
3. *Religion*
4. *Sex*
5. *Handicap*
6. *Familial Status*
7. *National Origin*

Many local communities are adding sexual orientation to their local fair housing laws. It is your responsibility to know the rules and regulations if you want to rent property. I can't tell you how many times I locked somebody up for a criminal offense and the perpetrator said, "I didn't know that was against the law."

Fair housing involves a lot of other concerns. Ultimately, it really does mean being fair to all people. Here are a few examples of things investors may not immediately associate with fair housing:

- *Steering:* Trying to persuade tenants to go to a certain neighborhood or trying to prevent them from going to a specific neighborhood
- *Available units:* Not showing all available units to prospective tenants or disclosing all available units
- *Qualifying standards:* Not having written qualifying standards for your property

For details straight from the horse's mouth, here's HUD's web site address for complete information on fair housing: http://www.usdoj.gov/crt/housing/title8.htm.

FIGURE 7.1   HUD Logo

Make sure the Equal Housing Opportunity notice is plastered all over your forms. Put it on your application, rental agreement, move-in and move-out forms, and even the front door and wall of your office and your web site. In my town, this is a major concern of enforcement officers.

This logo (Figure 7.1) is available for free on my web site at www .MikeButler.com; you can also get it free from HUD's web site. Use it on your forms.

The Americans with Disabilities Act (ADA)

Here is HUD's web site address for the housing concerns involving the American Disabilities Act: http://www.hud.gov/offices/fheo/disabilities/index.cfm.

Some of the highlights involve the definition of *service animals*. In the past, you and I might have thought of dogs only as pets; however, if a person has a medical necessity for an animal of some kind, it can be labeled a service animal, and not a pet. You might put yourself in a legal quagmire if you have a no-pets policy and refuse to rent to an applicant who has a service animal for medical reasons.

Another highlight involves the applicant's or tenant's request and desire to make the unit "handicap accessible." Your tenant in a wheelchair may want to widen the doorways, lower the bathroom and kitchen countertops, and perhaps install a ramp. The ADA pretty much says you must allow tenants to make these changes at their expense providing they return your unit to its original condition. I have not experienced this one personally, but I know some investors who have.

I bring this up because most rental agreements forbid tenants from altering or making structural changes to the property. Once again, you might be in violation of the ADA if you forbid this request from a disabled tenant. Ignorance of the law is not an excuse.

CHAPTER 8

CYA—Covering Your *ASS*ets

Asset protection and entity structuring are a critical part of your investment program.

Today, insurance companies are bailing out and backing off all kinds of coverage. Many old-timers and veteran investors have relied on insurance for asset protection. Just like many other forms of protection, those safeguards are fading away.

Watch TV commercials: Attorneys are advertising, "Please help us find somebody to sue!" What an ugly society. Bust your butt, work your tail off, and somebody wants to sue you. Accidents are almost a thing of the past. I guess people no longer are clumsy or uncoordinated, and kids don't slip or trip on things the way we did when we were growing up. Somebody's gotta pay.

As a real estate investor, you are *born with deep pockets*. This is the stereotype of the real estate investor. This label gets tattooed on landlords. Adapt now—stop calling yourself a landlord. Use the politically correct sign of the times. *property manager*. It puts you in the middle between the owner and the tenant. You are a problem solver. This really doesn't fix any problems, but it sure gives you an out when you are dealing with disputes, especially with local government agencies.

Because insurance is not a cure-all, we must plan to protect what we are growing. I have attended many seminars on this subject.

Here is the bottom line: There is only one way to avoid liability exposure.

Get Off the Planet!

You will always have liability on our planet. If you exist, you will have liability. Suppose you are driving your neighbor's car to the supermarket. In the store's parking lot, you run over Little Sally Shopper, who is pushing her grocery buggy. Who's gonna get sued? Probably your neighbor (the owner of the car) and you, because you were driving the vehicle.

There are basically two ways for folks to come after you: the front door and the back door.

The Front Door

- Something causes an injury and the injured party sues the owner of whatever caused that injury.
- Tenants who go after owners are usually using the front door.

The Back Door

- You do something personally (like running over Sally in the parking lot).
- Now the attorneys will sue *you* and go after everything you have an interest in.
- There is not much you can do about the back door, except get off the planet.

True Nightmare Story

At a real estate investor conference in Columbus, Ohio, a couple of years ago, I had the pleasure of sharing a dinner with a sharp aggressive investor from Illinois. He wanted me to tell his story as a warning to other investors. Let's call him "Jim."

Jim told me he set up his property management company as instructed and felt he had done a pretty good job in the asset protection battle plan arena; however, he had kept all his properties in *his personal name*.

Jim had a tenant who was angry about not receiving 100 percent of her security deposit after moving out of one of Jim's units. The tenant disagreed with Jim's cost of repairs and so on (normal stuff) and took her complaint to court.

Who got named in the tenant's lawsuit? The landlord was the expected defendant and was the property owner.

Jim was prepared to go to court and accept the charges as part of doing business as a landlord. He even took his checkbook with him. As expected, Jim lost the case. He wrote a check on the spot in the courtroom paying the money owed to the former tenant.

Whoa! It's not over. Remember, the judge made a *judgment* for the tenant and against Jim, the investor.

Okay, what's the catch? The judgment against the investor became a public record and ended up on Jim's personal history and his credit report even though it was paid in full.

Jim, an aggressive investor, was buying several properties a month and re-financing them to put cheap long-term financing in place. His credit score fell through the floor. No more A1 credit. No more cheap long-term loans. Whammo!

He told me he had several refinancings pending and he was relying on the cash from these refinancings to purchase properties for which he had already made cash deals. His entire operation had hit a huge stumbling block and rocked his world.

I am sure Jim can fix this mess with a lot of effort; however, he could have totally avoided it simply by using a land trust instead of taking title to property in his personal name.

You Can Fix It Now!

Here's the battle plan: I am a privacy nut according to most folks. In my previous life as an undercover cop, it was scary to see how much information is available to folks who could cause you some grief. Privacy is *not* protection. It is simply the first line of defense in a shell game or a smoke-and-mirrors game. Or you might say, it just helps to keep you off the radar or allows you to fly below it.

Don't advertise the number of properties you own or bump your gums about your success, especially to tenants and others who might envy you.

Technology improves almost at the speed of light. Any computer-competent person and most attorneys can research legal documents, county courthouse records, entity ownership, and much more without leaving their desk. This is the power of the wonderful tool called the Internet.

Let's just make it a little more challenging for them.

Use a *land trust* to help in the privacy department. If used in a simple manner, it provides no protection against liability. Yes, there are folks who argue against my comment here, and they could be right; however, this is part of the beginner basics, the foundation for a good solid plan of landlording on auto-pilot.

Simply put, the land trust is an instrument used to hide, not protect, the beneficial interest of the land trust.

Depending on the computers in your county clerk's office, each field may be limited to a certain number of characters. In my town, it used be 28 characters maximum. The above example where a tenant sues both the landlord and the owner, used properly, burns up 28 characters before the first comma.

Get your free downloadable "All Those Questions You Forgot to Ask about Using Land Trusts" complete four-page report at www.MikeButler.com (click on the Free Information Bar on the left side of the screen).

Entities

My attorney has thoroughly researched an entity that is available for real estate investors. Check with your experts in your town to see if the *single member, manager-managed limited liability company (LLC)* will work for you.

This entity is awesome. If you structure your entities properly by the kind of liability exposure of each, you can have the same benefits as the highly valued limited partnerships of years ago.

For those who have been around, you may recall the term *charging order*, which was used if the limited partnership got a judgment against it in court. The same applies to the single member, manager-managed LLC.

So, if somebody tried the back door after you ran over Little Sally Shopper in the parking lot and got a huge judgment against you, they would receive a charging order from the court against the single member, manager-managed LLC involved. Here is the interesting part: The manager of your single member, manager-managed LLC controls the disbursements of profits or dividends paid to the member (you). Your manager may choose to elect, for sound business purposes, not to disburse any funds to the member at this time.

Depending on the number of properties and the risks or exposures associated with them, you might want to have several single member, manager-managed LLCs. Before pulling the trigger on this, check it out with your expert in your state. In my state, it costs $48.00 to file new papers at the state capital to create an LLC and a $15.00 annual filing fee to maintain its status. Last year, a new state law took effect in Kentucky requiring each LLC to file a corporate return with a $175.00 fee. Prior to this new local law, we could choose to have the LLCs *not* exist for tax purposes, and we still have this choice for federal income taxes. I have heard some states have a $300.00 start-up fee and annual filing fee. Just do your homework and check out the law in your state.

Entity Structuring: How Do I Set It Up?

Let's keep it simple, as best we can. Let's look at a scenario for 25 owned properties. Let's say we have 14 high-quality properties and 11 low-end properties. Review the following assets to get an idea:

Entity	Assets
LLC 1	14 Rental Properties
LLC 2	11 Rental Properties
LLC 3	$100,000.00 in Cash
LLC 4	Your Property Management Company/Dealer

Now, remember, single member, manager-managed LLCs do not exist for federal tax purposes. To be proper and actually get the liability protection as intended, you must have a bank account for each LLC and be able to document (by bank statements) the activity of each LLC.

If you can't prove this, you will probably lose. Don't scream; just use LLC 4 as your property management company, and it can simply "settle up" with each LLC at regular intervals, perhaps at as seldom as once a year settling-up. No need to make things cumbersome and complicated by creating monthly reports or settlements. Since you own and control the owner and the management company, just make a one time annual settlement to each owner. Life can be so much simpler this way.

You can carry this over into vehicles owned, boats, planes, and more; however, this is a book about laying a good foundation as a landlord and investor.

What if You Have Zero Properties Today?

This involves passive and earned income concerns. In the beginning, you probably should not be structured with 25 rental properties, as in the preceding list because the property management company income is considered earned income.

When starting out, you might want to have two single member, manager-managed LLCs. Give one of them the name you want all your tenants to know and use when making and mailing their rent payments. In the beginning, this will be your buy-and-hold LLC.

Your other LLC will be your dealer LLC. As you grow, you will simply make amendments to the LLC allowing it to become your property management company and dealer, perhaps allowing it to be treated as a C-corporation with more benefits to you if used properly.

Asset protection should be an integral part of your landlording and investing program. It doesn't need to be superexpensive or as complicated as many experts recommend. A simple plan should not beat you up unnecessarily with extra tax returns that you must file or cumbersome hoops that you must jump through.

To get the same version that I use in my business today, visit www .MikeButler.com and click on the link to CYA-Protecting Your Assets. This in-depth home study course was researched and developed specifically for real estate investors by real estate attorney Harry Borders of Borders and Borders Attorneys in Louisville, Kentucky, and includes my input and concerns.

Fatal Mistakes Involving Asset Protection

- Listening to bad advice
- Thinking you can set it up and forget It. (Work and specific duties and responsibilities are associated with creating entities; you gotta do stuff.)
- Comingling funds (credit cards)
- Creating entities and never opening bank accounts for them because your wonderful advisor never told you to do so (This actually happened to me. They [expert advisors at the time] took my money to create an entity and never told me I had to open a bank account! This one misstep eliminated all my protection. The sad and

absolutely terrifying thing, when looking back at this huge mistake on my part, is that I was operating without any protection while being led to believe I was almost bullet proof. I didn't know anything about it.)

- Transferring title from personal to entity without realizing that it destroys all your asset protection
- Failing to understand how an entity's existence is *proven* (bank statements in addition to records)
- Ignoring filing of annual renewal reports, fees
- Total ignorance of must do's involved with each entity—minutes, reports, and so on
- Keeping your insurance agent in the dark (Insurance agents should not be your enemy. They should be part of your team.)
- Using your own property management company without having a signed management agreement and fee and paying the fee for the service
- Playing games with a land trust's beneficial interest *after the fact*

This list of fatal mistakes was developed by my attorney, Harry Borders, based on the mistakes he has observed investors commit frequently.

The Six *Must* Questions to Ask Your Expert Advisor about Asset Protection

Q1: What's best and how many for privacy, asset protection, and taxes?

- What are the costs of each entity, plus annual fees?
- Does each require another tax return?
- Are balance sheets required?
- What stuff must I do to keep the entity in good legal standing and in good solid sound "bullet proof" status as far as "operating the entity"?

Q2: What are the pros and cons of having your own property management company?
Q3: Is there a difference between "real estate investor" and "real estate dealer?"
Q4: For tax purposes, how many ways can I sell real estate?
Q5: Are Land Trusts:

- Good, bad?
- How do they work?
- How much do you charge?

Q6: (Tax advisor question) Explain the Passive Activity Loss Rule. Can I offset my rental losses against other income?

PROVEN WAYS TO CAPTURE HIGH-QUALITY LIFETIME TENANTS

This is your meat and potatoes. Picture yourself having high quality tenants like June and Ward Cleaver in all of your units.

Odds are it's a very safe bet you will have minimal trouble and problems, if any, like the nightmare stories told by all of those other landlords.

As a rule of thumb, "the quality of the unit parallels the quality of your tenants." Good tenants usually aren't attracted to nasty, dirty units.

This section gives you a buffet or smorgasbord of tips and techniques to capture and keep great tenants for a lifetime!

CHAPTER 9

Marketing and Advertising Including a Zero-Dollar Budget

In discussing this topic, I begin with the same zero-dollar advertising budget I had when I started and progress up to a full-blown office with a full-time office manager:

- *Homemade yard sign:* I used plywood, some old paint, and my pager number.

- *Handmade or computer-generated flyers and posters:* I placed them in the window of the vacant property, which meant prospects had to get out of their car and walk up to the house to see the rent, deposit, and contact information. Use bright paper—yellow or neon green. Do not use white. Do not use those clear or plastic flyer boxes that hang on a yard sign. Applicants steal them to keep other prospective tenants (their competition) from getting your flyers.

  Place flyers in the neighborhood of your rental:

    - Grocery stores
    - Coin-operated laundries
    - Pawnshops
    - Restaurants
    - Any retail outlet with a community bulletin board
    - Apartment community vending or laundry area (be prepared for phone calls if you do this one)
    - Apartment community parking lot
    - Church bulletin board
    - Hardware stores

- *Section 8:* When I was getting started in my town, I pretty much had to take on some Section 8 Rental Voucher tenants to fill vacancies. It was a necessary risk when I was a novice investor. This government agency would let us put available properties on the list that they gave to would-be tenants. It was a free service at the time.

- *Business cards:* Odds are you will get some business cards announcing that you are an investor who buys property. Let people know what you intend to do with the properties you buy. I developed the slogan for my company: *VISTA— We Buy Houses, We Rent Homes!* You can get free business cards at www.vistaprint.com which is no kin or relationship to me (see Figure 9.1).

FIGURE 9.1   Business Cards

- *Peel-and-stick business card magnets:* I tried the laminated business card magnets and was disappointed. They were shiny, but the colors looked dull, not bright, as originally ordered. The peel-and-stick business card magnets I found at Staples and Office Depot work great. They are easy to use. Just peel the sticker off, and apply your business card. Whammo!

  I kept a stack of them in the door pocket of my truck. Every time I visited a home for sale, I would slap a magnet on the fridge while telling the seller it was a free gift. I never asked for permission to do so. Easier to ask for forgiveness.

  Our tenants also got one of these magnets for their fridge. It was right under their nose, with our web site and phone numbers readily available, reminding them and all their guests, We Rent Homes!

  Send them out in your marketing pieces, letters to sellers, and so on.

- *Referrals:* These are the number one source of effective advertising. Let your tenants, your sellers, your buyers, your real estate agents, and your attorneys know you rent homes. Offer to pay them a referral fee if a lead becomes one of your tenants.

When I graduated to a small budget for advertising, I used a bit more expensive marketing pieces:

- *Professional yard signs:* You can get these signs reasonably priced and design your own custom sign at Dee Sign Company in Ohio. Their phone number is (800) DEE-SIGN. Figure 9.2 shows the first yard sign I used before I had the web site:
  —*Sign 1,* with removable 6-inch by 24-inch inserts, allowed for easy changes in management decisions from pager numbers to cell phones, to hiring a disabled person to take phone calls.
  —*Sign 2* promotes both buying and renting as well as my web site.
- *Corner signs:* These direct prospects to available rentals. They are created from crack-and-peel neon colored paper, which is available at most printers. I don't recall seeing this kind of paper at office supply stores.
- *Classified ads in the newspaper:* As a typical tightwad investor refusing to spend a lot of money on almost anything, I combined these ads into one classified ad. Classified ads are very expensive! The ad would be placed in the "Houses Unfurnished" classified ad category and would read something like the text shown in Figure 9.3.

  The phone number listed in the ad was a pager number. While working a full-time job, I found this to be a great tool. Not only did my pager have the pager number used to contact me for my job as a police officer, but I discovered I could add up to two more numbers on one pager. That's pretty neat.

FIGURE 9.2   Rent Signs

- *Web site:* This is by far, the number one marketing tool today. Although these were not yet popular when I was getting started, web sites today are an absolute must. If you have average computer knowledge, you should be able to get your own web site up and running for about $20.00 per month, providing you have patience and enough creativity to design your own web site (see Figure 9.4).

FIGURE 9.3   Classified Ads

South, East, West

123 Main St.	3BR	$599
321 Maple	3BR	$749
1412 Oak	4BR	$799

2,3,4 Bedroom Homes
Rent & Rent w/Option

www.VistaKy.com

502-896-2595

FIGURE 9.4   **We Rent Homes! Screen Shot**

Perhaps you could hire one of your kids to put it together. Kids today know a lot more about computers and the Internet than most parents, and your son or daughter probably would enjoy the challenge. Technology is blazing in our society!

—Musts for your web site. (Try to kill as many birds with one stone mind-set. My web site promotes We Buy Houses, We Rent Homes.) To help market your rentals, include a list of expected vacant units. Don't wait until they're empty.

- Give the folks who visit your web site the opportunity to fill out some kind of form that will allow you to call them back. I call this our Call-Back form.

- Check out my real estate web site at www.VistaKY.com to see it in action. We get dozens of these forms weekly from folks who are looking for homes to rent.

- Don't even think your kind of tenants don't use the Internet. Baloney again. They surf the Internet while they are at work!

- The flip side to this web site thing is to also have a page or two describing how you buy property; once again, provide a form for potential sellers to complete that will be automatically e-mailed to you. Today, this is my number one lead generator for buying property. In fact, I have stopped running my classified ad about buying property.

- Include your web site in your classified ads. Most newspapers have a web site where readers can search and view the classified ads online. If you have your web site in your classified ad, they can click on the link and go directly to your site.

- Include answers to all those questions prospects will ask. Address and spell out your qualifying standards, how to see a unit, security deposits, restrictions for pets, who pays utilities, renter's insurance, and so on. The more information I put on the web site, the fewer questions people ask on the phone.

- Include photos of your properties, inside and outside.

- Include a map. You can copy and paste a map from MapQuest or Google right into your web site.

- If you're not savvy enough or do not want to build your own site, Jeff Adams, a good friend, a Los Angeles Firefighter, and fellow real estate investor, has a great turn key web site product for investors and you can get more information about Jeff on my website at www.MikeButler.com and click on the resources navigation bar.

- Another great resource to get your properties on the Internet is my good friend Rob Massey at www.Rentalhouses.com. We advertise on this web site with links to our web site.

—Some don'ts for your web site:

- Don't encourage applicants to communicate via e-mail. Use the phone.

- Don't allow your tenants to communicate via e-mail. Use written correspondence.

- Your web site should be the place to go if you're looking for a place to rent or if you have a property to sell. Everybody else, including your tenants, should be directed to your office or virtual office.

- Don't make your web site address too long; create something short. I have the web site www.VistaPropertiesInc.com, which is a very long address. It costs more to advertise in classifieds due to the extra lines it takes up. I created www.VistaKY.com as a short, easy-to-use web site address. Perhaps the initials of your property management company along with your state identifier would be short and to the point.

- *Calendars:* These cheap peel-and-stick calendars were placed in almost all the Louisville police cars and almost all the Yellow Cabs in my town (see Figure 9.5). Attorneys and real estate agents got them, too. These were supercheap, effective ads to keep under people's noses all year. If I were still doing this today, I would include my web site. These cost about 29 cents each when ordered in quantity. I ordered them from Viking Office Supplies.

- *Grocery store receipt tapes:* These are also an effective advertising media. You could target the receipt tapes for specific neighborhoods. Prices will vary depending on the size and number of stores you select. When I used this media, I again advertised "We Buy Houses, We Rent Homes" and included my web site.

- *Local stock cars:* This was an eye-opener for me. Rick Heine, a police buddy of mine who is in the K-9 unit, had a hobby of racing Figure 8 cars on the weekends at our local track. Rick phoned me one day asking if he could talk to me about sponsoring a car. Uh-oh, I'm thinking, here comes a bottomless pit cash-eating machine. I had heard war stories about how expensive those Nascar and Winston Cup cars were, and I expected local cars to be just a few notches below those guys. (It can't be cheap to build a car, drive it crazy tearing wheels and tires off, crashing it, and doing it all over again next weekend.)

To my surprise, I was able to get the whole car sponsorship for the entire year for a flat $1,000. They put my company logo, web site, and phone numbers on the top, the sides, and the hood of this car. A neat thing happened when the announcer at the race track identified the car and the driver. They were designated as the "Vista We Buy Houses We Rent Homes number 26 driven by Rick Heine." This was blasted over the loudspeakers, all through the

FIGURE 9.5   Calendar

grandstands and the clubhouse during the race, provided they were somewhere near the front or were the leaders.

When they won a race, they were identified in this manner and had a Winner's Circle photo made (see Figure 9.6). We have several of these photos in our office today.

This was awesome because the people sitting in the stands were the profile target of most of our tenants and most of our sellers. I got a lot of comments about this car.

- *Two-sided key tags:* These things work (see Figure 9.7). Get bright yellow with reflective blue lettering. Give them to every tenant and use them with your Key Sign Out Program for viewing your vacant units. Once again, today I would also work in my web site address.

- *Door hangers:* Your local print shop probably has these prepunched cards ready to go. Create your own and use them in place of business cards (see Figure 9.8). They are great to keep in your car or truck and pass out to bird dogs and your maintenance crew. Use them in your property management business for reminders of missed work order appointments, nasty notes to tenants to do this or that, or even a positive mention to tenants for doing a good job on their flower boxes.

FIGURE 9.6   Race Car

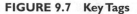
FIGURE 9.7   Key Tags

Door hanger cards are precut with a loop at the top to fasten to the door. They are cheap and sure work more efficiently than trying to tape or slide a business card into a storm door.

- *Coffee cups, mugs:* It's okay to get a few. I have a good relationship with my closing attorney Harry Borders. He has them on every closing table in their office to hold pens. Awesome. Imagine the seller's perception of your real estate business when your coffee mug is sitting on the closing table at the attorney's office (see Figure 9.9). Also give them to your vendors at the holiday party and to your tenants. Coffee cups last a long time.

- *Baseball caps:* They work great providing you only give them to people who wear them. If they're not wearing a baseball cap, don't give them your baseball cap. My siding guy, Ed Weck, would keep two or three of my Vista We Buy Houses, We Rent Homes! caps around. He had a dirty old work cap, and he had a formal or dress baseball cap for nice functions.

- *Golf shirts, T-shirts:* I used black golf shirts and T-shirts screen printed with our company logo and slogan and phone number. Our rehab guys wore them, too. For the hot days of summer, I got them some light gray T-shirts and tank

FIGURE 9.8   Door Hanger

FIGURE 9.9   Coffee Cups, Mugs

tops. The shirts looked professional and loudly announced what our company is about.

- *Jackets:* We used them in the same manner as the shirts. Most of the time, our rehab guys would wear the windbreakers in cold weather. It instilled a sense of professionalism on our part, and the tenants liked them too.

- *Real estate show on local cable TV:* I developed a 15-second color spot pitching Vista We Buy Houses, We Rent Homes! I included our phone number and our web site. This worked very well, and when I was tracking my marketing, many tenants reported that they remembered seeing our ad on TV although it hadn't been shown for almost two years. These things stick in people's minds.

- *Bus benches:* Ads on benches are expensive, and I witnessed many local investors get their clocks cleaned on this one. I did not want to be in the business of buying advertising to make bus bench companies rich. The rate, by the way, when I checked into it was about $60 per month, per bench.

- *Billboards:* When I priced them, they were outrageous. The same local investor who used bus benches signed on with a large billboard company. Although he got great exposure, he sure pulled the plug on billboard advertising pretty darn quick.

These are some of the marketing ideas I've used to rent properties and buy houses. Pick and choose the methods that fit your budget and that appeal to you. Some will work and some probably won't. A lot also depends on your market and your region.

What Can You Do When Your Market Has Too Many Units and Not Enough Tenants?

Does this sound familiar? Is your town going through one of these painful cycles where there are too many rental houses and not enough tenants? Are you left with trying to select your tenants from the "cream of the crap?" What happened? Where did all our good tenants go?

Not that long ago, I simply put up a yard sign and Whammo! The phone started ringing, and wanna-be tenants began swarming all over my property like hornets from a disturbed nest; things weren't too bad. All I had to do was dot my i's and cross the t's when I processed rental applications.

Back then, perhaps I'd have an open house to create a frenzied competition and sense of urgency among the applicants to take action now. This allowed them to see other folks who wanted the same unit and the race was on. Many times, six or more applications were turned in after one open house.

My open houses were never like those held by a traditional real estate agent. In the beginning, I made the mistake of promoting or announcing an open house say on Monday, from 5:00 to 6:00 P.M., or, worse yet, on Sunday afternoon. But here's what happened. The bozos all showed up at 5:50 P.M., 10 minutes before 6!

This prompted an almost immediate change. Here's the result, and remember, this was done while I was working a full-time job. Suppose I had three vacant units (at this time, I was primarily renting single-family houses), our ads would promote:

House 1, open at 5:30 P.M.

House 2, open at 6:00 P.M.

House 3, open at 6:30 P.M.

This allowed me to be more efficient and move from unit to unit without having to sit and wait, and wait, and wait. This technique forewarned the applicants that I couldn't stay and hang around because I had another open house scheduled.

During the good ol' days, the promotion and advertising consisted of some simple effective techniques:

- Yard sign promoting
  —We Buy Houses, We Rent Homes!
  —Rent with option to buy
  —Web site
  —Phone no. (for my pager)
- Classified ad

Your Ultimate and Cheapest Virtual Office

My pager was the core of my virtual office allowing me to operate 75 rental properties before hiring a part-time office person for five hours a week. Today, you can carry one pager with four separate phone numbers. (In fact, you can have three phone numbers and never carry a pager if you don't need one for your job.)

Pager 1 was for my job as a police officer: As a detective and a member of the bomb squad, I was expected to be on call pretty much all the time unless I was on vacation.

Pager 2 was for vacant units: Here is where it gets better. Contact your pager company and ask to speak to a supervisor. Odds are, the generic customer service representative (CSR) won't be able to pull this off. Politely, professionally, and in a very friendly manner, ask for assistance to extend the greeting time on your second, third, and fourth phone numbers. Greeting times can be adjusted from 9 seconds to over 60 seconds, at no additional cost, and you can edit and change your greeting by following some simple phone prompts.

The pager greeting on Pager 2 used for vacant units would say something like:

123 Main Street is a nice three-bedroom, one-bath, Bedford stone ranch home located just one block over from Home Depot. . . . Rents for $599 with a $639 security deposit and will be open Monday at 5 P.M.

321 Maple is a great three-bedroom, one and a half story home with one bath, basement, and huge fenced rear yard. It rents for $749 with a $799 security deposit and will be open Monday at 5:30 P.M.

1412 Oak Street is a huge four-bedroom, two-bath, brick ranch with a basement, 2-car garage, Rents for $799 with a $849 security deposit.

These homes are ready now. To see photos of these homes along with upcoming homes and answers to most of your questions, please visit www.VistaKY.com.

Thanks for calling Vista, We Buy Houses and We Rent Homes!

Pager 3 was used to capture seller's name and phone number and had a typical generic greeting: "I'm on the phone, away from my desk, or with a customer . . ."

Pager 4 was the emergency contact number for current tenants and thus required somebody to carry it. In those days, it was me.

Chew on it for a moment, especially if you've got a job and your time is precious. Even if you don't have a job, your time is still precious. Depending on your own comfort level, this one technique might be an easy way to rent your units without answering any phone calls!

I used this system for years while growing my little empire. Today, we're larger, with a real office, and we've graduated to never showing vacant units. I could never find anybody who would show vacant units to prospective applicants for free. Odds are, you can't either unless you're beating up on some relatives or in-laws or outlaws.

Here are some methods I tried and rejected:

- I had my help do open houses. This was expensive and cumbersome. On Mondays, I would ask a couple of my workers to travel and conduct the open houses for prospective tenants and applicants. This was a disaster:
  —The labor meter, their hourly rate, was cranking the whole time.
  —It took them away from the current rehab projects causing us to miss goals, deadlines, and objectives for those projects.
  —The guys had to receive training in fair housing and landlord laws because they were now representing me, and I was responsible for what they said or promised. Ouch.

—It diverted their skills and interest from rehabbing to marketing, with a clipboard and paperwork.

- I found a disabled woman who was very good on the phone and created a yard sign insert with her phone number. I faxed her a list of available properties, and she would pitch these properties by answering all the phone calls and mailing applications to prospects. She was paid by results. Whenever we rented a property that she pitched, we paid her a fee. This program just seemed like too much work, was too slow in processing applications, and finally fizzled out.

- Years ago, thinking I had another sharp idea, I invited one of my tenants who was on disability to help me out by showing vacant units so my rehabbers could stay focused on their tasks. Good ol' George is still with me today. He wanted to do a good job, and he worked cheap. I paid him perhaps $5.00 or $10.00 per open house. Several challenges surfaced including that George couldn't read or write. He also made absurd promises, was often late, and lost applications.

Here is the way my system works today, and it actually makes money. Applicants travel to our office:

- They sign out a key.
- They pay $20 cash for a key deposit.
- Applicants must produce a valid photo ID that we enlarge and copy.
- Applicants complete a simple one-page, fill-in-the-blank form and sign it.
- Now they can visit the unit all by their lonesome without our labor expense meter running to conduct an open house.

Whoa! Stop right now! You might be thinking like a tenant. You might ask (and we do get asked), "How in the world can you convince a tenant to drive 20 miles across town to get a key, drive another 20 miles to see the unit, and drive 20 miles back to the office?" Here is our powerful, stop them dead in their tracks, answer:

Applicant: I'm interested in the home at 123 Main Street. When can I make an appointment to see the unit?

Property Manager: You can see this home anytime you wish. When would you like to see this home?

Applicant: I'd like to see it today after work, about 5:00 P.M. or so.

Property Manager: We've got a unique, special program designed just for you to see this home. May I ask you a question?

Applicant: Sure.

Property Manager: Have you ever looked at a rental home in the past with a pushy landlord or leasing agent almost breathing down your back wanting you to hurry up and make a decision?

Applicant: Yes, that's not good.

Property Manager: You're absolutely right! This is going to be *your home.* Wouldn't you like to have plenty of time to walk through the home, picture how your furniture will fit, and get a feel for the inside and the outside of this home? This is going to be your home, and we want you to make the right decision, too. Wouldn't you like to see this home without any pressure and take your time?

Applicant: Sure (they always say yes).

Property Manager: Well, to give you this special benefit, it simply requires one little step on your part. Just stop by our office, at your convenience, and sign out a key, that's it.

When the above-average prospect, who is pretty darn serious about renting our place, shows up at the office, we have the person sign our Key Sign-Out form, pay a $20 cash key deposit, and provide a valid photo ID or operator's license that we enlarge on the photocopier before releasing a key.

Tip: Use a specific key just for your vacant units and only for your vacant units. Never use a key for an occupied unit that is soon to be vacated. This safety precaution reduces your liability if the key is not returned. Now you know the applicant's identity, and you are missing only a key to a vacant unit. When it gets rented, you will change the lock.

What if you don't have an office yet? Try this—borrow space from somebody who does have an office in the neighborhood where you invest. An insurance office, local hardware store, dry cleaner, a sign company, or your attorney's office could be your "virtual office." Cut a deal with them to be the location for your applicants to stop by and sign out a key. Be creative.

Almost everybody has access to a digital camera today. They are even built into cell phones. If your office is on wheels, you can use your camera to snap a photo of the applicant and snap a photo of their photo ID or driver's license.

Okay, so let's get to the meat and potatoes. How do you choose desirable tenants to fill your vacant units?

Here is my discovery for operating with next to no competition. In my town, investors are screaming the blues. They are trying to hang on to market rents when market rents have actually declined due to the imbalance in supply and demand.

So, What's a Poor Investor to Do?

Many investors have lowered their standards in qualifying tenants. It is ludicrous and stupid to do this. Just do the math. It does not work. It never will. These investors are jumping on the first applicant who can flash some cash with little regard for the applicant's track record, credit report, and recent evictions.

Believe me, a tenant who has been evicted four times in the past two years is almost guaranteed to become a nonpaying dirtbag in your property, and you will be filing an eviction notice.

Here's your solution for keeping high-quality tenants in your properties with almost no competition from other investors.

If You've Gotta Good System, Just Lower Your Rents!

Don't wig out! Remember, this is for markets where you have too many units and not enough tenants. Believe it or not, hard-working folks and responsible tenants still exist in the United States today. However, they are shopping for bargains, just like you and me, the tightwad investor.

With an effective system in place, you can lower your rents and still blow the doors off your competition. An efficient landlording system will allow you to earn much more than market rent when all is said and done.

One of my best techniques to attract good tenants is to advertise lower rents—as much as $100 to $150 cheaper than all the other guys. This is how it works: Suppose market rent is (or was) $800. Advertise and promote your unit with a "special" rent of only $699* (note the asterisk, same as the big retailers use for fine print in their ads.) The asterisk allows me to state: "Special Rent $699 rent program is good only with a coupon and expires Friday at 4 P.M."

Long story short, your prospect completes your rental application, gets qualified, and is ready to complete your lease or rental agreement. Your lease or rental agreement lists the real market rent of $799. (The lease shows monthly rent of $799. Now, if somewhere down the road, the tenant stops paying rent, you will be in a better position to enforce the real rent of $799.)

During the signing of your rental agreement or lease, your tenant may balk or squall that the rent was advertised as $699*. This is where you produce your "Vista Bucks" Rent Coupon. We go a little overboard on ours, but here's the way to set up the program.

Go to an office supply store and get one of those goofy little finger-pinching corporate seals (paper masher) with your property management company name on it. It costs about $20.00. Get some heavy almond or beige paper or card stock and using your computer create your own *Bucks Coupon.* (see Figure 9.10).

FIGURE 9.10 Vista Buck

Each "My Company Name Buck" coupon has a specific "good for date," your signature, and the impression of your seal, or paper masher. The fine print reads "your account must be current, paid in full, with no lease/rental agreement violations." In short, each individual coupon is good only for the month named specifically on the coupon. It also states the tenant's account must be current and have no rental agreement violations. This may seem cumbersome, but it is done one time when starting out with a new tenant. This is just another creative method to cherry-pick desirable applicants and keep them from your competitors.

Many investors using Tenant Tracking are getting well over 100 percent of their rents. In fact, we get 110 percent of our rents and we regularly get "atta-boy" and thank-you letters from investors all over the country who are doing the same. The magic happens when you implement a system. You are in business. Treat it like a business and operate like a business.

To get the Key Sign-Out form and the simple two-sided Rental Application form, go to www.MikesForms.com and download both in Microsoft Word and PDF format.

CHAPTER 10

What to Do When You Have Too Many Units, Not Enough Tenants

Understanding market conditions and having that sixth sense of what is going on allows the successful investor to stay out in front of the pack and operate where there is no competition. Just like the book *Who Moved My Cheese?* (Spencer Johnson, New York, G. P. Putnam, 1998) screening tenants for your rentals is now more critical than ever. This simple book references the simple life of four mice and how two of them make immediate changes when the cheese is moved or gone. This could be very similar to changes in our market conditions. Two other mice sit and wait and worry wondering when the cheese will return. Many small market indicators have crept up on us over the past few years. Although each condition by itself is not too serious, when they occur at the same time, they have a major impact on our rental market.

These factors include the nightly news reminders of a bad economy, high unemployment, jobs leaving the United States, and home ownership at all-time highs. The nonstop new home construction far exceeds the growth of our local household census. Other contributors to the challenging market of *supply and demand* are new apartment construction; availability of free money to first-time home buyers (including our own long-term tenants); all-time low interest rates; access to easy money from lenders; and an influx of stock market jumpers who have seen the light, realize real estate is the place to be, and are investing in it. The result: too many houses and not enough quality tenants.

While surfing the net, I found a web site (www.badlandlords.info) devoted exclusively to educating tenants on how to negotiate better terms with landlords and giving the inside scoop on how to beat up your landlord. They even promote the same by selling T-shirts with the logo, "Kill the Landlord." This web site harps on the abundance of vacant rental properties and encourages tenants to go after two to three months of free rent. Locally, we have apartment communities that are experiencing a 25 percent vacancy rate although their profitability is projected at a maximum 5 percent vacancy rate. We have a large apartment community where 40 percent of the units are empty. These apartment communities are offering blow-out specials, low prices, and free rent to fill vacancies.

Last month, my brother purchased a home I would rent for $800. His total PITI (principal, interest, taxes, and insurance) payment is $543. Be aware of how this can affect you. Mortgage brokers and lenders are targeting our sometimes overlooked, but valued, long-time tenants and are pitching this same opportunity. They pound our tenants with "Why are you paying $800 per month rent making your landlord rich when you can buy a home just like yours or bigger for $250 per month less?" The sad reality is that we learn this too late. We receive our tenants' notice to move because they are becoming home owners. (Perhaps you would have sold your tenant the home they are renting from you.)

Congratulations to tenants who become home owners. Almost anyone who can breathe can buy a home (think about who is left—an ugly thought). Although they are excited about home ownership, many get zapped with outrageous fees resulting in the tenant paying well over 100 percent for their home. In addition, the former tenants do not receive any financial education on how to manage a household budget. When the roof, furnace, or water heater breaks down or needs replacing, the new home owners will have to dig into their empty pockets to make repairs; previously, a phone call to the landlord resolved their problem. Now we are in the beginning or perhaps the middle of a cycle that will eventually rebalance supply and demand. Sadly, many of these homeowners will go belly up, lose their homes, and return to being tenants. In the meantime, we are short a boatload of quality tenants.

New investors have added to the current problems. Poor financial decisions from the recent bygone days of easy cash-out refinances have allowed some of these new investors to live the good life on borrowed money. These types have now run out of cash, and their rent income barely covers the mortgages, let alone repairs or lost rent from vacancies. These people are going bankrupt by the dozens locally, and lenders have shut all their doors on loans involving nonowner-occupied property, including the seasoned veteran cash-heavy investor. The pendulum has swung the other way.

The investor with *cash is king*. If you do not have cash, you must have resources for acquiring cash to stay active. The gravy train days of pay cash, make it right, refinance, and cash out—getting your money back on 30-year fixed to do it again—are almost gone. Focus and polish your education on seller financing, negotiations, and develop your own network of private lenders. Cash in on private lenders whose certificates of deposit are paying 2 percent. Make it attractive to the private lender and you will always have cash resources at your fingertips. Private lenders who have cash network with people who have cash.

CHAPTER 11

Your Answering Service

My peers still ridicule me about my answering service. This simple tool that costs eight or nine dollars a month has been instrumental in my real estate investing. (Never call it a pager, call it your *answering service*. Perception is reality.)

Let's begin with getting the pager. Here are the features you need. Start with a voice mail pager. Make sure it has a greeting and plenty of space for voice messages. Unknown to many, the greeting can be extended from the usual 8 seconds up to 20, 30, or even 60 seconds at no additional cost. Get the most greeting time possible. Put a little effort in this process. You will only need to do it one time. The challenge is setting it up properly.

The second step involves another pager feature. Again, most folks are clueless. You can have up to two additional phone numbers on one pager. Each number can be used for a separate purpose. The important part in setting this up is placing an identifiable mark on your pager display for each number as it receives a message. For example, pager number 1 should be displayed when you receive a voice message for that phone number, pager number 2 should be displayed when you receive a voice mail message for it, and so on.

When I had a job as a police detective, I had to carry a pager as part of the job. I simply added two additional numbers to my pager. If you don't have a job-related pager, you may have to spend $8.00 to $9.00 per month for the service.

Answering Service Number 1—Vacancies

When you use the pager, you will have a specific purpose and greeting for each pager number. When I had a job, I used pager 1 on my yard signs, in classified ads, and to pitch or take calls on available homes. This allowed me to see what kind of activity I was getting on my advertising, and I could function uninterrupted at my full-time job (I kept it set on vibrate). If you have a job, you understand the perceived tension from your coworkers who emit ill feelings toward you concerning your real estate activity. I don't want to use bad words here, but it seemed to me that some coworkers almost wanted to see me fail instead of succeed. I tried my best to keep my real estate activity "off the job." This tool allowed me to project a full-time real estate image with a part-time availability. It was a great feeling knowing my real estate was cranking while I was unavailable. Open houses were scheduled immediately after getting off work.

The greeting for pager number one to promote vacancies would be something like:

> *123 Main Street is a sharp three-bedroom, one-bath brick ranch with a basement, two-car garage, fenced yard located in the Highview area off Preston Highway. This home will be open Monday at 6:00 P.M., rents for $900 with a $950 security deposit. See you there.*

Do *not* ask callers to leave a message because they will. The serious prospects will make arrangements to show up at 6:00 P.M.

If you have more than one unit available for rent, use a slightly different greeting. Begin your greeting by announcing that a number of units are available for rent so that callers don't hang up thinking they have called about the wrong property. With more than one unit, your greeting could be something like this:

> *Thanks for calling my properties. Several homes are ready now, please listen to the entire message.*
>
> *123 Main Street is a nice three-bedroom, one-and-a-half bath brick ranch with a full basement, fenced yard, two-car garage, rents for $950 and will be open at 5:00 P.M.*
>
> *1519 Western Parkway is a sharp four-bedroom, two-bath home with a full basement, fenced yard, rents for $500 and will be open at 5:30 P.M.*
>
> *21 Cross Creek is a four-bedroom, two-bath home with a family room and two-car garage, rents for $1,200 and will be open at 6:00 P.M. See you there, and thanks for calling.*

I really liked this arrangement when I had a full-time job. It gave me peace of mind about getting in trouble doing real estate stuff while I was on duty and allowed me to "answer" phone calls about my vacancies 24-7. An additional benefit was that this method triggered a sense of urgency on the part of those who showed up to see the home. *Do not use* "open from 5 to 6 P.M." It will be very painful for you, because people will show up at 5:50 P.M. Just say, this home will be open at 5:00 P.M. period. If they are going to arrive late to see the home they want to rent, odds are, they are going to be late when paying their rent. If several prospects show up at the same time, it will create an exciting sense of urgency and competition among the prospective tenants. This is to your benefit.

Answering Service Number 2—Emergencies

You use the second number on the pager as an emergency answering service. Many local ordinances require emergency contact information to be posted prominently on the front of rental property. If your local government requires this notice, your pager can be helpful. Make sure your rental agreement notes the emergency number, and if you have an office with a real answering machine, mention the emergency number there as well. The greeting used for this emergency answering service is as follows:

> *You have reached the emergency answering service for* my properties. *After the tone, please leave your name, your address, and a brief description of your emergency, along with your phone number. Please speak slowly, clearly, and say your number twice. Thanks for calling* my properties.

This powerful little phrase will allow you to prescreen your emergencies. Do *not* let your service person carry your pager. You want to make the call whether to send someone out after hours or the next day. It is surprising how few calls you will receive. Again, you are training your tenants. In the beginning, the messages they leave are not emergencies at all and can be handled the following day. One of my favorites involves hearing the pager go off at 1:00 A.M. Yes, call the pager, retrieve the message, and learn about the tenant's emergency. It usually is not a real emergency. For example, in the summer, the message may be that the air-conditioning is not working properly. (I don't consider this an emergency, but tenants do.) Do *not* call the tenant at 1:00 A.M. Train your tenant. Phone the tenant promptly at 5:30 A.M. or 6:00 A.M. when you start your day. (This can be entertaining. You are responding promptly to their emergency, right?) Guess who is asleep at 5:30 A.M. or 6:00 A.M.? Your tenant is horizontal and still has his eyes shut. Inside, you will chuckle when you call at 6:00 A.M. to ask about their emergency. Amazingly, the emergency doesn't exist at that hour of the morning.

If you receive a voice mail message stating, "This is Bill Smith, my phone number is 123-4567," bite your lip, even if you know your tenant and where he lives. Remember, this is your answering service. The greeting plainly instructed the caller to leave name, address, description of emergency, and phone number. If callers do not follow the instructions, do NOT call them.

Don't give tenants your cell phone number: They *will* call you. If it is too late, get another cell phone number now. You will be thrilled. Always hit *82 before phoning your tenant, and your cell phone number will not be displayed on their Caller ID.

Do not dodge your responsibility of being a landlord, but promote responsible behavior by your tenant. *Train your tenants.* If you say "How High?" when a tenant tells you to jump, then the tail is wagging the dog. You are enabling the tenant to be a pain in your neck. You are causing your own grief. This attitude can be carried over into almost every aspect of landlording.

Answering Service Number 3—Finding Sellers

If you have an aggressive "We Buy Houses" campaign, especially with a full-time job, use the third pager number and your pager greeting to give instructions to sellers who call you. Put this number on your business cards, classified ads, yard signs, flyers, and "bandit" signs. Bandit signs are a slang term referring to all of those signs you see nailed on telephone poles and placed in medians along roadways. Your greeting could be as follows:

> *Hello, this is Mike. I am on the phone right now. Your call is important. Please leave your name, number, the address, and sale price of your house. This will help me get your answers quickly when I return your call. Please say your number twice. Thanks.*

Motivated sellers will have no trouble leaving messages and will ramble on telling you a boatload of information about the property and situation. Although many people get pissed off at answering machines and voice mail, you must weigh the odds here. You can pitch and promote, "Call me anytime, 24-7."

With today's rapidly advancing technology, you may soon be able to do the same with a low-cost cell phone.

CHAPTER 12

Your Application Is Your Crystal Ball

In this chapter, I put a great deal of emphasis on the application process. This is your only opportunity, your one shot, to land a high-quality tenant for a long-term relationship. Screw this part up and you'll end up being like all the other landlords.

A lot goes into this process. Take some time with it. Study it. Learn the powerful multipurpose and in-depth reasoning for using the detailed specific questions exactly as they appear. These folks are trying to get the keys and move into your investment property. Do you want it destroyed or well maintained? Do you want your neighbors to be furious with you, or do you want your rental property to blend in with all the owner-occupied properties on the street?

Think about all the effort, time, energy, and money you may have invested to capture this investment property. Surely it's worth a focused effort on your part when opening the door and searching for a new tenant.

If you are an experienced investor and landlord, think about these questions: Who have been your absolute ultimate best tenants? What made them your best tenants ever? I'll bet you some of these things are high on your list:

- They always paid their rent.
- They never complained or called.
- They took care of the property.
- They never caused any problems.
- And maybe, just maybe, if you were lucky, they stayed for years.

What prevents you from repeating this? Think about how you rent your properties today? Do you make an energetic effort or do you waller through it to get homes filled?

There really are tenants with the traits I have listed here in your town today. The market has meant big changes for all of us. All the little things as well as changes in ourselves make the search for good tenants seem so much harder. In 1993 when I started attending Kentucky Real Estate Inspection Association (KREIA) meetings, old-timer investor James Blair would whine and cry the blues about how tough the times were (in 1993). He would say, "Man, oh, man, Mike, do you know how many houses for rent were in the Sunday paper? I counted 152 houses for rent. Man, there's so many people jumpin' in this real estate stuff. It's really getting hard."

His comments never stopped me or slowed me down. I rock and rolled and grew our little empire.

I saw James Blair at our December 2005 monthly meeting. Take a wild guess what he told me: "Mike, did you see how many houses for rent were in the Sunday paper? I counted over 175 houses for rent. Man, oh, man, everybody is just jumpin' in this real estate stuff. It's so much harder now."

The point I'm trying to get across is that things do change; however, *we are also part of the change.* Maybe we slow down and get lazy. Maybe we are not as aggressive as we used to be. *Good tenants* still exist in our world.

Let's start implementing the beginner basics you learned in Section I of this book and we will graduate to using the title "property manager" instead of "landlord." Managing tenants effectively builds your wealth and it all begins with screening your tenants properly before and when they submit an application. Most property managers use applications and charge a fee. My objective here is to give you a smorgasbord of screening tips allowing you to select items of your choice to work into your system.

I have spent quite a bit of time on this rental application and the process. Do this part correctly, and you will have fewer headaches, nightmares, and expenses. Do it wrong or half-assed, and you will immediately join the landlords who constantly cry the blues.

Remember, this is your applicants' job application.

As you learn about different aspects of my *Landlording on Auto-Pilot* system, you will see that many of my procedures, forms, and policies have multipurpose goals and objectives.

My one-page (two-sided) rental application functions as:

- A lead generator for finding motivated sellers of properties
- Authorization to release Information about the applicant allowing me to fax the back page to employers, previous landlords, and so on
- Immediate Identification of qualified lease/option candidates
- A method for tracking my advertising and marketing

- Identification of trades (roofers, electricians, auto mechanics, landscapers, plumbers, painters, etc.)

Rental Application

First, make sure your application is properly worded and legal, and does not violate any fair housing laws or local laws. On the back, include a section with a few lines where the applicant can write comments. Also include a small section of text briefly detailing your qualifying standards and requesting permission for the landlord to check all sources in evaluating the application for tenancy. Also state that a "false or incomplete application" is a reason to be disqualified or not approved. The applicant's signature line is below this bit of text.

The first section on the application asks for full real name, date of birth, Social Security number, and phone numbers to contact the applicant. Ask for several phone numbers—home, work, cell, pager, and so on. After attending a class by an enforcement officer of the Equal Housing Commission, I learned to my surprise that it is permissible to ask for the person's date of birth, for identification purposes, but you can't ask for the applicant's age—baffling, but true.

My rental application and the application process are strategically designed to give me as much ammunition as possible for my team, without making it dangerously simple for dirtbags and professional tenants to weasel their way into my properties. Additionally, I don't want to handle a cumbersome and complicated multipage form. Many gurus seem to be in some kind of contest to see who can come up with the most questions and the longest form; it must make them feel clever. I'm just the opposite. Let's *power pack* this form into one piece of paper. Yup, I'll use both sides, but it's still one piece of paper (see Form A.2: Rental Application, in Section III).

Rental History

The next section deals with rental history for the past five years, including addresses, owner/manager contact information, and dates of residency, along with reason(s) for moving. This part has developed amazing leads for buying property. Some of the reasons for moving have been:

- Landlord is selling property.
- Landlord died.
- We're losing it to foreclosure.

- I lost my job and am losing my home.
- I had problems with landlord (and many other nice-to-know things).

Employment and Income

The next section, Employment and Income, demonstrates the applicant's ability to afford and pay the rent. Information about employer, wages, and other source(s) of income are entered here.

I made a huge mistake just a couple of years ago, and one of my local friendly competition investors captured a good tenant that my office turned away. Here's how it happened. Shirley, my office manager, while working up the application, realized the applicant's income fell way short of our qualifying income standard to afford the rent on the property (remember that the purpose of this section is to evaluate the applicant's ability to pay the rent). This applicant went to our competitor and *paid a full year's rent in advance* when asked to do so. Never forget this: Keep the big picture in mind. One of the purposes of the application process is to make sure the person(s) can pay the rent . . . duh, they paid a year in advance. . . . I think they qualified on the income stuff.

Additionally in the Employment and Income section, we're looking for stability:

- How long have they been on the job?
- If they have changed jobs recently is the new job in the same field?
- Do they have a good occupation/profession?
- Do they have a full-time or part-time job?
- Do they work a second job? (I prefer tenants who have jobs. Those who don't work, except for older retired folks, seem to be a magnet for bad news in the neighborhood.)
- Do they have any additional income or assistance? This one might surprise you. One might expect child support, alimony, and so on, but I've discovered additional income from severance packages from a lost job, and a biggie is income from a trust fund left to an applicant as part of an inheritance.

Section 8

If you don't participate in HUD's Section 8 program, you can remove this line from your application and skip over this section. When I got started, participation was a necessary evil. Section 8 in many markets pays top-dollar rents in low-income neighborhoods. The federally subsidized housing program is well intended and is actually a useful program helping many American families today. I have families on the Section 8 program who are as responsible as, or better than, many of our straight-rent tenants. The problem is not with the families. Section 8 has a bad name because it is operated by a government agency, allowing us—the taxpayers— to see our taxes at waste.

Many landlords are frustrated and fed up with how local agencies operate the program, along with allowing any family, including the worst of the dirtbags and tax eaters, to participate and benefit from it. I had a pretty shocking experience a couple of years ago in my town. Our local Director of Housing, who also is in charge of our local Section 8 program, agreed to meet a small committee of leaders from our local investor group. I was president at the time. Perhaps a dozen or so of us attended this meeting. These were not necessarily mom-and-pop operators. Our representatives included the past president of our Board of Realtors and property managers for small, medium-size, and large investment companies.

Section 8 leaders had told many in our group that if a family screws up, they get booted off the Section 8 program. Instead, we learned that some families who screw up and are booted actually get back in the program. To our amazement, the Director of Housing pretty much told us, they go back to the end of the line, receive a new tenant number, and are allowed to open a new file with Section 8. His justification for this was simply: Where else can these folks go for housing? He pretty much acknowledged the Section 8 program takes everybody—dopers, criminals, drug dealers, tax eaters, and all the low lifes in our society.

This is not fair. Many wonderful families who need and have earned the right to get some help are lumped into this group of bad tenants.

So what can a property manager do? Before jumping into the Section 8 program in your town, contact other landlords and get their feedback. How do you find them? Go to your Section 8 office and ask for a list of available properties. They will give you the list along with the contact phone numbers. Many Section 8 offices have available properties listed on a web site, where you can let your fingers do the walking.

By contacting other landlords in your town, you discover the pitfalls, the pain-in-the-butt factor, and problems with the operation and participation in the program. Here is one rule of thumb I've discovered: The smaller the town, the better the program. If you live in a large city, you'll probably hear many complaints and horror stories. If you live in a small town, you'll probably find they run a pretty tight ship with a helpful attitude toward landlords and tenants.

The line on my application about the Section 8 program is designed to "cut through the bull *now*." Applicants come from all walks in life. Some are sharp; some are not the sharpest tool in the drawer, to put it nicely. Years ago, many times we worked up rental applications involving a Section 8 family only to learn they were merely on the list waiting to be contacted to actually begin the program. The waiting list at the time was over a year.

This was not the fault of the families. The Section 8 representative gave families a packet of information explaining how the program worked and that they could shop for a home of their choice. This is what they did. So we learned the hard way. Today, as you can see on the application, we ask:

- **Are you on Section 8?**

- **If yes, have you had your briefing?** The briefing is the meeting where a Section 8 representative gives misleading information to new participants on the details and the process of the program. They leave this meeting with a large envelope filled with forms and information. It includes:

—The list of available homes and apartments for rent

—A map detailing the density of Section 8 participants in our community, the bulk usually being in low-income neighborhoods.

—A local fair housing complaint form

—A federal fair housing complaint form

—The EPA publication, "Protect Your Family from Lead in Your Home," information pamphlet.

—A HUD-approved mandated lease agreement (which is tenant friendly)

—A HUD-approved mandated Move In Inspection Form

—A HUD-approved worksheet for allowances for utilities, and so on.

—A HUD-approved voucher for X number bedrooms and dollar amount

—An assortment of other informational flyers if they are on the program:

  - New investors and landlords always get jackpotted by accepting applications from families who think they're on the Section 8 program, but are not yet participating. In my town, the family cannot get approved or rent a unit until they have had their briefing and have their packet in hand.

  - We will not allow any applicant who states they are on Section 8 to submit a rental application unless they have had their briefing.

- **If yes, I have a _____ bedroom voucher.** Once again, because of the misleading information given to participants during their briefing, most families leave their briefing and begin their search for a home. At this time, the Section 8 Program is a voucher program based on *number of bedrooms*. There are changes in HUD coming down the pike that will terminate the voucher program and local agencies will have the authority to manage the program as they feel best for families and their community.

In the meantime, we have to deal with the voucher program. During the briefing, the families are told they have an X number of bedrooms voucher allowing up to X number of dollars in benefits.

Let's use one of the frequent headaches we experience: A family has a two-bedroom voucher with a maximum dollar amount benefit of $725.

The frustration begins right here. During their briefing, the family is told they can go shopping for a two-bedroom home or unit and if the landlord supplies all the utilities across the board, their rent cannot exceed $725. In this example, this would include not only rent as we know it, but water; heat; air conditioning, cooking, whether electric or gas; trash; personal electric and unit electric; and hot water. Using the HUD utility allowance chart, dollar amounts for each of these vary based on number of bedrooms. Therefore, if the tenant has to pay for all the utilities in a two-bedroom single-family house, the maximum allowable rent after utility allowances might be in the neighborhood of $500 to $550.

Unbelievably, this family with a two-bedroom voucher is told that if they can find a three-bedroom home and not go over $725, they can rent it. So guess what the poor family pursues? They go out shopping for a three-bedroom home with their two-bedroom certificate. Assume they find a three-bedroom home where the rent is $700. The family think their search is over and get totally frustrated when *we* have to school them on how the program works. When they shoot for a three-bedroom home, they must use the HUD utility allowance chart for a three-bedroom house, not a two-bedroom house. Common sense dictates utilities across the board will be significantly higher on a three-bedroom home than on a two-bedroom home. This results in about $300 left for rent if they desire a three-bedroom home and the tenant must pay all the utilities. Why can't the Section 8 representatives conduct the briefings properly and give families accurate information?

- While I'm on the Section 8 bandwagon, I'll point out a couple more things you can benefit from. In my town, landlords are required to use the HUD-mandated forms for the voucher, lease agreement, utility allowances, and move-in inspection. Usually at the end of the lease agreement, you will find a section titled "Additional Provisions." Years ago when getting started, I would handwrite all my additional provisions onto the carbonless HUD (Section 8) lease agreement form. Today I've gotten a whole lot better by including my Section 8 Additional Provisions form detailing perhaps as much as two dozen additional provisions on my part and they are *landlord friendly* (see Form A.22: Section 8 Additional Provisions).

  It is imperative for you to understand as much as possible about the Section 8 program before an applicant submits an application to you. In my town, two of our consistent headaches involve getting started with the paperwork and the Section 8 property inspection procedure:

  —*Headache number one:* The applicant fails to return the completed forms to the family's assigned worker. Sometimes a family will simply sit on the packet and not deliver it to the caseworker for several weeks. In the meantime, the poor old landlord is waiting for Section 8 to quit dragging their feet and get on with the program. Rent payments don't start until the property has passed the Housing Quality Standards (HQS) of the Section 8 program.

- Section 8 adds to this headache because for some unknown reason the Section 8 office in Louisville, Kentucky, will not allow families to submit completed packages on Friday. I'm totally baffled by this one. I can understand banker's hours, but a four-day work week with banker's hours for a government agency is mind-boggling. But, we must deal with it.

- Headache number one is motivating the family to return their briefing package to their caseworker immediately. We motivate them by giving them 24 hours to submit their completed package of paperwork to their case worker at the Section 8 office or *they* can be cancelled and we can move on to the next tenant. Years ago, some of these families would drag their feet for unknown reasons in returning the paperwork to the Section 8 office. This slows down *everything*. The inspection process and getting *rent*. Everyday the unit sits empty is lost rent you can never replace.

—Headache Number Two involves the HQS inspection. Once again, I'm relating the process as I know it in my town. Once the family submits the paperwork to their case worker, a very slow pipeline moves the paperwork from the caseworker to the Inspection Department. This department must then schedule an "initial inspection" of the property to ensure it meets HQS along with the requested rent.

- There have been situations where the department schedulers have drug their feet for over a full month. This means the landlord is out another month's rent. If you contact a Section 8 office and get a real person on the phone, you'll hear that the inspection occurs within three days. (Baloney)

- By the way, the landlord is also at the mercy of the almighty, all-knowing, never-does-anything-wrong Section 8 inspectors. If they discover anything is not up to code or not to their liking, they have the authority to fail your property.

- *Solution to headache number two:* I created an *Additional Provisions* addendum to include with every Section 8 Rental Agreement. I took it a step further, and had a HUD-certified Section 8 representative approve my additional provisions form acknowledging the date and time of his approval. You can do the same. Check out my addendum (see Form A.22: Section 8 Additional Provisions, in Section III) and see if the additional provisions could benefit you as well.

This is important information if you want to be involved with the Section 8 program. Once again, I do not have issues with the families on the program. We screen them with the same standards we use for all our tenants, and we have wonderful Section 8 tenants. Nevertheless, Section 8 used to play a larger role in our rental program, and I look forward to the day when we are 100 percent Section 8 free. But, I will not turn our back on our good families.

Additional Questions on the Front Page of the Form

- **How long will you live here?** _____1 year _____2 years _____3 years+
I'm not in the hotel business. I want all our tenants to stay forever. It just makes everything so much easier. We are communicating a big subliminal message to applicants with this question. What box do you think most people check?

  Most check the three-years-plus box. This is awesome. We're grooming them mentally for our long-term relationship. In fact, as far as marketing and conversation at first contact, we can offer less than market rent for our residents because we don't have the turnovers other landlords and apartment communities experience. Those costs are passed on to the residents.

  If an applicant for a single-family house checks the one-year box, we frown on it greatly. However, almost all apartment applicants check the one-year box; we accept it for apartments only.

- **What is your attorney's name?** Having this question on your application is powerful. Many leave it blank (which is great). Those who fill it in the blank might give you some insight about your applicant. It might be one of those attorneys who advertise on the Jerry Springer show in your town," Help me find somebody to sue."

  Another revelation with this attorney question is that it conveniently reminds applicants of any pending lawsuits. I can't tell you how many times applicants have scribbled a name of an attorney in this blank and it reminded them of their pending lawsuit involving "one of their previous landlords." Hmmm, pretty good stuff—many actually scribble summary information about their lawsuit on the back page under the Comments section.

- **Is the total move-in amount available now?** Pretty simple question, but does the family have all the funds needed to pull this off *now*? Many times, they will say no or they expect to have enough money the following Tuesday.

- **Have you broken a lease?** This is a pretty generic question. Nothing fancy, but it forces them to think about being responsible. It's also another opportunity to capture another piece of ammo for your team in the qualifying process. The majority of applicants will answer this question *No* hoping to convince you they're responsible. If you discover they have broken a lease in the past, this could be deemed false information on their application.

- **Are you a convicted felon?** Crime is a hot potato today and can be a source of serious liability for property managers if not handled properly. For example, in a large nice apartment community on the taxpayer side of town, a resident tenant was the victim of a burglary, rape, and robbery. The on-site managers were made aware of this crime and knew that the perpetrator had accessed the victim's apartment through the sliding glass doors on the first floor patio,

A short time later (I don't recall if it was days, weeks, or even months), the bad guy struck again and repeated almost the same behavior.

The second victim (along with the entire apartment community) was never notified of the previous criminal offense. When she found out about the earlier attack and the management's failure to issue a warning, she initiated and pursued a civil lawsuit against the apartment community management and owners and whoever else could be tagged.

The victim was awarded a multimillion-dollar judgment against the apartment community and others. This lawsuit sent shock waves not only locally, but throughout apartment associations on a national level.

Don't freak out and make this real complicated. My first tenant was a convicted felon, and he is still with me today. The majority of applicants who answer this question yes are decent folks; they screwed up in their past and have a strong desire to explain what happened. The applicant who writes *yes* with no explanation needs further research.

You have several resources at your fingertips for checking yes answers. The Internet allows you to make a basic search from your home or office. Get online and check out your local sex offender web site. I recommend you should do this for all applicants anyway, especially if you have multiunits.

The nature of the applicant's offense, when it occurred, conviction and sentence, and performance since release are all factors in working through an application. A convicted felon is not the most promising prospect, but in my state, a third conviction of DUI (driving under the influence) is a felony.

- **How many evictions have been filed on you?** This one is huge! I repeat: This one is *huge* because your applicant has trouble reading the question properly. For some reason—I assume because every other rental application on the planet asks, "Have You Ever Been Evicted?"—that wording seems routine and comfortable to them. They answer the question: "How many evictions have been filed on you?" as if the question were, "Have you ever been evicted?"

  While working up the application process, when we confront an applicant about the false information on the application involving our discovery of three filings of starting the eviction process from a former landlord, the applicant who answered this question *zero* or *none* will almost always respond "But I've never been evicted!"

  That is not the question. Read the question again, if you need to. This question puts another bullet in your gun; it provides more ammunition to protect you. This entire application process is designed to help you and me, the investors.

- **What kind of animals do you have?** Do not ask, "Do you have pets?" This phrase almost automatically implies the landlord does not accept animals, and your applicant will usually answer this question with a "No." The first question implies it is okay to have animals. From the tenant's perspective, the question, "What kind of animals do you have?" implies a pet-friendly landlord, whereas "Do you have pets?" sends a message to your applicant that you probably have a No Pets Allowed policy. Many folks treat their animals better than other folks treat their kids and are prepared to pay extra to keep their pets. It is an opportunity to bump up your cash flow by increasing the rent perhaps $25.00 per month per animal in addition to requiring an animal deposit.

- **What may interrupt your income or ability to pay rent?** Don't laugh at this one. I've had applicants write, "I'm losing my job in two months." Some write remarks such as "If I get sick, die, or in a bad car wreck." I've also discovered scheduled serious income-zapping surgeries. Other things listed have been "I'm getting divorced after we move."

- **If approved, the following people will be living with me.** Household composition is the next section. You cannot use the word *family* or *children*. Think of those words as lighting fuses to cause you trouble. If you're doing it, *stop it now.* Substitute the phrase, "How many people are in your household?" If their response refers to children and a spouse, you're in good shape because they volunteered the information. You did not ask it. Yes, it seems like a play on words; however, the fair housing mystery shoppers (investigators) looking for landlords who violate the federal laws will call and record your phone conversations. Be aware.

  Notice that this section on the application simply has six numbers with a line or space for the applicant to write down names. Many times, because of everybody else's rental applications, the applicant, without being asked, will write something like this:

—Shelly Smith, girlfriend

—Tommy, 6 yr. son

—Sally Jones, 12 yr. daughter

If your applicant completes your application in this manner, you're okay. Just do not instruct applicants to tell you anything about the relationship of those who will be living with them. This would or could violate the Familial Status of Fair Housing. It is the application process that is so sensitive and critical with fair housing. Once qualified and approved, you can require names, ages, date of birth, and relationship of all those who will be occupying your unit. The important thing to remember is that the fair housing regulations are critical in the application procedure.

- **Credit references.** This one is simple. It simply helps us identify other monthly payments the applicant is responsible for. Most of the time, we'll see car payments, credit card payments, and student loans. I'm not the least bit interested in taking up space on my rental application for lenders' addresses and account numbers. Phooey on all that. You can still get a lot of insight into your applicant by what they write in the blank. Suppose you see car payment and student loan? Not too bad, but you sure would consider and factor in the dollar amount of their monthly payment(s) against their income and your rent.

  Suppose you see Alrenco payment for TV and a pawn shop payment? Hmm? Totally different isn't it?

- **Do you have a checking account?** Just a simple yes or no question is all I need. Many applicants do not have a checking account or savings account. It used to boggle my mind, but I've gotten used to it. There's just a segment in our society that believe in using money orders. My gut feeling says they hate banks because they don't know how to keep track of a checkbook register.

  When I worked at Winn-Dixie years ago, Tammy made me sell my old black Lincoln town car. She hated it, saying it looked like a gangster or Mafia car—shiny black with tinted windows and red leather interior. I think this was a 1974 model, and I was selling it in 1983. Anyway, I sold this car and financed it to a fellow who worked for me at the grocery store. Poor ol' Jeff would give me his weekly payment usually with a personal check. I would, when I remembered to dig it out of my wallet, hand it over to Tammy. She took care of our finances at this time. It was common for me to have several, perhaps as many as five of Jeff's checks in my pocket. Tammy would lump them together and deposit them into our checking or savings account.

  I arrived at work one day and Jeff was absolutely furious. He was so excited and borderline screaming that it was hard to understand his high-priority problem. After venting for a short bit, he informed me that I had just cost him over $500! Naturally, I was dumbfounded. Jeff, please tell me how I cost you so much money?

  Jeff began his short story. He told me he would always check his bank account with the bank teller or on the ATM (automated teller machine) whenever he deposited his Winn-Dixie paychecks. Based on the teller's answer or the balance displayed on the ATM, Jeff would proceed to write checks and pay his bills. *Never* did he keep a register of checks written. He relied solely on his bank balance at the time.

  So I got blasted because I held on to five weekly car payment checks and deposited them weeks, or even a month, after he wrote the check. First of all, I reminded him that I didn't do this to him, Tammy did it.

  Jeff's method of tracking his funds had a snowball effect. He had written checks assuming his bank balance was his real balance and didn't allow for uncleared checks that he had previously written. His checks to retailers began to bounce and triggered overdraft charges and bad check fees. He really did have over $500 in fees from this activity.

What is truly amazing, is that to this day, Jeff honestly believes I (Tammy) screwed up his bank account, and the bank just spanked him hard in fees because they wouldn't accept his explanation about us not depositing his weekly car payments in a timely manner.

This is a true story. Now you can see why some applicants and people will never open a bank account. They don't trust them.

- **Do you have a savings account?** Moving on down the list. More applicants have checking accounts than savings accounts. If an applicant has both a checking account and a savings account, you probably have a responsible application in your hand. If you notice, I don't ask for bank names or bank account numbers. It is simply a waste and takes up valuable space on my one-page rental application.

- **Do you own real estate?** This is another lead generator for the investor/landlord still looking and searching for deals. I have stumbled and tripped over many good deals with this one question. Just a thought, perhaps you could trade some rent for a property?

- **Emergency contact(s).** This section includes the phrase *"including nonpayment of rent."* Nonpayment of rent is an emergency to me and I'm letting applicants know my definition of an emergency. I also include this phrase right above the emergency contact information section in our rental agreement. This is powerful and allows you to contact these folks if the tenant gets behind on the rent. Yes, your tenants might throw a fit the first time you send a notice to the contact, but you remind them that they instructed you to do that on both their application and rental agreement. Usually, the emergency contact is someone applicants respect, admire, and hold in high regard—a parent, a favorite uncle or aunt, a reverend, or some other relative.

When tenants screw up and drag their feet paying their rent, I send a copy of their late notice (7-Day Pay or Quit Possession Notice in my town) to their Emergency Contact(s). Most of the time, Mom or Dad coming after them with a skillet is 10 times more powerful than an attorney, a court paper, or a sheriff's deputy.

Having to endure some embarrassment can be a powerful training tool for tenants. They will make sure to pay their rent on time to prevent their emergency contacts from receiving notices. I recall one tenant in particular whose mother would go off and attack and slap her son over his irresponsible actions. We need more moms like her. Don't think you have to do this all the time. Just a few late notices will usually to get them trained.

- **List vehicles and trailers your household will possess.** Many towns have local laws and ordinances to regulate the number of vehicles allowed on a property. Many have strict laws for inoperable vehicles. The bylaws of many neighborhood associations and subdivisions detail specifically what can and cannot be on a property or driveway. Suppose you have a great rental property in a well-established upscale development and your tenants list a tractor trailer rig, a mammoth motor home, or a houseboat.

Don't simply ask for cars that the applicant owns. They might not own the car they drive. They could be borrowing it. It also leaves them the opportunity to say, you didn't ask about trucks, trailers, or houseboats.

This part of the application can be critical if a tenant begins to turn your property into a car lot.

- **How did you find this home?** This question is self-explanatory and helps me track my advertising and marketing along with referrals and referral fees earned by those who advertise and pitch homes for us. I also use the word *home* for apartments. Remember, our slogan is "We Buy Houses, We Rent Homes!" I am convinced that the word homes has a warm fuzzy feeling.

- **Your requested move-in date.** Don't get fooled here. Responsible applicants might write in a date five months down the road. Irresponsible tenants will write "Now." This immediately gives you an idea what they are shooting for. Most responsible tenants will enter a date several weeks in the future.

- **Do you want to "rent with option to buy" or "rent to own"?** What's wrong with asking this on an application? It is a great opportunity to encourage and promote a long-term relationship with your tenants. Offering an avenue to homeownership is appealing to many tenants. Some prefer to remain tenants and never own their home.

- **How much cash do you have?** Very seldom do applicants get their feathers ruffled about this question. Most seem to answer the question pretty honestly. I've seen this question answered with "None Now" to "$25,000." It may get you pumped up a little if a large number appears here.

Suppose your applicants are a little weak in the income arena, but are sitting on $15,000 cash. Couldn't you continue processing their application, while informing them about their shortfall in the income department; however, you have a solution just for them. How about paying a year in advance?

Or better yet, with a good chunk of cash available, could you interest them in purchasing an option to buy on their home. You can be creative: More cash now might equal smaller monthly rent payments for them. All these creative opportunities can never be discovered or explored if you don't ask them how much cash they have.

If they've happened into a chunk of cash and having a bankroll doesn't fit the profile of your applicants (perhaps they won a lottery, or received an inheritance or money from a lawsuit), odds are that they will lose every bit of that pile of cash.

Did you know that most million-dollar jackpot lottery winners are broke and file bankruptcy after about three years? They can't manage their money. If they're sitting on a chunk of cash, you might as well help them and get some of it, because they're probably gonna give it to someone else. At least with your program or an option to buy, they'll be investing toward the purchase of their home.

Back Side of Rental Application

- **Other comments or explanations:** This small section allows applicants to explain anything they want, to vent, to blast their current or previous slumlords, or to write anything they choose. Interesting stories have been scribbled in these few short lines. One in particular, I recall, detailed the ongoing lawsuit the applicant had with her current landlord over mold and mildew under her kitchen sink.

Here's the fine print on the back side:

- **This agreement made this date by and between Vista Properties, Inc., manager for the Owner, hereinafter "Landlord" and the below signed, hereafter "Applicant." The Applicant shall pay to the Landlord nonrefundable fee upon the execution of this agreement in the amount listed on application to cover the administrative costs, expenses, and time of the Landlord to verify information submitted by the Applicant.**

This identifies the parties involved in this application agreement, to ensure compliance with our landlord/tenant laws and informs the applicant the fee is nonrefundable and is used to cover the expenses of processing their application.

- **Applicant authorizes the Landlord, his employees, agents, or representatives to make any and all inquiries necessary to verify the information provided herein, including but not limited to direct contact with Applicant's employer, landlords, credit, neighbors, police, government agencies and any and all other sources of information which the Landlord may deem necessary and appropriate within his sole discretion.**

This simply means the applicant gives the landlord permission to contact *anyone* he deems necessary.

- **The Applicant represents to the Landlord that the application has been completed in full and all the information provided for herein is true, accurate and complete to the best of the Applicant's knowledge and further, agrees that if any such information is not as represented, or if the application is incomplete, the Applicant may, at the Landlord's sole discretion, be disqualified.**

This protects you by stating that false information or just an *incomplete application* is enough reason for the landlord to disqualify the application.

- **The Applicant provides the information contained on this form.**
This means the person signing this form, the applicant, is the same person who completed the application. This removes any opportunity for someone to say, "but my brother filled it out for me."

- **Landlord is not liable to the Applicant, his heirs, executors, administrators, or assigns for any damages of any kind, actual or consequential by reason of the verification by the Landlord of the information provided by the Applicant, and Applicant hereby releases the Landlord, his agent, employees and representatives from any and all actions, causes of action of any kind or nature that may arise by virtue of the execution or implementation of the agreement provided herein.**
Although a lengthy bunch of words, this paragraph is simply a CYA for the landlord should any kind of harm come to the applicant from the landlord's processing of the application. Say the landlord contacted the applicant's employer to verify income and job position and the applicant was then fired for receiving a personal phone call. Even in this extreme example, the wording of the agreement would nip in the bud any opportunity for the applicant to sue the landlord for the loss of employment.

- **This property requires a security deposit equivalent to one month's rent plus $50.00 that must be paid in full before any rental agreement is made.**
This formula and language allows us to use a universal application for all our rental properties without having to provide special rental applications for specific properties. I also highly recommend that you always have your security deposit or damage deposit slightly more than a month's rent. If it is the same or even less than a month's rent, your tenant may move on saying "Keep my deposit for last month's rent." If your security deposit is more than a month's rent, it gives you the opportunity to hold out a carrot while saying "You've got to play by my rules to get this back."

- **Animal deposit(s) are in addition to security deposit.**
This requirement is simple and to the point.

- **Applicant, once approved, must obtain renter's insurance**
This speaks for itself, but renter's insurance is your first line of defense in your asset protection program. Insurance companies are getting pretty slick these days. They have access to computers, too. Whether you realize it, you have an insurance record, much like your driving record. Claims, inquiries, and even certain properties can gig your insurance score and result in higher premiums or even cancellation. Insurance is something we gotta have, but better never use.

Suppose a tenant has a grease fire in your property while cooking bacon on the stove. Without renter's insurance, your insurance will have a claim and repair your property. With renter's insurance, your tenant's policy will have the claim, leaving your record clean and slick as a whistle.

- **Landlord will attempt to contact the Applicant by the phone numbers listed on this application**

This doesn't say *must* contact. It says, once approved, the landlord will *attempt* to call the applicant using the phone numbers provided on the application.

- **Applicant has 24 hours from time of approval to fulfill rental agreement by producing all monies required and signing all rental agreement papers. If Applicant fails to perform within 24 hours of Landlord's approval, Applicant may be disqualified and Landlord may rent this home to the next qualified Applicant.**

This is huge. I can't tell you how many times in past years we approved applicants and set up a time to do the rental agreement and turn over the keys, and they pulled a George Jones . . . no show. I would feverishly try phoning them, calling them at work, and even their Emergency Contacts with no luck. After a day or two of this, I would move on to the next application and get the home rented. Guess what happened then? Low and behold, after three or four days, the original approved applicant miraculously appeared wanting to rent the property. At the time, I had no policy, and it was not a good feeling. I inserted the 24-hour rule to solve this problem.

Our required standards for qualifying to rent a home are simple and fair. They are:

- **All homes are offered without regard to race, color, religion, national origin, sex, disability, or familial status.**
This is the Fair Housing thing.

- **Each adult occupant must submit an application.**
This allows us to charge an application fee for each adult who will living in the unit. If another adult is listed on the application, we will work up an application on that person. When it comes to adults, don't permit an applicant to house a criminal or dirtbag in one of your properties.

- **Your gross monthly income must equal approximately three times or more the monthly rent.**
This is a starting guideline. In the old days, I was raised to believe that your rent or house payment should never exceed one fourth of your monthly income, or one week's income. One third is still pretty conservative, believe it or not, as many folks can get a home loan providing their house payment doesn't exceed 41 percent of their gross monthly income. Scary, isn't it? No wonder foreclosures are at an all-time high.

- **A favorable credit history.**
Don't hold your breath on this one. Odds are, your applicants wouldn't be here if they had good credit because they could buy a home. There is such a thing as

"good bad credit" and *"bad,* bad credit." We also tell folks "Bad credit will *not* prevent you from renting a home."

This is an example of *good bad credit:* In reviewing their credit report, you see late payments on credit cards, perhaps a student loan in default, and all kinds of medical tragedies and collections associated with those tragedies.

This is an example of *bad, bad credit:* In reviewing their credit report, you see collections on local utilities, judgments, and garnishments and evictions from previous landlord(s).

See the difference?

- **Be employed and be able to furnish acceptable proof of the required income.**
  This is pretty simple.

- **Good references, housekeeping, and property maintenance from previous landlords.**
  This is your silent sleeper. Your knuckle ball. Your curve ball. Your home run with bases loaded. This sets the stage for you to not only ask previous landlords about the applicants, but to do a housekeeping check on the current residence if it is a local address. This is powerful. We do not blare this phrase out loud everywhere. As you can see, it is contained in the fine print on the back side of the application.

- **Limit the number of occupants to 2 per bedroom.**
  I'm not sure really where I got this. I probably stole it from another landlord; it allows me to enforce the number of people living in a household. For example, if you had a two-bedroom unit or home for rent, and a person submitted an application with six people to reside in this household, you could cite this qualifying standard as a reason for not renting to them.

- **Compensating factors can include additional requirements such as double deposit or rent paid in advance for applicants who fall short of above criteria.**
  This is the landlord's weasel clause allowing us to make exceptions to the preceding qualifying standards set forth in our application.

The Applicant authorizes release of all information to Vista Properties, Inc.

APPLICANT: _____ **DATE:** _____

The applicant signs the application and this back page becomes your AUTHORIZATION TO RELEASE INFORMATION signed by your applicant. If your applicant has scribbled some sensitive information in the comment section, simply cover it up before faxing this page to employer's and previous landlords. Note HUD's Equal Housing Opportunity logo needs to be everywhere.

CHAPTER 13

Submitting the Application Is Your First Critical Step

The first couple of contacts with an applicant are critical. You must be on your toes. You must make sure you comply with all the rules and regulations involved in this business. This is not a great concern if you are doing this yourself, but as you graduate into true auto-pilot landlording, you will delegate this job to someone who represents you and your business. This can be overwhelming at times.

I don't care where we get started here. Let's pretend we are at the vacant unit, showing it to prospects and they acknowledge they want to fill out an application. You pull out the simple, one-page, two-sided, fill-in-the-blank rental application, and instruct your applicant:

Please fill out this entire rental application completely; remember that we need your signature and date on the back, too.

If an applicant wants to leave your property with the application, don't worry—this is okay. I used to almost freak out and say, "No, you can't leave with my application." This is what many gurus instructed me to do. Once again. No need to worry. Here's what I've discovered. I will bend over backward to help good tenants. What I'm talking about are perhaps the Larrys and Daryls of the world. On the old *Bob Newhart Show*, the hotel maintenance crew, Larry and Daryl, weren't very bright. They were still good people. Although you may find this a bit hard to swallow, there are many wonderful people in our society today who cannot read or write but who would make excellent long-term tenants.

Their request to take your application with them to complete at home just might be their way of concealing their inability to read or write. Knowing this today, I would never refuse to allow an applicant to take a rental application home.

Okay, back to the ones who can read and write.

Turning in the Application

You handed them an application and instructed them in a calm voice to fill out the application completely. If you have an office, make a copy of their valid photo ID and enlarge it so you can see the picture and information better. If you're doing this at the house or while showing a vacant unit, use a digital camera and photograph the applicants and their valid photo ID. Many people are victims of identity theft; you don't want to get a trashbag posing as a responsible person.

When they hand back the application, quickly review the top section to make sure you can read the name, date of birth, Social Security number, and the phone numbers to contact them. Here's the hard part: Skip everything else. Flip it over, and make sure they signed and dated it.

Before you part with the applicants, I encourage you to try a new aggressive approach to prevent the loss of potential responsible tenants. In the past, we heard the warning, "Beware of the applicant waving cash; odds are, the cash they're waving under your nose belongs to their current landlord." Many times, I've have worked up an application and called the applicants to let them know they're approved only to discover that they've already rented another home. Ouch! Back to ground zero.

Now, when an application is turned in, we encourage the applicants to put a *Deposit to Hold* on the unit (see Form A.3: Deposit to Hold with Application, in Section III). It must be close to or exceed the dollar amount of the normal security deposit. The language on this form states the applicants put up X dollars to hold this property pending the approval of their application. If they're approved, these funds will be used and applied toward funds needed to start their tenancy. If they're not approved, the funds will be returned to them within 30 days.

If they want to receive their money sooner, we charge an $85 processing fee. If the applicants are approved and refuse to rent the unit, they forfeit the entire deposit. The objective here is to prevent desirable tenants from continuing their search for a rental unit while providing stiff consequences to the undesirables hoping they can slide through the cracks and get one over on us.

Also, so applicants are not caught off guard, I inform them of our 24-hour notice to perform when approved. How many good tenants have you lost because an applicant was approved, you made arrangements to do the rental agreement on Friday, and your approved applicant becomes a no-show whom you cannot contact by phone? Puzzled and frustrated, do you give them a couple of days? Do you rent to your next qualified applicant only to have the original approved applicant reappear and challenge your process? You can prevent this headache with the simple 24-hours-to-perform rule. The small print on the back of the rental application states that the landlord will use the phone numbers listed on the application to contact and inform applicants of approval. This is the start of the 24-hour rule. Period. If there is no answer or voice mail, I may keep calling, but I sure start working on my next application. I shoot straight with the new applicants and tell them another person is in front of them and will have until 3:00 P.M. today to perform or my newest applicant can be in the driver's seat.

This next part is where a lot of landlords and professionals make fatal mistakes. Do *not* worry about seeing blank spaces in the rental application. An incomplete application is wonderful. This is good and very powerful for you.

Before you start to process, or work up, their application, make a copy of the front page. Even small home fax machines have a copy feature, and many of the all-in-one printers can do the same. Stop by your local Office Depot or Staples store and buy two cheap rubber stamps. One should say "ORIGINAL" and the other should say "COPY."

Stamp the original rental application submitted by your applicant with the ORIGINAL stamp in two places on the top and the bottom.

Stamp the copy of the rental application you just made with the COPY stamp in several places on the front side. Now you can staple or paper-clip the two together placing the copy on the top of the original. Do not write on the original in any way, shape, or form. Do not scribble on the original or fill in any blanks. Do nothing to the original, and safeguard it because it may become evidence to support your decision later. The stamped copy is now your work copy for processing this application.

Work through your application process with this work copy. You can write on it and fill in the blanks on the fields of information they failed to fill. I get more worried about the 100 percent completely filled-out application than about an incomplete application. The incomplete application gives you another bullet in your gun or more ammo, because an incomplete application is one of the reasons you can disqualify an applicant. You can telephone the applicant and fill in the blanks on your work copy, and not their original. (Remember, an incomplete application is a reason to disqualify.) I've found that two types of applicant leave blanks on their applications: the dirtbag professional tenant who's trying to put one over on you, and the person who doesn't know any better. I'll go out of my way to help qualify a person who doesn't know any better because they usually end up being great long-term tenants. If you help dirtbag professional tenants by filling in all the blanks on their original application, you're just making it more difficult to disqualify them; in fact, you're actually helping them to get qualified.

Many tenant screening services complain that processing incomplete applications is one of their most challenging problems when dealing with landlords and providing services. J. R. Hutto with National Tenant Network (NTN), would give short seminars or classes to landlords and apartment owners telling them how difficult it is for him to pull or run a tenant check with an incomplete application. In fact, he would instruct them to take a few extra minutes to make sure every blank was completely filled out. J. R. is a great friend and a good guy, and he was shocked when I told him this was the absolute worst thing a landlord or apartment owner could do. After I explained the preceding process, he agreed, but I think he's reverted back to his original presentation because it's just easier for him and staff.

CHAPTER 14

Protect Yourself by Never Disqualifying an Applicant

If you never disqualify an applicant, it is harder to get a complaint. Nobody, even a dirtbag, likes rejection. Folks who are thorough, document everything, and dot all their i's and cross their t's, can still get slammed on discrimination complaints. Even if they've done nothing wrong, other than disqualify an applicant, the disgruntled applicant can wreak havoc on the landlord with a formal discrimination complaint. It doesn't matter whether it is valid or unfounded, it will still be treated with a full-blown expensive, time-consuming, and intense investigation. The investigation is conducted by a government agency that seems to have an attitude of "You're guilty until proven innocent."

Don't get me wrong. As a cop, I was a government employee, too; and I witnessed many tax eaters in the criminal court system who used the system to their benefit.

Another protective action is to implement a safe, solid method for processing your applications. Do not get caught in the trap of reviewing all the available applications in front of you and choosing the best one. This system would be illegal because if you have more than three rental units, you must rent your unit to the first *qualified* applicant.

So who is a qualified applicant? Now we're right back to the basic challenge of having a "system" or a policy or a procedure. It is safer to have it in writing also—like right on the back of your rental application.

I highly recommend you have a simple procedure for processing applications. The no-brainer procedure is the good old-fashioned, first in, first processed. How do you protect yourself when you use this procedure? You must document the *date and time* the application was submitted. At the bottom of the back of our rental application is a blank to write in the date and time the application was submitted.

If you're at an open house and show a vacant unit to six applicants, you have a system to properly and fairly document the submissions of your applications.

With this system, you must process one application at a time. Suppose you got six applications at an open house. They now include documentation establishing the chronological order in which they were received.

You process Application 1 first. You run it through your entire application process without sneaking a peek at any other applications. If Application 1 meets your qualifying standards, the applicant is approved and becomes your next tenant. If he or she fail in some area or get disqualified, only then may you move on to Application 2. The process for the available unit continues in this pattern. If you operate in this manner, you should be pretty safe with processing applications fairly and having the documentation and evidence to prove your actions.

Additionally, when processing applications, take your Application Worksheet and fold it vertically in half to create a column to document, in chronological order, the activities you perform in processing the application:

Feb 25, 11:30 A.M., credit report.

11:40 A.M., phoned previous landlord.

11:44 A.M., faxed authorization to previous landlord.

11:55 A.M., received landlord reference reply by fax.

12:05 P.M., phoned employer and left voice mail.

12:50 P.M., phoned applicant about incorrect previous address. Blah, blah.

Establish and implement good solid procedures like this and you'll reduce risks and loopholes for folks who try to attack your system.

Try this on for size: If you have a goal of never disqualifying an applicant, it should greatly reduce your odds of a discrimination complaint.

The simplest way to achieve this goal is to always present a challenge or hurdle to applicants that prevents you, the application processor, from moving forward with their application. Put the ball in their court. Show a friendly attitude by offering a helping hand or guidance toward possible solutions that would fix or cure their newly discovered problem.

The *applicants* need to take action to correct *their* problem that you found for them. You project an attitude of helping them by explaining how they can work through this obstacle. Being friendly and giving your unqualifiable applicants a couple of big hoops to jump through almost always causes them to forget about renting from you. This gives you the liability-free position of not having "disqualified a person for housing."

If you insist on disqualifying an applicant for whatever reason, never do it over the phone or in person. Always do it in writing so you have proper documentation.

In the old days, I fell victim to the method that the gurus taught investors. I tried it for a while. When an applicant was disqualified, I would tell the person on the phone that to protect the privacy of the applicant and to prevent any opportunity for any misunderstanding or miscommunication, the applicant must mail a stamped, self-addressed envelope to our office to receive a written explanation of the cause for not being approved. On a couple of occasions, I did receive those stamped, self-addressed envelopes and they did not give me a good feeling either. I came out okay, but it was still cumbersome. How could I get rid of this unpleasant task? My answer today is that I simply avoid disqualifying applicants, and I don't have to deal with these problems.

Let's say a horrible applicant, Tim Smith, has no chance—zero—of renting a unit from me for reasons 1, 2, 3. I'll telephone Tim explaining I need a little bit of help from him working up or processing his application. For example:

Mike: Is this Tim Smith?

Tim: Yeah, this is Tim.

Mike: This is Mike with Vista Properties calling about your application for the house at 123 Main Street.

Tim: Okay.

Mike: Tim, while working up your application, we found on your credit report an address at 123 Daffodil in the Mountain View Apartments in July 2005. . . .

Tim: Oh, yeah, I forgot about that one [*or* I thought I had that on my application].

Once he admits he lived there . . . ,

Mike: Tim, I discovered a little problem that put a stumbling block in moving forward with your application. . . .

Tim: What is it?

Mike: Well, Tim, in August 2005, Mountain View Apartments filed an eviction on you. . . .

Tim: I did not get evicted from there!

Mike: Hold on, Tim, I didn't say you got evicted. I said they filed an eviction on you.

[Once again, he'll usually deny getting evicted.]

Mike: Tim, you don't understand. I'm stuck here and can't move forward with your application as it stands now, but if you believe somebody screwed up, I'd like to know about it.

[He'll ramble on just a bit about how somebody screwed up.]

Mike: Tim, would you like to know how to fix this so we can move forward on your application?

Tim: Sure.

Mike: Grab a pen or pencil and a piece of paper.

Tim: Got it.

Mike: Write this number down. It's #05F25879. This is your District Court Case Number for the eviction they filed on you in August. Did you get that number, Tim?

Tim: Yeah, I got it.

Mike: Now, Tim, here's what you need to do. Keep that number, it's important, and take it with you to District Court. Explain to them your situation and what's going on and they'll help you. You need to get this case and number removed from your record and then I can move forward with your application. How long will it take you to do this, Tim?

Tim: Uh, oh, a couple of days.

Mike: Okay. Here's what I can do for you, Tim. Do you have my phone number here at Vista?

Tim: Yes.

Mike: When you get this done, give me a call right away and I can get right back on your application, but in the meantime, I'm gonna have to put it on the shelf until I hear back from you. I've got to move on to the next application until you get back with me.

Tim: Okay.

I can't tell you how many times I have had similar conversations. Remember, the question on our rental application is "How many evictions have been filed on you?" This is not what Tim read. He assumed the question was "How many times have you been evicted?" and he answered "zero."

After pulling his credit report, we found another address and an eviction filing. At minimum, this set the stage for false or incomplete information on his application.

The simplest and easiest way to never disqualify a tenant is to offer him a helping hand. Give him an out, give him an example or a course of action on his part to fix the problem, Another red flag could be a bad landlord reference. Do not go into details, but explain there's a problem with his rental history and *he can fix it* with a letter from the landlord explaining his situation and how it was resolved. If he does this, it will allow you to move forward with processing his application.

Implementing this approach in our application process has largely removed liability on our part because very few applicants get "officially disqualified." They just get "parked on the shelf" until they contact us showing they have resolved their issue.

Some applicants try tactics that you need to nip in the bud. Instead of focusing on old-fashioned generic steps 1, 2, and 3 in processing these applicants, you need to squash their attempts to lie to us, the landlords.

Always use your work copy application and never write anything on the original application submitted.

If you ever choose to disqualify an applicant for false information or an incomplete application and you have scribbled all over his original and altered it, you probably have no proof, no acceptable evidence, because you have destroyed it.

Hiding Previous Addresses

A frequent flyer tactic is trying to hide previous addresses when listing addresses for the past five years on the application. Also amusing is noting that the top of our application reads:

> *Only Clean and Responsible People Who Pay Rent on Time May Apply, with a Valid Photo ID.*

After submitting her application, the applicant is asked to produce a photo ID, and amazingly another address is listed on her ID. Do not confront the applicant at this time. This is another bullet to put in your gun.

On occasion, some professional tenants just seem to self-destruct. If they have given you a bunch of baloney on their previous addresses, you may ask them again later when using your work copy of their application. . . . So you lived at 123 Main Street for the past three years? If they reply Yes, and you've already discovered another address during the same time period, then you can ask them about the newly discovered address. They will start to backpedal and will realize you are serious about working up their application. They may even move on and search for a dumber landlord. You may choose to slow-walk the conversation on the telephone by making a big deal of the first issue (asking for their help to get them qualified), and then expose the second hurdle, the third, and so on. Most of these folks then just evaporate.

Phantom Owner/Manager

Have you received applications where you suspect the current landlord is a relative or friend trying to help them rent your place? If your gut feels this, here's a good method to expose the loser.

Call the owner/manager listed on their application and ask, "How much is the rent on the place you have for rent?" Be careful and don't expose yourself on Caller ID. This question usually catches the phantom wannabe landlord off guard and the person will usually reply, "I don't rent houses or apartments!" . . . Aha, now the cat is out of the bag! This would be an excellent candidate for false information on an application. It doesn't necessarily mean automatic disqualification, but it sure gives you the authority to do so, and it shows them this ain't no kid's game.

The *previous landlord,* not the current landlord, is your most powerful reference. Do yourself a favor and do *not* burden the previous landlord with the long list of 26 or 32 questions you got at some seminar. Be nice and friendly. Remember, you're a landlord, too. You don't make a plug nickel on tenant reference checks and neither do they. Don't waste their time. Tell them you have four easy questions. Remember, this tenant is gone! You are taking up their time.

Ask these questions:

Did they pay their rent on time?

Did you receive any complaints?

Did they damage your property?

Would you rent to them again?

An efficient property manager or landlord may do the legal thing and request an authorization to release this information on the part of the tenant. If they request this, no problem, fax them the back page of your application and the Previous Landlord Verification Worksheet allowing them to check yes/no on these same four questions and fax it back to you. Now you have better proof, because it's in writing. The challenge with working up applications today is that everybody wants an answer *now*.

Most of the time, I can get mom-and-pop landlords to answer these four questions on the phone. I just convince them I don't want to waste their time, I need to get an empty unit rented quickly, and I have authorization from the tenant because it's part of our application.

I say, "If you can answer just four simple yes/no questions for me right now, I promise I'll fax their authorization to your office as soon as I get off the phone with you." This usually results in me getting my answers *now*.

Think about this for a moment.

How would you feel if you got a phone call from another landlord who started down a list of 25 questions about your former tenant?

What if you received a fax with a list of 30 questions or more about a previous tenant?

I can tell you when I get a fax from another landlord with a long list of goofy questions, yup, it goes into File 13, the trash. This is reality, folks.

Current Landlord

Be careful here. Think about it for a moment. Have you ever had a bad tenant and you got a phone call from maybe their new prospective landlord? What did you really tell him? Did you say he was average or okay, or he was really great and you hate to lose him? I've had some of my good friends and local competition tell me the same things when a tenant they were evicting was trying to rent a place from me.

Credit Reports

It seems that more than 90 percent of all applicants have no credit or bad credit. How can we find good tenants? Remember, anybody who can breathe can buy a house. Most good tenants have become homeowners. What remains is the ugliest of the ugly. How can we make lemonade out of lemons? There is no need to stand by and hope for A1 credit. It's not going to happen. You will have extended vacancies. You must make adjustments.

Almost all applicants today have poor credit (that's why they're tenants!) so don't expect to find wonderful credit scores. Expect bad and poor credit. How can they get qualified? Your answer is: By using compensating factors. Here are some solutions:

- Use the phrase, "Bad credit will not prevent you from renting a home."
- "We have ways to help you get qualified. For example, you might be able to double your deposit."
- Provide a good credit cosigner.
- *Buy down* his rent to help him qualify with his income. For example, a house rents for $800 a month. For $2,500 today, your applicant can buy down the rent to $600 for the next 12 months.
- Encourage an option to buy: Get educated on it first in your state and jurisdiction. Many landlords using options improperly are jackpotting themselves.
- Ask for a *full year* paid in advance. Just like an aggressive investor, train yourself to ask this question, it costs you nothing, and some applicants have resources to pull this off. We sometimes focus on income to ensure their ability to pay rent. I missed the boat and lost a good tenant to one of my business friends because he asked this question and the applicants paid a full year of rent in advance when they signed their lease. Who needs a job or income if they can do this? It costs us nothing to ask the question even if we may feel uncomfortable or think it is useless.

Housekeeping Check

This is your best screening tool for use with local applicants. This is your last and final step before approving an applicant. Do this with no phone call and with no notice to your applicant. You must do this step unannounced. If you tell him about this in advance it defeats the entire procedure and you would be wasting your time.

This step is your crystal ball allowing you to see your property in the future.

After working up his application on your work copy and on the phone—get out of the office. Your final step before approving him is to ride by and see where he lives. If it's ugly—tall grass, cars in the yard—no need to stop. If it looks okay from the street, then stop and knock on the door. You need to verify he actually lives in this pretty home.

If the outside looks acceptable, stop by and knock on the door and ask for your applicant by name *before* you identify yourself. Many times, the person who answers the door says, "He doesn't live here. He lives over there."

If your applicant answers the door, then you can identify yourself and say: My property management company sent me here to do two things:

1. To verify you really live here.
2. To see how you take care of the place.

I used to do this housekeeping check myself; however, I have passed this task off to my maintenance supervisor. He now does the housekeeping checks. Here are his guidelines. After stepping into Sally Applicant's living room, he asks himself:

Q1: "If Sally fixed me a bologna sandwich, would I eat it?"

If Answer is: No, she is not approved.

If Answer is: Yes, go to Question 2.

Q2: "Do I want to clean up behind Sally when she moves?"

If Answer is: No, she is not approved.

If Answer is: Yes, she is approved.

Okay, suppose Dan, my maintenance supervisor, discovers a horrible pigpen, animal-infested, urine-smelling house and he answers his questions *no*. My experience has been that these folks almost never call anymore. They got the message. Remember the top of our application reads:

> *Only Clean and Responsible People Who Pay Rent on Time May Apply, with a Valid Photo ID.*

There have been a couple of occasions where an applicant just didn't get it. He didn't have a clue he was a pig. I had the gazoongas to tell him on the phone he was just too dirty. I even had one of these applicants try to file a complaint telling the complaint taker he was disqualified for being too dirty. I got a chuckle because he was not allowed to file his complaint because "dirty people" are not *a protected class and we had this properly noted on our application.*

Protected Classes

You can also choose not to rent to certain individuals, but you should spell it out on your qualifying standards. You could have a policy stating you don't rent to cops and this would be perfectly legal. Cops are not a protected class. You could do the same with attorneys. They are not a protected class. You could pick on school-teachers, or football coaches, or even preachers providing you won't rent to any preacher. I'm exaggerating this a bit, but the point I'm trying to make is that a lot of people confuse being fair with being discriminated against.

As discussed in Chapter 12, there are seven protected classes (race, color, religion, national origin, sex, disability, familial status) you cannot use as a reason to refuse to show or offer housing. Outside of these seven, providing you are fair, have a written policy, and adhere to it 100 percent, you could choose, for example, not to rent to cops.

Preventing tenant turnovers is your number one method of avoiding vacancies. Do something special and create loyalty from your tenants. Financial incentives and benefits to your tenants that cost you zero are home runs. Keeping good tenants in units would eliminate all the hoops and hurdles discussed earlier.

CHAPTER 15

After Three Years, March 31 Is a Good Money Day

Who started this stuff you gotta rent your properties for 12 months (or 1 year)? Are you in the hotel business? I'm not. I want my tenants to stay forever! Chew on this and start doing this now.

From now on, for all your single-family properties, your rental agreements or leases with tenants will be for a minimum of 36 months, with all of them expiring on March 31, *after* completing 36 months.

For example, a new tenant moving in on December 10 will complete a lease with an "anniversary date" (lease expiration date) of March 31, three years down the road, which would give you a 40-month lease. Don't start crying or thinking like a tenant, saying nobody will do this. You are nervous and jumpy because you're not used to seeing it.

Keep in mind, you've been grooming your applicants and tenants for this all along with these ticklers:

- On your rental application, you asked, "How Long Do You Want to Live Here?" _____1 year _____2 years _____3 years (odds are they checked the 3-year box).

- Your Bonus *All-Star Plan* offers rent discounts including *free rent* when they've been with you for three years.

- You pitched below-market rent because you offer long-term housing, whereas other landlords usually do 12-month rental agreements.

Sometimes tenants ask a question about an expiration date of March 31 when moving in on December 10. We just kindly ask them and remind them, "Do you really want to move again right before the holidays, during the school year, and in bad weather?" This usually prompts a thank you from our tenants for this consideration. Besides March 31 is a better time of the year.

From our perspective, March 31 is the day before April 1. Before long, school will let out for summer vacation.

Most tenants seem to have kids. It's a fact. Responsible tenants usually begin their search for a new home several months *before* they want to move.

What kind of tenants do you find between Halloween and January 1? I'll bet not many responsible tenants are looking to move in this period.

How many tenant turnovers do you want to deal with? Ideally, all of us landlords really love to almost shut down during the winter holiday season. If we have tenants moving out during this time, it just causes more work for us.

Ask yourself during what season, or month, of the year the biggest pool of responsible tenants might be searching for homes. I suspect most of these good tenants start looking a month or two before the school year ends. How about March or April?

This also coincides with the time when many tenants get their tax refund checks, giving you the opportunity to pounce on doing rent with an option to buy.

It also works wonderfully well for all our current tenants. Responsible families do not want to move during the school year; therefore, current tenants will feel compelled to renew their rental agreement to avoid moving in March and jerking their kids out of school. Not a 12-month lease, but a brand-new 36-month lease.

There are many reasons to have your leases expire on March 31 after their third year. It just makes good *cents*.

Also with our All-Star Plan, tenants can get Month 37 absolutely free, providing they sign a new 36-month rental agreement.

CHAPTER 16

Let's Have a Little Rent Talk First

The Rent Talk is part of our New Tenant Indoctrination. It is a flip chart presentation contained in a one-inch, three-ring binder. Each page is enclosed in a transparent sheet protector. You open the binder completely, almost reversing it, allowing it to serve as an easel while sitting on your desktop, kitchen counter, or hood of your car or truck (see Figure 16.1).

You flip one page at a time over the rings and discuss the topics on that page. This is your opportunity to school and train your tenants before you give them the keys to your investment property.

This powerful and professional flip chart is a great training tool to help both you and your tenant get off on the right start. Earlier, I mentioned how much training I received before I was allowed to bag groceries, you need to invest an hour or two in training your tenants to care for your property. Don't shoot yourself in the foot, take their money, say "Sign Here," and give them the keys. You are just asking for problems.

FIGURE 16.1 Ring Binder

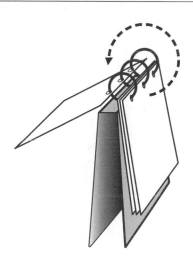

If you do not train your tenants, I promise you, they will perform and behave based entirely on what they have been conditioned or brainwashed into believing about acceptable tenant behavior. I'm proud to say we've helped many tenants become more responsible individuals.

This training tool also has nipped future problems in the bud. We've had approved applicants, money in hand, waiting to sign their rental agreement and get their keys, who—after the presentation—actually said, "Nope, this is too darn tough for me." They backed out of renting a home. Having this happen is much better than getting a problem tenant in one of your properties.

Especially with single-family homes, l stress that they have qualified to rent one of our homes. There are responsibilities and privileges involved with renting a home. It's much different from renting an apartment.

Figure 16.2 shows "Rent Talk." Just imagine giving your presentation while using your one-inch binder flip chart as a visual aid. Some of the topics covered in rent talk include:

1. Paying rent on time and how important this should be.

2. Encouraging tenants to set up an "emergency fund."

3. Responsibilities and duties of being a resident in a single-family house:
   a. Lawn service
   b. Trash
   c. Cleaning gutters
   d. Changing air filters
   e. And many more jobs

4. Responsibilities and duties of being a resident in an apartment community detailing such things as building rules and respect for fellow residents.

5. Explaining to tenants the life of the property and the life of things in a home, for example, storm doors should last 10 or 15 years, not 3 months.

6. ALL STAR PROGRAM explained in detailed.

7. Our help in working toward home ownership.

8. Maintenance repair requests or work order requests:
   a. Single-family homes: Tenant MUST be home and be present.
   b. Apartments: Tenant must complete a maintenance repair request form.

9. Renters insurance is for the tenant's protection and is a bargain (plus it is the landlord's first line of defense in asset protection).

FIGURE 16.2   Rent Talk

We Buy Houses!   We Rent Homes!

Congratulations!

- YOU are an important part of our business.

- We are proud of our performance & the many referrals received – we want your experience to be the same.

- Remember, We do more than rent homes – excellent "seasoned" people like yourself may become a homeowner sooner and easier than you think.

- Thanks for choosing us for your housing needs.

(continued)

FIGURE 16.2   (Continued)

Useful Life

• Interior and exterior paint should last 7-10 years. If you drag your hands along the walls or grab door jams causing handprints, then you are responsible for cost to paint. Smoking also shortens the life of paint.

• Carpet should last 10 years +. If stained or damaged and it is less than 10 years old, then you are responsible for replacement cost of new carpet.

• Windows, doors, light fixtures, and plumbing fixtures should last 20-30 years.

Reasonable Wear and Tear

• Defined: Needs replacing or repair because it has been in use longer than it's normal life expectancy.

• Nothing has a life span of less than 5 years – (except light bulbs and furnace filters)

• If all items are in good working order now, then all items should be in good working order in 5 years.

• If you live in a home for less than 5 years, and it needs repairs or cleaning, then you are responsible for these expenses.

FIGURE 16.2   (Continued)

Our Mission Statement

To provide housing for clean responsible people who always make their payments on time, take care of their home and property, and stay for a minimum of 5 years.

We intend to find and keep these people by providing:
- A quality home
- Excellent service
- Competitive rates
- Opportunities for upgrades
- Assistance to homeownership

What Is a Rental Agreement?

The promise from the Landlord to provide a home in reasonable cosmetic shape, with safe working mechanical systems for the full term of the rental agreement.

AND

The promise from the Tenant to treat the property with care, by maintaining its good condition and paying the rent on time for the full term of the rental agreement.

(continued)

FIGURE 16.2 (Continued)

Living in a Single-Family Home
Your Responsibilities

Congratulations on your move into a single-family home! You have maintenance responsibilities with your home for the full term of your rental agreement.

You must maintain the exterior of your home. This includes proper lawn care, cleaning out the gutters in the spring and fall, trimming tree limbs keeping them off of your roof, and covering crawl space vents in the winter to save on your utility bill(s) and prevent water pipes from freezing.

All this is in addition to regular home care maintenance such as changing furnace filters monthly, smoke alarm batteries twice a year, and minor repairs including small leaks and faucet repairs. Your responsibilities help maintain your home's good condition and prevents costly major repairs.

This equals affordable rent for YOU.

Remember, we are responsible for these systems:
- Roof
- HVAC – Furnace & Central Air (not window air units)
- Hot Water Heater
- Water supply from meter to house

Maintenance Guarantee

We are responsible for the mechanical systems in your residence, and promise to maintain them in good working order for the full term of your rental agreement.

We employ professional, friendly service people and utilize several licensed trade professionals to service your home.

We are responsible for these systems:

- HVAC – Furnace & Central Air (not window air units)
- Hot Water Heater
- Water supply from meter to house

We understand that many other people complain about their Landlord's repair problems; however, we can NOT repair something we know nothing about...Please call.

FIGURE 16.2   (Continued)

Maintenance Requests

If repairs are needed that are your responsibility, we can help you.

Your cost during business hours is $_____ per hour for labor (including travel time), plus material. After hours includes a $_____ service call charge. *(These prices are subject to change without notice.)*

If you have a maintenance request, please call the office. A service person will contact you promptly to coordinate the scheduling of your work order request. Our company policy prohibits any service person from entering your home unless you are present.

Please do not contact our service people directly. They will only respond to authorized work orders from the office and have instructions to refer any additional requests to the office for approval.

> Remember, we are a business and have never found someone to work for FREE. Excessive repair requests *almost guarantees you will get* a large rent increase. Please help yourself and work with us to hold down your costs.

Your Repairs

- **Clogged sinks** – from food that should have been placed in trash
- **Clogged toilets** – from flushing items other than human waste (pads, toys, excess paper, clothing, or cleaning products, even a ham hock bone)
- **Leaks** – from shoving items under the sink (This knocks water and drain lines loose.)
- **Faucet knobs** – from using too much force, causing broken knobs and leaking faucets (I do not have this problem at my home)
- **Broken** windows, doors, glass, or locks for any reason.
- **Storm doors** – storm door on my home is 30 years old?
- **Malfunctioning HVAC**: usually due to failure to keep clean:
  - A/C units gets clogged with grass clippings and weeds in summer.
  - DIRTY filter will cause A/C to freeze up. (I know, this did happen to me)
  - Furnace filter not cleaned or replaced monthly causing higher utility bills.

> YOU WILL BE CHARGED FOR THESE KINDS OF REPAIRS

(continued)

FIGURE 16.2　(Continued)

Have an Emergency Fund

- All financial advisors recommend that YOU should have an "Emergency Fund" of not less than $1,000.

- It is better to have 3 to 6 months of pay saved at all times.

- This way, when "Life" throws you a curve ball, there will already be money set aside to handle the problem.

- You should ALWAYS have $1,000 in reserve.

(Need help with this one? Ask how we can help.)

No Excuse for Not Paying Rent

We're NOT cold and mean people; however, We're in the business world–

Financial obligations are taken seriously;
unfortunately with ZERO TOLERANCE for excuses.

Imagine this phone call:

Property Manager: "I'm sorry . . . Our Tenant got sick and did not work for 4 days this month and has not paid the rent yet."

Banker: (You can guess what the answer is . . . .)

FIGURE 16.2 (Continued)

If You Do Not Pay on Time

- *You will cause* yourself grief for late or non-payment
- *You will cause* late charges, attorney fees, & court costs
- *You will cause* your credit to be destroyed
- *You will cause* your own eviction
- *You will cause* a judgment against you & everything you own.
- *You will cause* your wages to be garnished.
- *You will cause* yourself to be chased & hassled until paid.
- *You will cause*.....

    ALL THE BAD STUFF

The Rule of Ten

Any action you take, positive or negative,
will come back to you **tenfold**.

- If you always pay on time and in full, you will have a credit rating in the **top 10%** of the population.

- If you do not pay on time and in full, odds are you will end up with a judgment and garnishment of **10 times** your original monthly rent payment.

(continued)

FIGURE 16.2   (Continued)

CHAPTER 17

The Cookie Cutter Move-In and Paper-Signing Process

Now it is time to tee off and get your approved applicant graduated to Active Tenant in your program.

1. Prior to your "Sign the Papers" meeting, set up a one-third cut, letter-size manila file folder for your new tenant. On the tab of the file folder, write the following: Your Rental Property Street Name, Unit Number, Tenant Last Name. (If you file all your folders in alphabetical order, it will be easy for you to find any tenant file you're searching for.) Your file folder should contain everything you have collected since your first meeting: your key sign-out form, if you use it; a photocopy or digital photo of the tenants' IDs; the rental application and all the papers involved with processing it; and the documents in a new tenant package.

2. Prepare a goody bag and a packet for your tenants containing all their papers. Be professional and take pride in your business. When new home owners attend their closing, they often receive a nice bag from their real estate agency to keep all their important papers together. You don't need to get custom-printed bags or folders. I use plain colored-paper pocket folders from my office supply store. Inside the pocket folder, there is a prepunched place to insert your business card. This works just fine and costs less than a dollar. This professional attitude will carry through many things in your business. Your goody bag could contain such things as:

- Your peel-and-stick calendar
- Refrigerator magnet with your phone number
- Coffee mug
- Welcome flyer or page
- Utility, phone, cable, Internet contact information
- Community packets (free from your local chamber of commerce or travel agents)
- School information

- Key tag
- Coupons and whatever else you can come up with

    3. Have your New Tenant Office Checklist in your tenant's file folder to make sure you dot your i's and cross all your t's (see Form A.10: New Tenant Office Checklist, in Section III).

    4. Plan and schedule an appointment for the indoctrination of your new tenants. Let them know it will take no longer than two hours. If you get finished in less time, you'll look like a hero. Tell your tenants what to bring:

- *Certified check:* They should get this from a local bank for the amount of funds needed to sign the papers and get started. Tell them exactly what that amount should be. (Never take a personal check when starting a tenancy, and do your best to stay away from cash for safety reasons.)
- *Full-year renter's insurance policy:* Premium must be paid in full. If they don't have the policy handy, let the tenants know you can contact their insurance agent to fax a declaration page or proof of insurance to your office. I highly recommend that you try to help your own insurance agency by referring your tenant as an insurance customer. It will make your insurance agent happy and will give you better control of the big picture.
- *Required signatures:* All those signing the rental agreement must be present. If there are two adult applicants, both must sign and complete your starting process before they get keys.
- *Security deposit:* Make sure your procedure is in compliance with your local landlord/tenant law. In my town, we must keep this money in a separate bank account (not an escrow account). As a licensed real estate broker in my state, I'm required to have an *escrow* account for deposits made by buyers of real estate plus another bank account that is used exclusively for tenants' security deposits.
- *Animals:* Tenants with animals must bring in photos of those animals and proof of any shots and licenses required in your town/state.

    5. When your tenants arrive, think of them as *new employees*. Don't tell them that—just think this way. How would an employer greet you if you were a new employee?

    6. Go through the Rent Talk with them first (see chapter 16).

    7. Then go over your rental agreement or lease agreement in detail, line by line. You must do this to properly train your "new employee" (tenant; see Form A.12: Rental Agreement, in Section III).

    8. It is your responsibility to get your tenants started out on the right foot. Don't get lazy. Do it right. Ask them if they understand every part of the agreement.

9. Make them initial each page.
10. Make them sign and date each form properly.
11. Treat your new tenants with respect and make copies of all documents for them. When I got started and did this at the property, I would simply make two packages of blank forms and then let the tenants keep a blank set.
12. Your move-in inspection form must be properly completed and signed.

Move-in inspection forms can be a sensitive issue. This one form is all over the planet. I've seen some move-in inspection forms with five pages *per room* for each property.

The purpose of a move-in inspection form is to properly document the condition of the property at the time the tenant moves in. Its secondary purpose is to protect the interest of both the landlord and the tenant. Many states require the move-in inspection to include existing damage or items in need of repair along with the cost at that time.

Here's my let-the-dust-settle reality check. No move-in inspection form is the ultimate, absolute perfect, landlord-safe, tenant-proof form. Any competent attorney who had a passion to attack a move-in inspection could go after the very best form and chew it up causing the landlord to lose the case in court. I truly believe this. Remember, it's ultimately up to the judge.

Therefore, if I can't incorporate a bulletproof form, why not use the next best thing—the KISS (keep it simple, stupid) method—my one-page fill-in-the-blank move-in inspection form. I admit, it's not perfect; however, I have used it in thousands of move-ins and move-outs including very few involving lawsuits and have never been challenged on it. Plus, not once (knock on wood) has my move-in or move-out form been challenged by those tenants who end up in collections after their tenancy and go to court with judgments, garnishments, and more.

If it has worked 999 times out of 1,000, I'm sticking with it. The move-out and move-in inspection forms are identical. Only the title at the top is different. When a tenant moves in, we include digital photos of the property both inside and out. We use the Windows Fax and Picture Viewer to put nine photos on a page, handwrite the property address and the date, and allow the tenant to sign and date each page. This can be done in our office without having to travel to the property again.

Unless the home is a newly renovated or rehabbed property, we mark everything "Good" and draw a line on the left column with "All Good." On the move-in inspection form (see Form A.15: Move-In Inspection, in Section III), we check the good boxes down the left column as well. We instruct the tenants to look over the property again, and odds are, they're going to find some small things when they move in.

We ask the tenants to please call us within seven days to report any problems they discover. We will add them to their move-in inspection form and send someone out to make any needed repairs we may have missed. This has worked fine for us.

Ask the tenants for their new phone numbers and congratulate them on their new home.

1. With single-family homes, we instruct the tenants to transfer utilities, and we document our request to terminate service on our Utility Log.

2. *Lead-based paint:* For houses and residential rental property constructed prior to 1978, the Environmental Protection Agency (EPA) requires you, the landlord, to give tenants the EPA Publication: "Protect Your Family from Lead in Your Home" *before* they rent your property (see Form A.23: EPA Publication, in Section III). You are also required to give them this pamphlet again if you ever do any repairs to their unit or a common area that disturb a painted surface of more than two square feet. Not many landlords are aware of this requirement.

3. *Due date for rent:* Getting your tenants set up to pay their rent on or before the first day of the month helps to get your landlording on auto-pilot. The twentieth day of the month determines how they get started. For example, if your tenant moves in on the twelfth day of the month, just charge them rent from the twelfth through the end of the month to get started. You will be sending them a bill on the twentieth for next month's rent. This gets them set up for paying rent on the first:

- Other landlords pitch creative strategies to enhance your system. Some experts encourage landlords to have their rents due on the twenty-fifth of the month, supposedly to put the landlord in a better position to get the rent before making a mortgage payment or renting to another tenant. Phooey!

- About 99 percent of society believes residential monthly rent covers a calendar month. Guess what—those folks in the courthouse also think this way. The courts, as a rule, aren't very landlord friendly. If I go into court and try to explain to a disgruntled judge my newfangled, supersharp creative rent program that says rents are due on the twenty-fifth or the second Tuesday after the third blue Wednesday, the judge will probably get an attitude toward me before I ever get started. *Keep it simple,* and when in Rome, do as the Romans do. If you want the court system to be a last resort or tool for your benefit, don't irritate the judge and shoot yourself in the foot. Keep your rent schedule as the rest of world knows it, by the calendar month.

4. *Animals:* Use your animal addendum form to document the number and type of animal. Ten species of dogs are forbidden because of insurance company regulations:

1. Pit bull
2. Rottweiler
3. German shepherd
4. Husky—Alaskan malamute
5. Doberman pinscher

6. Chow
7. Great Dane
8. Saint Bernard
9. Akita
10. Wolf hybrids

We enforce this rule and have seen other landlords' property insurance get canceled when an insurance representative has found any of these animals on the insured property.

Providing the tenant does not have these animals, we charge $25.00 per month additional rent per animal along with an animal deposit. Three animals will crank you another $75.00 per month in rental income.

You Really Can Teach Pigs to Sing

My wife, Tammy, frequently reminded me of one of her favorite phrases; she claimed she discovered it in a Beatles song years ago:

Never teach a pig to sing, it wastes your time, and annoys the pig.

Most of the time, she is right. But on occasion I'd hear one begin to hum a tune.

Case Study 1—Inherited Tenants You Intend to Keep

As an aggressive investor, I was buying, and buying, and buying property. I purchased four single-family, shotgun style houses from a slumlord named Joe. This guy never did anything properly. He replaced broken furnaces with used furnaces and didn't worry about the quality of his tenants.

Joe used to tell me one of his favorite investor truths was that the properties he was most embarrassed to admit he owned were usually the properties producing the most cash flow and profit. Perhaps for Joe, but his program was not for me.

I negotiated a pretty good deal with Joe on these four houses. They were all in a row on the same street and had *his* tenants in them. Horrible. We put the deal together and scheduled the closing.

In the meantime, we moved forward discussing the arrangements with his existing tenants. Joe informed me he had to stop by every Saturday morning knocking on their doors to collect rent. I boldly told Joe I would never knock on their doors to collect rent. These tenants would mail their rent payments monthly. He then gave a thigh-slapping, gut-wrenching belly laugh. And then another one, saying, "They will *never* mail their rent. They don't know how."

Joe told me he'd had these properties for years and not once, never, ever, had any of his tenants in those four houses mailed their rent. He promised me this could not be done, but he still wished me good luck.

Before the closing, and before purchasing the properties, I made four copies of my Tenant Information Sheet (see Form A.9: Tenant Information Sheet, in Section III) and New Tenant Packages, which include the Move-In Inspection, Rental Agreement, and lead-based paint pamphlets and arranged a meeting with each of the "inherited" tenants. The purpose of this meeting was to have a thorough "cleansing" from the previous landlord and transition these folks 100 percent into my system.

But, what if your inherited tenants have a signed rental agreement or lease with the previous owner? Use your great people and communication skills. It simply takes the agreement of both parties involved—the landlord/owner (you) and the tenant. You can agree to terminate and kill the existing agreement effective on a specific date. You both can enter into your rental agreement with a new effective date. The exception would be any kind of government program such as Section 8. You would then be forced to step into the former owner's shoes.

I took their folder(s) and a clipboard and visited each tenant. These tenants did not have telephones or cell phones, so I had to stop by unannounced. I gathered information from each tenant about the property, their past financial relationship with their landlord Joe to verify their rent, security deposits, and so on. Doing this prior to the closing allows you to take it up with your seller (in my case, Joe) before buying the property. It is much easier to work these bugs out on the front end than after your closing.

Suppose a tenant says he paid a $600 deposit to the landlord, and your seller says he's got a $300 security deposit. Wouldn't it be best to discover this prior to buying this property and inheriting the tenant?

I stopped by and visited each tenant to identify myself as the probable new owner. This was their opportunity to vent and blow off steam about anything they chose including the soon-to-be previous owner.

Remember, these folks didn't need an application to rent from me. They were already in the property.

Letting these tenants vent made them feel important and valued. They probably hadn't been treated this way in a while. While I had them eating out of my hand, I completed all the paperwork to transition them completely into our system, including my new rental agreement.

At this time, I schooled them on our great new program for them. I let them know our property management company would mail them a bill on the twentieth of each month. Inside would be a monthly statement detailing charges on their account, an addressed envelope for mailing their payment, and a monthly newsletter just for them with all kinds of tips and coupons.

Here came the static; they started bucking. They never mailed their rent before. Joe always came and collected weekly or several times a month. I told them this would never happen again. They *must* mail their rent payment.

I held their hand mentally, let them calm down, and showed them how easy this would be: "Nobody will knock on your door early on Saturday morning. You can sleep in now. All you have to do is get some stamps. You can get them at the grocery store. Put your money order or check into the envelope, put a stamp on it, and drop it in a mailbox."

Some of these tenants balked, stating that they had no bank account, or didn't get their check till the third of the month.

Rent is due on the first of the month. Period.

Guess when it's late? It's late on the second. Period.

Late Charge: 10 percent of the monthly rent.

Daily Late Charge: $5.00 per day, in addition to the 10 percent charge.

Here's how I handle those wanna-be problem children. Suppose you acknowledge their checks arrive in their mailbox on the third. You offer a simple solution. Remind them that their monthly rent bill is mailed to them on the twentieth. Tell your tenants to put their payment in the envelope and mail it before the first of the month.

We use the postmark date on their envelope as the payment received date.

I sometimes receive payments in the mail on the third or even the fourth with a postmark date of the first. This means the tenant does not have a late charge.

No competent judge in any court will refuse to use the postmark date as a payment received date. This totally eliminates those stupid tactics by tenants who mail a check on October 5 but handwrite September 30 on their rent check thinking it will prevent a late charge.

Back to the tenants who got their check on the third of the month. I told them to put their payment in the envelope and mail it in before the first with a note, "Please hold until the third." If we receive their payment with this note before the first, they will not be hit with a late charge. This works great.

Joe saw me a few months after I bought his houses, and he asked me how things were going. He also asked how I liked knocking on doors weekly to get the rent. I told him I never knocked on tenants' doors and they were mailing their monthly rent payments as instructed. He was shocked and didn't believe it. He went over to see his old tenants to verify my story, and they told him the same.

Joe thinks I'm the best landlord on the planet because he sure would've bet $1,000 I could never get these tenants to mail their rent payments monthly.

So, yes, you really can teach pigs to sing.

Case Study 2—Inherited Tenants You Want Out Now

No need to make this difficult. The current tenants and occupants have your sellers pulling their hair out. For whatever reason, you want these tenants gone and gone now. They don't fit into your program.

Here's what I've done many times. First, you must coordinate your activities legally and safely so you never throw out money before you have control and own the property. One of the worst mistakes you could make is to take your expertise and make the problem tenant leave quickly before you buy the property. You might have just fixed the seller's problem, and he may change his mind about selling you the property. You made it nice again. So, be careful not to do this before you actually buy the property.

You own the property and you want to get these idiots out fast. You have two avenues to get them out:

1. Figure out how to do it yourself.
2. Use the court system, attorneys, and legally evict them.

I can tell you Plan 1 is the best for you.

Plan 2 can be expensive; it makes money for the attorneys and drags out your access to the property. You can't start working on it, your overhead meter for taxes and insurance is running, and the tenants are just making the property worse. Plus, you can bet they're gonna leave you a huge mess when they finally get evicted.

How much money, time, and effort will you be out with Plan 2? In my town, I could easily spend $1,000 to get these tenants out using the court system.

Here's my solution: After you buy the property, stop by and visit problem tenants. As hard as it may be, bite your lip, and try to be friendly and sincere while maintaining your firm professional attitude. Here's how the conversation goes:

Landlord: Hey, Billy, I might have a deal for you. Can I talk to you a minute?

[Billy, even if an idiot, will usually agree.]

Landlord: Here's the deal Billy. My name is Mike. I know that you and Tom (your seller) aren't getting along right now, but I don't have any problem with you at all. Do you understand this?

Tenant: [Billy may start to blab about Tom. Don't tell him to shut up. You'll piss him off, too, just like Tom. In fact, it would do you some good to agree with Billy by shaking your head in acknowledgment of his situation.]

[Let Billy vent a little, continue calling him by his name, and then tell him about your deal.]

Landlord: Here's the deal, Billy. First of all, I have no issue with you at all. You understand that, right? But I've bought this property and I've got plans, and unfortunately you're gonna have to move. We can do this as friendly folks and I can help you out, *or* you can make it difficult and you and I will both lose and the attorneys will win. They just want to always make a mountain out of a molehill and make us pay for it. So here's your deal in a nutshell, Billy. I can give you money to help you with your move or I can let the attorneys have your money. Are you interested?

Tenant: Tell me more.

Landlord: Here's the deal, Billy. If you get all your stuff, and I mean all your stuff, out of here by 4:00 P.M. on Saturday, have it "broom clean" with all your trash hauled off and not stacked up anywhere, I'll give you $600 cash on the spot. All you have to do is call me and let me know you got it done, I'll show up here to see you've really done it, and you'll get your money, no questions asked. This might help you get a truck or help you with getting a new place.

[Most of the time, Billy will jump on this. He might say 4:00 P.M. on Saturday is impossible. Acknowledge it and ask what will work for him. You want this to be a win-win situation. Suppose he says 4:00 P.M. on Monday will work for him.]

Landlord: [That's still good. And I'd remind him]: Remember, Billy, this means nothing in here, broom clean, no excuses about anything. All out, all gone. Not a chair left behind or even a fork. You got it and do I have your word on it?

[If Billy agrees to this, I know he will do as agreed—I've never had a tenant who didn't. Pretty amazing isn't it?]

Use Written Correspondence

Since you are using my Tenant Tracking system to bill your tenants monthly, this sets the stage for you to incorporate written correspondence into your program. It is amazingly simple to implement once you start billing your tenants. You are already mailing them a monthly statement (a piece of paper), and many times when they mail their rent payment to your post office box, they scribble some kind of note.

Don't get me wrong. I'm not saying this happens all the time. I'm guessing perhaps one or two out of a hundred tenant payments will contain a written note of some kind. It could be anything from a complaint to a work order request to miscellaneous information that they deem important for you to know.

The important thing is you did not waste time on the phone, and now you have it in writing. Use your RECEIVED date stamp on their written notes and save it in their file folder.

Late Notices

Most states require landlords to give tenants who haven't paid rent a specific Pay or Quit Possession Notice of X number of days. Doing it right and legally will save you a lot of grief.

Tip: Most states include language stating that if a landlord accepts any partial payments of rent after the landlord has started the eviction process, the accepted partial payment of rent will *kill* and cancel the landlord's pending eviction action.

Therefore, we don't accept partial payments once the eviction process has started.

Also, suppose a tenant has a monthly rent of $800 and your late charge is 10 percent ($80.00). Using my Tenant Tracking system of billing our tenants, a chronological order of events might occur like this:

			Balance
8-20-06	Rent for next month	$800.00	$800.00
9-2-06	Late charge	$80.00	$880.00
9-3-06	Payment received from tenant	($800.00)	$80.00
9-20-06	Rent for next month	$800.00	$880.00

Now if my tenant mails in a payment of $800.00 and we receive it on the first of the month or before, we will refuse the payment *and return it with a late notice and a late charge.*

You must stick to your guns and be firm and fair. If you accept an $800.00 payment when you mailed a bill for $880.00, you are training your tenant that this behavior is acceptable. Don't do this! It might be difficult to get started, but it works in the long run.

CHAPTER 19

Removing Bad Apples the Safe Way

Just like computers crashing, a tenant dealing dope is simply a matter of *when* it will happen to you and not *if* it happens. There are no boundaries. Although the media tries to portray it as occurring primarily in low-income neighborhoods, dope is everywhere and dope dealers are part of our society at all levels. Your rental properties are not immune. I don't care whether the rent is $100 a month or $5,000 a month, dope dealers live in all areas.

This dope-dealing animal is something that can sneak up on you. You can have the best tenant-screening program in the world; however, tenants are people. People have relationships. Some work out and some don't. Jerry Springer, Maury Povich, and many other talk show hosts have made fortunes capitalizing on the hidden aspects involved in relationships. Why are your tenants any different? They are not. Tenants can start off down the right path with you, have a falling out with their significant other and get swept off their feet with their newfound _____. (You fill in the blank.)

Because your tenant has a good track record, you may or may not be aware that the old significant other has moved out and another person has moved in. Your good tenant is responsible, has a job, and shows no signs of any pending or brewing problems.

The point I am trying to make is that no landlord is immune from having dirtbag dope dealers as tenants. Therefore, this is for all landlords of A-, B-, and C-quality rental units.

Next, you get the dreaded phone call or a note from the good tenant in Apartment 3 who "confidentially" reports that the tenant in Apartment 2 is selling dope. If the landlord doesn't fix this problem yesterday, they will be moving out. This is contagious. If this information has made its way to you, you'd better believe it has saturated the entire building. You should thank your good tenant for letting you know.

This tenant lives close to the dope dealer. I am shocked at how landlords ask this good tenant for help. Landlords repeatedly, thoughtlessly, "drop in" on the good tenant who gave them the bad news.

Never ask your tenants who give you this information to help you by putting them out front as your source for information about the suspected illegal activity. It took great courage and loyalty to you to tell you about the problem. The easier path for your tenants is to simply move from your building.

If one tenant is reporting this to you, it's likely that many more good tenants are fed up, scared, and ready to move at a moment's notice if there is no any visible action on your part to correct the suspected dope-dealing problem.

The Challenge

The eviction of a tenant suspected of permitting dope dealing is a monumental task. Dope dealers usually have cash. In most states, it takes two months or more to forcibly remove tenants from a unit *without* a legal challenge. This is way too long to satisfy your good tenants—they will be gone before the bad apple gets evicted.

Let's run the numbers for a standard eviction process. First, if the bad apple is paying rent on time, you must find another reason to evict them. Assume they are on month-to-month. Isn't it fair to assume two months might be average before they are 100 percent gone and you have possession? This means a minimum of a month of ugliness, and they will not pay rent if you are pursuing legal action to make them move. (There is a month's rent lost.)

How many good apples may take action and move because they see no visible action on your part to get the bad apple out quickly? (Now, there is month number two of lost rent, along with two vacancies and tenant turnovers . . . yuk.)

The entire eviction process costs are usually in the neighborhood of a month's rent with attorney fees, court costs, sheriff department fees, and the labor costs involved with the physical set out, or removal, of their personal property from your unit.

All combined, it is fair to assume that with this traditional process, you can expect to lose at minimum, three months' rent along with two vacant units and a label in the neighborhood of being the building that has dope dealers.

Barney Fife—"Nip It in the Bud"

Take action, the right way. After evaluating the information received from your good tenant, and realizing they are probably right, it is time for you to take action before the bad apple ruins the whole barrel.

Remember, the three months of rent. Do not forget it.

Listed next are some tips to put in place. Each depends on your comfort zone. I have used all of these in certain situations with good results. I am presenting these tips in a smorgasbord fashion and you may select the best for each situation as you see fit. The objective is to get the bad apple out *fast* while preserving the good apples.

Stuff to Do

Hit with a 2×4. Confront them face to face and ask them to move. This takes some skill and tact. My background as a cop is definitely helpful when using this tactic. There are some do's and don't's, including:

- *Never* accuse them of dope dealing.
- *Never* mention your "good apples."
- Present yourself as a problem solver and helper, with a solution for their problem. "What's the problem?" they might ask.

    "Well, it's just not working out." They may respond, "How," or "What?"

    Your answer again is, "It's just not working out and I want us to settle up on good terms."

- Avoid setting the stage for getting into a debate or a "he said, she said" story. If you know for a fact, 100 percent sure, that traffic in and out of his unit has increased, then you may choose to say, "I have noticed a lot of people in and out causing noise to others." This is a risky statement because it can open a can of worms and he may ask you, "When did you see this?" If you know your stuff, you can recite it back to him, but be careful using this one.
- Offer a win-win solution for the bad apple with a comment like—"Look, it is not working out and I have an opportunity to help you that will allow us to settle up on good terms. If we both are stubborn and attorneys and the courts get involved, we both lose, and the attorneys win. You find a place to move and be out of here by next Saturday (select a reasonable time) and have this place broom clean and I will pay you X dollars." (I usually gear it toward a dollar amount close to a month's rent).
- Do not allow your principles to confuse you about good business sense.
- If you can pull this off successfully, you win big time across the board because:
    —You have removed the problem.
    —Good tenants label you a hero.
    —You saved two months rent or more.
    —There were no eviction headaches or attitudes.
    —You have preserved the integrity of your building.

It takes special people skills and tact to use this action properly. If you have a quick temper or are hot-headed, you may want to avoid this face-to-face procedure. You must appear firm, fair, and helpful to the bad apple regardless of how close your blood is to boiling.

Effective Results with Police

Yes, still do the traditional "call your local police department," and in larger communities, phone the narcotics unit; but let's put a different twist on getting effective assistance from law enforcement.

Many large apartment communities offer free rent or discounted rent to a police officer who will live in their apartment community. This is nothing new and happens all the time. The real problem with this scenario comes from the police officer. These officers are generally hungry for money, fairly new, and are not homebodies. They work as much overtime and as many off-duty jobs as they can find resulting in very little visibility in the community.

After determining the prime time for the suspected dope-dealing activity, contact the officer who rides the beat of your problem tenant during the hours of peak activity. If you have established that peak activity is Friday and Saturday night between 10:00 P.M. and 2:00 A.M. (which, by the way, is a very busy time for uniformed police), you should make arrangements to meet the officer who rides your beat during his scheduled shift. Ask to meet him somewhere other than your rental property. This causes you inconvenience, but it sure demonstrates to this officer the seriousness of your concern.

Never tell the officer that he or she has a problem at your property. Police are people, too. Many taxpayers talk down to police officers with comments such as, "You work for me, I pay your salary." This flips on the *us-and-them* mind-set and you have already lost. Most police officers really do want to help. Use this motivating factor to get results for you.

Start your conversation with an attitude of "I need your help. I have a problem." Do more listening than talking. They feel better if they talk. They will like you better if they talk. If you do all the talking, you will feel better and they may be tuning you out. They hear this stuff all the time. Be patient.

As a rule of thumb, the longer you let police officers talk and demonstrate their knowledge to you, the more apt they are to offer out-of-the-ordinary assistance to your problem while working their shift. Your property will get extra attention and patrol.

Do not ask them to ride by, stop by, or sit on your property. The challenge here is to get the officers to offer this to you as a way for them to help.

Offer the police officers a way to contact you if needed. Ninety percent of the time, they won't call, but offering 24-7 availability means a boatload to officers working the late shift and shows your level of concern about the problem. Offer your cell phone or home number confidentially.

Following are some ways your tax dollars can help you solve the problem of the bad apple.

Signs

Make *No Loitering, No Trespassing* signs and position the signs in visible locations on your building and premises. Before doing this, make sure to contact your good apples and ask for their assistance. Explain to the good apples, once the signs are in place, they, too, cannot hang out in the parking lot or porches. A short-term sacrifice on their part now can help run off the bad apples. When peace and tranquillity return to your property, no one will complain if peaceful people are loitering on their porches.

Hiring Off-Duty Police

Many landlords have been encouraged to hire off-duty police. Some communities have take-home cars for their officers.

Be careful. This off-duty income opportunity for officers is greatly abused. Many schedule several off-duty jobs at the same time. For example, construction site A, shopping center B, and apartment community C are all paying for an officer to patrol their property between 9:00 P.M. and 2:00 A.M. and the officer schedules all three jobs during the same hours because they are within three minutes of each other.

I am not antipolice. I am propolice, being a retired officer myself, and I have two younger brothers who are police officers.

Empty Car, a Different Twist

If your town has take-home cars for officers and your peak bad-apple activity occurs after the sun goes down, contact an officer who works the day shift. Explain that you can offer a unique opportunity. Work out a deal to simply park the marked patrol car overnight right in front of the bad apple's unit. This can be done a whole lot cheaper than having an officer sit in the car. The results are usually spectacular. Who wants to buy dope from somebody with a marked car parked at the front door? You might get an officer to sit in the car for $25 to $50 an hour and you might get the car for a whole night for $50 or $100 depending on your negotiation skills.

The hidden benefit here is that your good apples see quick action on your part. The bad apple's business should immediately begin to suffer and send the message to move on down the road.

Technology

In addition to assistance from on-duty and off-duty law enforcement and no loitering signs strategically placed on your buildings, technology can be a great inexpensive tool.

Video cameras are cheap. I am talking about closed circuit television (CCTV), not the camcorders you see in retail stores. Check them out on the Internet at Supercircuits.com or use any search engine. Entire video systems with recorders sell for less than $300. Put them up high on corners of buildings (protective weatherproof and bulletproof casings are available).

In addition to the no loitering signs, add "Premises Video Recorded 24 Hrs."

This takes some effort to start up—running wires, installing a recorder in the resident manager apartment or office—but it has tremendous rewards.

Let your local law enforcement know about your effort and action of installing cameras. Your good apples will see your action. It will hurt the bad apple business but it will also be a powerful tool to prevent new bad apples from landing in your units.

Here in Louisville, a creative take-charge investor has a number of units in a high crime area. After learning of a similar situation in a visit to Chicago, he became involved with the local cable TV company and received permission to use their cable as the conduit for transmitting the video images to the recorders in the office. The cable company also installed video cameras on the utility poles. With new technology that I do not understand, police officers can use their laptops in their cars to "dial up" and view specific cameras. The point here is that you might not have to bear the burden of all the expense for security; your cable TV, phone, or other utility company may contribute resources to "help the community."

CHAPTER 20

You Really Can Get over 100 Percent of Your Rents

This is not a typo. It is a true statement, and you, too, can get these results. Before starting, let's clear up the definition here so we're both on the same page.

First of all, what exactly is rent? When holding seminars for groups, I start by asking, "We need an honest landlord with more than 15 units. Do we have one here?" After I have identified our victim for education (the honest landlord with at least 15 units), I ask this "led to slaughter in front of peers" landlord:

Of all the rent owed you over a 12-month period, how much do you really get?

Amazingly, the majority of folks answer honestly. By far, the number one answer is 85 percent. Asked if they're guesstimating or do they really know, they embarrassingly admit it's only a guesstimate. Keep in mind, this question deals only with rent owed over a 12-month period. It includes tenants who slow pay, don't pay, get evicted, and so on. It does *not* include lost rent on vacant units. If you know how to get rent from vacant units, I'll be the first to sign up for your class.

Therefore, if you have 10 units renting for $800 per month (all occupied = $8,000 per month), over 12 months you should get $96,000. Based on the previous guesstimate, most investors believe they're getting 85 percent. This means you're only getting $81,600 of the $96,000 owed to you. Lost income amounting to $14,400 is not good for the home team. Almost a month and a half of your rents . . . Poof! . . . gone! Adios!

Now some good news: Let's take the same scenario of $96,000 in annual rents, but at the end of your 12 months you've got $105,600 instead of $81,600. I'm not kidding. Not only would this be $9,600 above what was owed you, this would be an increase of $24,000 in 12 months if you operated like most investors—the $14,400 shortage + the $9,600 over = $24,000 improvement in cash flow. Would you want

$81,600 on the Rent Income line on your Schedule E or would you rather have $105,600? Not a difficult choice, is it?

These are not pie-in-the-sky numbers. In this example, the investor has only 10 units renting for $800 a month. Let's squelch any argument involving vacancies. If you want to argue a vacancy factor, no problem; let's use an investor with 12 rental units at $800 monthly rent who has two units vacant each month. The numbers would still be the same. Got it?

Failing to Plan Is Planning to Fail

"Shooting from the hip" seems to be the system of choice for most investors who try to focus only on benefits without effort or hassles. Although you might be guilty of micromanaging by doing everything yourself, it's really not the best system for you in the long run. Starting off this way to learn the business is great, but you should have a plan to graduate.

Implementing proven systems into your real estate investing business can turbocharge your results in several areas, not just in the financial department. It can literally quadruple the quality of your life allowing more time for yourself, family, and hobbies (and yes, provide more time for investing if you choose).

Proven Systems Are Time-Savers, Moneymakers, and Good CYA Programs

Here are some solid tips to get your systems in operation. If you want excellent results, you must have superior systems. If you want to quantum leap your investment returns, you must learn how to "work smarter, not harder." This doesn't mean you should get lazy. It simply means you should use more of the gray matter between your ears instead of using your back and arms to trade hours for dollars.

Are you painting and cleaning up properties because you have time and honestly believe you're saving money? Don't feel bad if you're doing this because I did the same thing when I was getting started. A lot of this behavior has to do with our comfort zone. We're simply too scared to take on a big risk and believe we're saving money by swinging a paintbrush or fixing stuff.

Here is where you're gonna get egg on your face. When you're busting your butt to fix up your property after getting off work at your full-time job, you're only saving the cost of the labor to do it. In my town, you could probably hire a painter for $10 to $20 an hour. When slinging a paintbrush or roller, you're indirectly saying your time is worth only $10 to $20 an hour. Stop it! Hire a decent painter (not one found in the Yellow Pages. Those in Yellow Pages are paying HUGE dollars for advertising and this expense is simply passed down to you. You will be paying for their huge advertising expense). Now you can get the painting done while you're working at your job. At the end of your workday, you can go home, spend time with your family, and use your noggin for intellectual activities instead of using your arms to wield a paintbrush.

On top of labor savings, additional expenses, and lost income, add to your money-eating overhead expenses. If you hired a painter, could you get your unit rented sooner? If so, especially on a single-family house, your expenses for utilities and lawn service would also stop quicker. Your rental income would begin sooner. I bet you've seen other investors lose over a month's rent because they nickeled and dimed repairs and decorating to save money. Better results can be achieved using your head and a cell phone.

Go ahead and say "easier said than done," but it's true. Look at successful investors in your town. Do you see them painting or working on properties? *No.* Many of them started out this way, but they quickly learned how to become business owners.

"Riding the bull" is a term you can use for landlording. Many investors feel this way dealing with tenants. Many get beat up so badly, they develop an attitude of "no more tenants, never again." Don't fall into this trap. Tenants are necessary to build your wealth, allowing you to crank it 24-7. The challenge is to reduce the pain and get there quicker.

Tenants are not your customers. Think of them as your employees. Good tenant relations begin before you ever meet them. Your rental application should be treated like a job application. The applicants want to live in your investment. They have responsibilities and you should train them properly. Would you haphazardly hire employees and cut them loose on a new job without training them? Odds are, they would rely on their past job experience and knowledge. It is *your responsibility* to select the proper employee for the right job and train the person properly.

Even McDonald's or your local grocery store won't turn a new hire loose without proper training. Why in the world would you turn one loose in your expensive investment?

Do You Treat Your Real Estate Investing as a Hobby or as a Business?

This challenging question separates the "girls and boys" from the "women and men." Here are some of the characteristics of each:

If you treat your real estate as a hobby:

- You're a micromanager.
- You're "hands-on."
- You're involved with repairs and maintenance.
- You buy weird things to save money.
- You knock on doors to collect your rent.
- Worse yet, you travel to get partial payments of rent when summoned by your tenant(s).
- You allow tenants to call your home phone and cell phone.
- You go to court.
- You physically help with your own evictions.
- You show your own vacant units.
- You cut grass to save money.
- You have trouble getting to the next level because you feel so overwhelmed.
- You lose the desire to get to the next level because you believe it can only get worse.

If you treat your real estate as a business:

- You have a business owner's attitude.
- You're hands-off and use systems.
- You assign or delegate repairs and maintenance.
- You never knock on doors for rent.
- You have trained tenants to mail payments.
- Tenants never call your home phone or cell phone.
- Tenants don't know the owner.
- You never go to court (that's for attorneys).
- You never physically participate in or even show up at your own evictions.
- You never show your vacant units.
- You never cut grass.
- You have no trouble getting to the next level because you have time to achieve objectives.

Once again, take a look at the serious, successful investors in your town. It doesn't matter what town you're in, these people have a common trait: They act like business owners because they are. They put themselves in a position to continue networking and learning, and they stay close to the action. They don't go to court, paint houses, collect rent, cut grass, or help set out evicted tenants. They have systems in place to handle this for them. They also seem to have time for fun. Most have hobbies. It may be golf, hunting, boating, music, or any number of things outside real estate.

They may have double, triple, or more properties than you, yet they seem laid back, happy, and free of stress. I'm not promoting or encouraging you to buy more properties, I'm pointing out the importance of having your own business system. It will make your life and investing easier and much more efficient. With a solid, proven business system, you can graduate to your next level or objective because you'll have the time to focus on achieving that objective instead of cutting grass or doing repairs.

Here's a no-brainer. Remember the earlier scenario of 10 units at $800 month? Picture yourself implementing a good system to produce a $24,000 swing in your annual income from real estate—$2,000 per month! Here's an example of working smarter and not harder. With $2,000 extra per month, you could hire a full-time handyperson at $500 per week, or how about a 20-hour part-time handyperson at $250 per week and a 20-hour part-time office manager at $250 week. Don't do it now, just start thinking in this manner.

When I started, I wanted aggressive safe growth. My question was, "How many houses would it take to pay for a 20-hour per week handyperson?" Keep in mind, Tammy and I lived off my police officer salary and her nursing salary allowing our real estate to grow. In the beginning, I didn't like unclogging toilets, so we hired a part-time handyperson pretty darn quick.

Work Smarter, Not Harder!

Implementing proven systems can offer you tremendous benefits in the long haul. A successful property management program educates and trains tenants from day one. You must explain in detail the tenant's responsibilities and the consequences for failing to perform properly.

You don't have to be a dominating dictator or an arrogant king. Remember, you play the role of a boss when training a new hire. You explain company rules, regulations and policies up front. It is much easier doing the education part on the front end because on occasion, you'll have a new hire (new tenant) who decides your rules and policies are just too much and the person chooses to move on. Wouldn't you prefer this now instead of later?

While schooling your new tenant, explain the process for making monthly rent payments. Tell them right now that you don't knock on doors. They must mail their payment before the first of the month because rent is due on or before the first. It is late on the second day of the month. PERIOD.

Use Written Correspondence

Mail monthly rent bills to your tenants on the twentieth of each month along with a self-addressed envelope for them to mail their payment to you. Training your tenants to use written correspondence will reduce your phone calls. Every month while opening payments from tenants, we find scribbled notes ranging from neighbor complaints, to repair requests, to atta-boys. Date-stamp these things and put them in your tenant file folder. It might turn into evidence for you one day. The point is: Develop your system. Office Depot sells a "RECEIVED" stamp with a date roller. Keep it on your desk just for this purpose, or use an ink pen and write the date received on your correspondence.

Be firm and fair with late charges. Our late charges consist of 10 percent of the monthly rent plus an additional $5.00 per day as a daily late charge. Be sure to check your local laws as some towns have legal limits on late charges and the dates to assess them. Hold on before you go bonkers over your late-charge policy. Jump into the real world with me for a moment. Two of my favorite phrases are:

It doesn't cost you anything to ask a question.
Shoot for the moon, if you fall short, you're not a loser, you're just a star.

Stop squawking. Imagine a tenant blasting you over your late charge and your daily late charges. This sets the stage for you to be a nice guy. You politely and professionally remind your tenant of his tutorial session explaining the rules when he came on board; however, just this one time, you might void the daily late charges to show him you're a nice guy and make him feel better. Now the tenant thinks he's won and you're a fair person; however, you still got your 10 percent late charge nailed down tight.

Consider your daily late charges as gravy or icing on the cake. They are your first line of defense to protect your 10 percent late charge. If you're thinking this is difficult, you need a bit more training yourself. Remind yourself that business owner is your role.

Well-trained tenants frequently mail in their rent along with the 10 percent late charge before they receive their late notice. This action should really make you feel good because it proves the system is working.

It takes a lot more than late charges to get 110 percent of your rent. In fact, late charges are only 1.3 percent of our income received. Where does the rest come from? Investors have boatloads of money falling through their fingers they can't even see.

For example, how many times has this happened to you? You have scheduled an appointment for a repair and your serviceperson phones you to report that nobody is home. What do you do? Do you phone your tenant and accept some lame excuse like, "I forgot." This is *your fault.* Train your tenants to abide by the rules of your system. Then charge them $25 for a missed repair appointment and stick to it.

Do not void this charge. If you void this charge, you have just enabled and trained your tenant to believe it is okay to behave this way!

Document tenant-chargeable repairs and have the tenant sign your work order form acknowledging the same. Now you have written documentation (evidence) to support your claim of a tenant-chargeable repair such as a ham hock bone that got stuck in the toilet when the tenant dumped in her leftover bean soup (true story).

Another powerful source of extra income for you is implementing a good, solid, move-out inspection process without having to worry about receipts, labor costs, and material costs. Set up a program giving every tenant the same set of instructions and a price list for failing to follow your instructions.

For example, you can charge $6.00 for a light bulb. There were light bulbs when they moved in and you expect working light bulbs when they move out. Your tenant may scream, "but I can get four light bulbs at Walgreen's for only 99 cents!" Your answer is, "That's my point. We want you to go Walgreen's and get light bulbs because we haven't found anybody who'll go to Walgreen's for free and buy those 99-cent light bulbs. We have to pay somebody almost $20.00 hour to go to Walgreen's to buy a light bulb, and it costs more than $6.00 a light bulb for us to do this. So, please don't take one light bulb, take them all."

Most landlords who treat their real estate as a hobby dread the move-out process and tenant turnover. They assume that if the tenant challenges their move-out charges by going to court, they must gather all their receipts and still expect to lose in court. They have no system. Plus the hobbyists do their own repairs and cleaning. They don't get a receipt for their own labor. How insulting when a judge orders a landlord to return all the security deposit to the tenant. Worse yet, the judge accepts only the receipts documenting cash-out-of-pocket expenses, with absolutely zero worth to the landlord's time, effort, and labor.

Here's a partial list of items used in Tenant Tracking to assist you in getting 110 percent or more of your rents. You can change prices, too:

- Re-rental charge, breaking lease (1 month rent)
- Filling out forms ($15.00)
- Electric off ($75.00)
- Water off ($75.00)
- Floor tile ($2.00 each)
- Cracked window glass ($40.00)
- Storm door chain ($15.00)
- Storm door pneumatic closure ($20.00)
- Electric cover plate ($2.00)
- Car in yard ($200)
- Trash piled at curb ($200 pick-up truckload)

- Smoke alarm ($25.00)
- Air filter ($20.00)
- Cleaning windows ($10.00 each)
- Deadbolt locks ($30.00)
- Payment plans and more payment plans

To see more of this list along with the system, check out http://www .wealthbuilding247.com/TenantTracking.htm. It includes such fees as:

- Payment plans and financing for those who've already moved out of your unit
- Good old late charges
- Daily late charges
- Missed work order appointments
- Fill out a form fee

Plus dozens and dozens more that are legal and allowed in your state and town. A good proven system is your foundation in implementing an efficient business operation for your real estate. It allows you to have a business owner's perspective. If you use it properly, you'll increase cash flow because you'll stay focused on the performance of your "forest" instead of one tree or bush.

CHAPTER 21

Increasing Your Cash Flow

Investors who go belly up all seem to share the same blueprint or game plan for failure. In almost every case, there are two problems. The common denominator and number one problem is *cash flow*. The other culprit is management. These two basic business fundamentals are the keys to successful investing.

Foreclosures are on the increase, not only for homeowners but for investors as well. Locally, investors are going belly up by the dozens. One could make excuses of market conditions and more, but it still boils down to good business management and cash flow to cover the bad times.

As an aggressive investor focusing on quick safe growth, I have become lazy business-wise for a month or two on several occasions. I didn't ignore day-to-day activities, but I failed to stay on top of the big picture. Simply handling daily activities and ignoring your monthly cash flow while driving an aggressive buying machine can sure knock you on your butt when you finally take a look at that cash flow.

Most honest, successful investors will admit having periods of hard times when there is "too much month, not enough cash."

How to Identify Cash Flow

This is not a stupid question. If it were a stupid question, so many investors would not be going belly up. You cannot use the universal formula of

$$
\begin{aligned}
\text{Rent} &= \$850 \\
\text{Payment} &= \underline{\$650} \\
\text{Positive cash flow} &= \$200
\end{aligned}
$$

This is dangerous and not good business. It is a good way to sell books and tapes and add to the hype of easy success with real estate.

The proper way to identify cash flow is to look at everything in your big picture.

You must be able to track *all your income* and *all your expenses*.

If you have an accountant or another office person do your books by preparing monthly reports for you, you must learn and understand exactly what is included and what is not included in those reports.

If you trust the reports without fully understanding what is going on, you might be placing faith in a guaranteed plan for disaster.

Ask questions. Is your report a cash flow or a tax summary report? Most accountants actually prepare a monthly tax summary report, and investors assume they are reading a cash flow report. If this is happening to you, you could be on the road to failure without knowing it because the report will be missing:

- Principal pay down (needs real cash)
- All capitalized expenses (uses real cash)
  —Roofs, furnaces, rehab, and so on

Just imagine how great a report would look without these cash flow expenses. If this is happening to you, you are operating your business on false and misleading information. You honestly believe you are doing pretty good and your bookkeeper is telling you the same when in fact you are walking around bleeding profusely with a cut throat.

Successful investors growing their business *always* keep their fingers on the pulse of their cash flow and they do it monthly, if not weekly or daily. Playing ostrich to avoid seeing the facts is not acceptable.

You must track all your monthly income and all your expenses.

Guesstimates Are Not Allowed

Use real numbers. Only after doing this will you begin to see the real picture. Do this every month. You will now see the universal formula shot down. Repairs, vacancies, advertising, phones, lawn service, supplies, unexpected stuff, and more unexpected stuff all eat up the phantom positive cash flow.

Baggage with False Information

If you have been living and operating by the universal positive cash flow formula or tax summary reports, your attitude may have changed allowing you to feel more comfortable as a successful investor. Because of your imagined earnings, you may even have started to enjoy the finer things in life you used to dream about.

We see this over and over. Cash-out refinancings are a classic example. People are spending future profits on toys for today.

My point is that if you start having faith in false information, it can affect your attitude and way of doing business. You will feel more confident while bleeding unknowingly.

How to Stop the Bleeding

You cannot stop the bleeding until you figure out where it is coming from. You must identify it first.

Plan of Attack for Reducing Expenses

If you discover you have a negative cash flow, You must take action now to turn it around. Correcting negative cash flow involves doing things now to stop the bleeding. It might conflict with a conservative long-term investment game plan but, remember, if you go belly up from negative cash flow, you won't need a long-term plan.

Evaluate Your Liabilities

Review your list of mortgages and monthly debt service:

- Do you have some 15-year loans? Changing them to 30-year loans increases cash flow now.
- Review interest rates. Have you played ostrich and ignored the terms of your existing notes and mortgages?
- Money is cheap now. You should not have any loans higher than 8 percent.
- Washington Mutual was offering an investor product starting at 2 or 3 percent. This is an adjustable rate loan, and yes, the payments could go up after seven years, but there is a heck of spread if you have 8 percent loans and change them into 3 percent loans. This will give you an immediate jump in cash flow.
- Do you have any seller-financed properties or private lenders?
  —Refinance them with the cheap money available, but before doing so, contact these seller financers or private lenders and ask for discounts if you pay the loans in full now. (I recently picked up a $18,000 discount.)
  —Contact each of your seller-financed lenders and be creative. Ask to pay 10 months payments now for 12 months of no payments. This gives you two extra months of no payments and more cash flow now.

—Ask them to subordinate to second position on other properties. This will free up a property to refinance and pay off other debt.

- Study your liabilities carefully. Ask yourself whether you can refinance one house and take the money to pay off X number of houses with smaller balances. Can one new loan pay off three old loans?

I am not encouraging you to create a boatload of more debt. The objective of this chapter is to *stop the bleeding*. If you wake up and realize you have negative cash flow, how can you fix it fast?

Review Insurance

Approximately four or five years ago, my insurance was increasing at a rate of approximately 30 percent per year. Although I had a good relationship with my insurance agent, I had to shop my insurance to stop the bleeding. With a few phone calls, I quickly learned I could get better coverage and reduce my insurance premiums by $32,000 annually. That's right, an almost immediate $3,000-a-month instant increase with a couple of phone calls.

And almost the same thing happened again last year. The insurance premium started going up: I made a few phone calls and received as good coverage with an annual savings of almost $20,0000.

My experience with insurance companies has been that to get your business, agents will quote wonderful initial rates. Then they start creeping up. I have seen this pattern with multiple insurance companies over the past 10 years. Now I expect to switch again in two or three years.

Contractors

Using *Investor Books Made EZ*® properly, I reviewed an annual report of dollar amounts paid to vendors. It was surprising to learn how much I paid to my HVAC (heating, ventilation, and air-conditioning) company in 12 months. I take care of my vendors and pay them as soon as their bill hits my mailbox or fax machine. They like doing business with Mike. I believe I also get good service.

I contacted my HVAC contractor and asked him if he had about 10 minutes to talk. (If he was in a hurry, he would become frustrated.) I asked him if I was a good customer and his reply was "one of my best." Then I informed him how tough our business has been lately and we are struggling. (My objective was to reduce the "service run" charge by 50 percent.) After he acknowledged that I am a great customer, I asked for his help for the next 12 months by waiving the $50 service run charge. Of course, he balked and talked about his increased gasoline cost and so on, but then I asked him if he could meet me halfway. He agreed. Now, service run charges are only $25.

Repeat this scenario with your regular contractors and service providers.

Advertising

Classified ads are expensive in my town. If you use them on a regular basis, most newspapers offer a significant discount with an annual or six-month contract. Maybe Sunday only for a year, or three times a week for a year, or daily.

Coat-tail on the advertising by others. Rentalhouses.com is a web site for land-lords. As a member of an investor club and for a special limited time, you can place your vacancies on their web site for free. Then create an insert for your yard sign that reads, "For information, visit online at www.Rentalhouses.com." You will also capture out-of-towners searching for homes in your town.

Advice for Reducing Debt

Using Dave Ramsey's concept of snowball debt reduction will increase your cash flow. Attack the lowest balance debts first and snowball the payment from the paid-in-full debt to the new smallest debt.

Plan of Attack to Increase Income

Tenant Tracking registered users are getting 110 percent and more of their rents. Missy and Bob in Cincinnati are getting 115 percent.

How is this happening? No, it's not just late charges. It includes all the money falling through your fingers that you cannot see or won't see:

- Late charges
- Daily late charges
- Light bulbs
- Air filters
- Missed work order appointments
- Tenant-chargeable repairs that you paid
- Smoke alarms and batteries
- Door locks
- Keys
- Filling-out-form fee

- Annual increase in rent. This is tough, I hear investors all the time state they have tenants who take care of the property and they are scared to raise their rent. This is playing ostrich because what will happen is that after a few years of no increases you will finally realize their rent is too low. Now you want to play catch-up; you increase it $75—and they will move when this happens.

Increasing monthly rent by only $20 can increase cash flow tremendously with a few units. For example:

$20 per month increase on 50 units = $1,000 increase a month

That is $12,000 a year. . . . Do It!

- Animal charge. $25 additional monthly rent for each pet.
- Animal deposit.
- Additional occupant. Increase rent $50 and include a phrase stating this charge in your rental agreement.
- Sell options now. Mail letters to your tenants offering them the opportunity to purchase an option to buy on their home for $500 or $1,000 before the end of the month. This is a big boost to cash flow for one month. Do not have the mind-set of doing rent with option to buy only as vacancies occur. Why can't you sell options to your present tenants this month?

Other Investors

Do you know some good people with jobs who pay their bills and are interested in real estate?

- You can become their resource for fast cash, which will allow them to buy properties without using banks.
- You can simply buy some cheap money and resell it to them for their purchases.
- Look for safe borrowers secured with first mortgages on real estate.
- Buy $100,000 at 4 percent and sell it at 15 percent; this makes you 11 percent or $11,000 annually for going to the mailbox!

Where can you "buy" money? Home equity line, signature loans, or even credit cards will allow you to "buy money" in single digit interest rates and "sell the money" at 15% or more. Remember, increasing cash flow is the way to turn around negative cash flow. Fixing negative cash flow requires an immediate drastic plan of action.

Making Your Landlording Business More Profitable

This section focuses on how you can get better results by doing less property maintenance for the long term. The quality of your property parallels the quality of your tenant.

If you have an ugly, nasty, stinky, dirty property for rent, it will difficult to convince a responsible tenant to call it home. Do not confuse quality with the dollar amount or price of the property. Quality refers to how you manage and maintain your properties. Trash bag tenants have a wide range of income and pay a wide range of rents. Don't assume they live in "wobbly boxes" as Jimmy Napier, the noted real estate educator, says. If you offer clean, sound, safe, quality housing at market rates, you will consistently be able to beat out your local competition. With proper screening, you can capture quality tenants because they will want to rent your home over your competition's offerings, regardless of the price range you operate in.

The challenge is to maintain quality while reducing expenses. Here are some of our money-saving techniques:

- *Flooring:* This can be a money-eating pit many landlords simply expect with tenant turnover. Stop it and change your attitude.

  —*Hardwood floors:* Do you have properties with hardwood floors and install carpet because it looks better and "newer"? If you have hardwood floors, it is by far more economical to sand and refinish them than to do the replace-carpet routine. No excuses allowed, "but it has stains [or black spots, or somebody cut the wood and patched this or that]." (I used to say the same things.)*

  Here's how we do it. Rent a drum sander and edger from Home Depot (about $20 a day and have your workers wear a mask to keep the dust from going in their nose and mouth). Use the sander to clean and smooth up the hardwood floors. If there are big holes, ugly plywood patches, and so on, get some like-size wood and patch it properly.

  After sanding and cleaning the floors, Danny applies a mahogany stain. It is not the prettiest, and I would not put it in my home; but it covers almost all the stains and blemishes. Unfortunately, if the existing hardwood floors are light-colored, the sander can't remove deep dark water stains or, in fact any embedded dark stains. The mahogany stain applied properly (start with the darkest wood blemish and work outward) makes the stains go away! Get used to the red stain when you start with ugly beat-up wood floors.

---

*I am not a hardwood floor expert. I assumed refinishing hardwood floors was a superexpensive time-consuming procedure and carpet was cheaper, faster, and looked better. I was wrong. I learned these hardwood floor tips from my maintenance foreman, Dan. His brother Donnie works for my "education partner," friend, and competitor Jay Long. Donnie is Jay's maintenance boss and used to maintain floors for bowling alleys. Thanks Dan, Jay, and Donnie.

Got a really nasty dark stain and you are getting ready with the "but, but, but . . ."? I came up with this idea while Dan was working in one of our rehab properties. A big nasty stain. Long story short, he sanded the badly stained area first, then took a capful of bleach and poured it directly on the stain. He let the wood absorb it and dry, sanded it again, and repeated the procedure. This did not 100 percent remove the stain, but it diminished its prominence tremendously causing it to blend in easier. To see Dan's photos of this procedure, visit www.VistaKY.com/stain. This is a hidden page for your use only.

The next procedure after sanding is applying the stain. Allow one day for the stain to dry. If the humidity is up, it may take an extra day. After the stain dries, apply a clear coat of polyurethane (two coats if you have time).

A three-bedroom home (about 1,000 square feet) takes about three days for this process: one full day for cleaning and sanding, a couple of hours to apply the stain with a day for drying, and a couple of hours to apply the finish coat with a day for drying.

The initial expense is roughly double the cost of carpet, mostly due to labor. But here is the wonderful part. With a tenant turnover, you clean it up; but let's take a worst case scenario. Your tenants move out and you have a great big stain, or they sat the clothes iron on high on your floor for five minutes. Danny simply "patch-sands" the spot, reapplies the same color stain, applies the finish coat, and it all blends in together.

As noted, the initial cost is not prohibitively expensive. It costs a little less than twice the cost of carpet, but you will never replace carpet in that unit again. Simply clean and patch-repair the damaged area. It really works. If you need more detailed information on this procedure, visit www .DoItYourself.com.

—*Carpet:* If you have plywood subfloors and must use carpet, use it wisely. Making it "carpet installer friendly" will save you time and money, and will get you better results.

Don't use vinyl sheet floor covering; use vinyl tiles. When the flooring gets damaged (not if it gets damaged, but when) from scooting fridges, chairs with no protectors, and so on, you can simply replace the damaged tiles. Use a floor tile that is suitable for any room in the house or apartment. My favorite is a vinyl floor tile that simulates a wood pattern. It works great for kitchens, baths, hallways, entrance foyers, closets, and more.

Here is the goal to make this work with carpet. Put a stand-alone piece of carpet with no seams in each room. Carpet installers hate seams. Installation requires a lot of extra time. They hate seams and it always seems to create scheduling conflicts. No seams and they'll stop by on the way home and replace it.

So each room will have a stand-alone piece of carpet with no seams. Put floor tile in the closets, hallways, bathroom, kitchen, and foyer. Now, you have no seams, and you can replace carpet only as needed.

—Floor tile: This choice can save time and money. As stated, the objective is to reduce expenses while maintaining quality. Properties with a crawl space or with a basement will have wood subfloors. You should use a thick high-quality vinyl floor tile for these properties. Be consistent. Use the same tile for all your properties. We use the self-adhesive peel and stick, but have found they pop up frequently because there is not enough glue on the back side. The fix here is to add some floor glue to each tile.

Properties built on a concrete slab are a different animal. Use high-traffic commercial tile. The challenge here is find a commercial tile that will look acceptable in a residential property. But they do exist. After finding the right commercial tile, put it everywhere. Instead of wall-to-wall carpet, wall-to-wall tile. This will polish up nicely if you rent a commercial floor tile scrubber/buffer with the big circular pads. With a tenant turnover, clean and strip the wax off, reapply new wax, and buff it to a bright clean finish. Again, rental of the machine is about $20, and the stripper and wax cost about $40 for a three-bedroom home. The results are phenomenal; it looks brand-new again.

Some folks locally try to use commercial tile on properties with wood subfloors. Plumbing is the downfall here. If water gets under the tile to the wood (from toilets, tubs, sinks), the wood swells and you have a mess. If you use the peel-and-stick vinyl tiles, you can easily remove the bad wood and patch it. The commercial stuff is more challenging in these situations.

Mark Schaffer, one of my previous and perhaps my best bird dog ever* used the peel-and-stick floor tile to cover the inside of base kitchen cabinets and vanities. It helps to protect from any leaking or dripping traps, drains, or supply lines and it makes them look superclean and new.

One last note on floor coverings. Everything mentioned here involves the inside of the home. Pay attention to what is outside the entrances. You can have all the wonderful interior programs in place; but if you have "unfriendly to floors" material outside your entrances, you are shortening the life of your floor coverings.

Homes with badly deteriorated concrete or blacktop driveways, sidewalks, and porches will destroy your floor coverings in short order. Look at the entrances and see what will be sticking to residents' shoes to be tracked inside your property. Resurfacing a sidewalk, porch, or all or part of a driveway may greatly extend the life of your floor coverings.

• *Door locks:* This tip may need to be adjusted depending on the local laws where you operate. Before adapting to this system, I spent a boatload of money on door locks and replacement keys. What a mess. I researched getting my own key-cutting

---

*Bird Dog simply means Mark would beat the bushes and find deals for Mike for a very small fee in exchange for learning and getting a powerful investing education from Mike.

machine and learned how to rekey locks; and now not only is this headache gone, but I have turned it into another income stream.

Here is the short version. I use locks from Ernie Riddle of Salem, Indiana. His web site is www. Landlordlocks.com. His unique system allows us to change locks in about two seconds without using a screwdriver or a bunch of parts. The system utilizes a "master control key" that unlocks the round cylinder allowing it to be removed; you then insert a replacement cylinder keyed differently. Fast, easy, and cheap!

Take it a step further. Instead of a great big pegboard system of keys for each property, now you will simply use five large finishing nails. Here is my system: My property management company is Vista Properties. I have four lock cylinders named VP-001, VP-002, VP-003, VP-004. I have a finishing nail for each and they are labeled in this manner. Tenant in property number one starts off with VP-002. When that tenant moves out, we simply swap out the VP-002 and replace it with our choice of one of the remaining three. This is repeated all across town. Of course, we document the lock cylinder changes properly in Tenant Tracking.

Before you say ho-hum, here comes the good part. If a tenant gets locked out or loses a key, you can sell the tenant another key for $10.00. Lock-outs are made easy (and tenant chargeable) with no need to go to the old pegboard to get a copy. No more headaches of making copies. We stack all the VP-001 keys on the finishing nail labeled VP-001. When it runs low, we call Ernie and order some more keys.

—*More money:* Home Depot, Barnett, and Maintenance Warehouse sell deadbolt covers that cover holes in doors after removing deadbolt locks. With each tenant turnover, all deadbolts are removed and holes are covered (your local laws may prevent this one). The cylinders are changed out and the property is rented again. During the Rent Talk while signing a new rental agreement with a new tenant, Shirley offers the new tenant the opportunity to have deadbolts installed in their home that match the door key they are receiving today. We provide this service to our tenants for only $30 for each deadbolt lock. We sell and resell deadbolts over and over and over. Remember Danny is going to the property to remove the yard sign anyway, why not make it an income stream?

—*PLUS MORE!* Handling your empties, vacancies, rehabs. We use the pretty polished brass locksets for residential properties. For unoccupied properties, we use our VP-007 cylinder which is a polished or brushed stainless steel. It stands out like a sore thumb when inserted in a polished brass lockset.

All unoccupied units get this cylinder, and we place a VP-007 key in a Sur Lok key box (also sold by Ernie). Do not confuse this with a Supra. This $17 key box is better than the Supra because there is a separate code to remove it from the door. One code for the key, one to remove the lockbox. Supras always got stolen. The VP-007 cylinder is used on all empty properties. Although I am blessed with an office today, we offer a unique opportunity to prospective tenants to view properties. They can see a property at anytime on their schedule without a landlord or leasing agent watching over their shoulder encouraging them to hurry up and make a decision (plus your inconvenience or cost of help showing property).

My fifth finishing nail has a stack of VP-007 keys for showing property. Prospect stops by the office, produces a valid photo ID, fills out our simple Key Deposit form along with $20 key deposit, and leaves our office with a key and a copy of the Key Sign Out form to view the property (see Form A.1: Key Sign Out, in Section III). This form clearly states they have one-time permission to view the property only, and no possession permission is given. Believe it or not, out of the thousands of keys signed out this way, I have only had one person actually move in over a weekend. He was a little short upstairs mentally and thought he had completed a rental agreement (he could not read). He moved out Monday without any conflict. But what happens if the prospect walks off with your key? Good news, you just sold the $1.00 key for $20.00 plus had zero expense and inconvenience of showing a property. Remember, all vacant units have the 007 cylinder. Do not tell your prospects (or tenants) about your key system. If they want to see two properties, they sign out two keys with two deposits.

This may not seem like much, but it all adds up. I went through a spell of having open houses after work, or hiring a person to attend open houses for $10 each time. Not only have I reduced or eliminated this expense, but I have done a 180—turning an expense into an additional income stream. If you have multifamilies with a common entrance, be sure to ask Ernie about his "vestibule system" for your tenants. His number is (800) 847-8729.

• *Oak cabinets:* Use solid oak cabinets in both kitchen and bathroom vanities. Solid oak cabinets wear better, last longer, and look better because they are solid wood with no particle board, or el cheapo laminated white or wanna-be wood look found at a lot of retailers. Barnett, Brass, and Copper is a wholesaler located in Jacksonville, Florida, with many locations across the nation. You can get a 5-foot starter set of Vista Light Oak Kitchen Cabinets consisting of a 5-foot base cabinet and two 15-inch-wide x 30-inch-high wall cabinets for only $306, direct from the manufacturer, delivered to your door with no shipping or freight charges! These are good cabinets with raised panel doors and look like twice the cost.

• *Bathrooms:* Many of us have bathrooms in our units with a small narrow bathroom sink area. Instead of putting the el cheapo narrow bathroom vanity and setting a cultured marble sink on top, try this instead. Install a wall-mounted sink or a cheap pedestal sink. This allows for easy access to the plumbing stuff in the future; it also prevents the tenant from throwing stuff underneath your sink that might knock supply lines and drain lines loose, causing leaks. "In the wall" medicine cabinets are always a pain. Replace those with a large mirror fastened to the wall using sturdy clips. Install an "above the toilet" solid oak cabinet. This Vista Light Oak solid oak cabinet is 36 inches high and is made of solid wood. They look awesome and cost only $52. The web site is www.e-barnett.com and Barnett's phone number is (800) 288-2000. Call and they'll send you a wholesale catalog with over 1,100 pages of things we use.

• *Mismatch paint:* This will save a ton of cash and preserve your property. Odds are, you get paint on a regular basis. We have used Devoe, ICI Deluxe, and for the past few years, Porter Paints. They created a color for us called "Vista White," which is an eggshell finish off-white. We use it for all interior walls in residential units and we get a good price. This finish and color allows us to patch-paint spots instead of repainting an entire house with tenant turnovers.

Mismatch paint happens in all paint stores. Talk to them about paint they mix up wrong or someone refuses to buy. Several times a year, we purchase all their mismatch paint for $1.00 a gallon! That's right, only $1.00 gallon, sometimes less. Save some of your old 5-gallon buckets and take this mismatch paint and mix it up to get the lightest color possible. Be careful with the dark colors; set them aside for a moment. Take all the light colors and mix them into your 5-gallon buckets and use this color to spray basement walls and basement ceilings or badly stained floor joists. Boy, talk about making a dungeon-dark basement look fresh, clean, and bright. Light colors reflect light well. Who cares what the exact color is—for $1.00 a gallon, you let loose a paint bomb in the basement.

Mix together the darker colors and use this paint for foundations, porches, garages, shutters, fences, basement floors, and so on. Whatever. Remember to keep paint close to room temperature. If it freezes, it is over. If you paint porches and sidewalks, be sure to throw a thimbleful of sand on top of the wet paint to prevent slips and falls when wet.

CHAPTER 22

Giving Your Tenant a Project Can Be a Good Thing

Is *project* a good word or a bad word in our world of real estate investing? Your mental knee-jerk reaction is probably "bad." Settle down for a moment, and you will learn how you can benefit with both your time and your money by creating projects. How many times has this happened to you?

One of your great long-term tenants contacts you with a request for new carpet for their living room (not the whole house, just one room).

Do you have thoughts like:

- Think about how good they have been by not being a pain.
- Son of a #$#@, why now, I don't have time for this problem and spending more money.
- Perhaps not giving in to new carpet may cause them to move creating another vacancy?
- How can I play ostrich, buy some time, postpone this expense for another year?
- The carpet was new when they moved in, they don't need new carpet if they would take care of it properly.
- Thoughts switch to greed or "business" . . . hmm, upgrade with new carpet = higher rent?

Well, sit down and get ready to knock yourself in the noggin with a big stick.

Good tenants are a rare breed today. They are on the endangered species list. I think I saw it on the Discovery Channel.

Your Life versus Tenants' Life

Your life: Do you have a busy schedule every day? Putting out fires, "riding the bull," doing deals, taking care of paperwork, insurance, taxes, phone calls, messages, bills, payments, evictions, late charges, late notices, work orders, Family, plus a job? . . . sound familiar? I found myself in this rat race for many years. If this is not you, you are a rare exception. Stick to it.

Let's switch gears and step into the tenants' shoes. If they are retired senior citizens, or tax-eaters, they watch late-night TV. Sleep late. Coffee in the morning, Jerry Springer, soap operas, gossip TV, gossip phone calls, pizza delivery, getting ready to wait for the mail carrier to arrive, two hours spent preparing a grocery list, . . . *way too much time on their hands.*

Now let's go back to the carpet story.

Your knee-jerk reaction is another problem. Wrong.

You should view this as an opportunity.

Especially with a good tenant, *your house is their home.* Do not forget this. It is a powerful tool for you.

When your good tenants contact you with the carpet story, the absolute most dangerous act on your part is to go "check it out." This good business practice on your part simply puts a bullet right between your eyes on the part of your tenant. Your good business behavior is actually calling your tenant a liar. Your actions are saying, I am not sure I believe you; let me come over and check it out. Even with good intentions on your part, you just went two steps forward and seven steps backward.

Hold on—there is more. . . . So, you go "check it out," and you agree with your tenant. Yup, it is worn and should be replaced. Mentally, your tenants have their arms folded across their chests saying, "I told you that earlier, stupid."

With good intentions on your part and a concern of saving money, you might tell your tenant something like, "Yes, I see you could use some new carpet. I will call my carpet guy and he will contact you to schedule putting in the new carpet."

Remember, you try to run an efficient rental business by using the same cheap carpet and the same installer with all your rentals. Putting systems in place really is a good business thing.

Your kind act and pride in showing your tenants that you have a system in place to take care of their problem totally disregards the concerns of the tenant. You just smacked them square in the face with a 2×4 by reminding them that they are tenants and are renting your house. All their thoughts about their home just evaporated with you bumping your gums about your system.

But wait a minute. You are trying to be a nice guy and a good landlord. Yes, this is true *by your standards.* You are taking time out of your busy day, spending your money, to do something for your tenant in *your house.* So when they view you as a greedy landlord, you remind yourself of your good intentions, good actions, and the money you spent, all for not even a simple thank-you. You are as guilty of promoting the *us* and *them* attitude as much as anyone else.

Switch gears and try this next time. When your good tenants contact you with a request for new carpet in one room, turn it into a win-win situation for both you and the tenants.

If you are discussing this on the phone, let the tenants talk for a while. Use their name when talking to them. It makes them feel good. After they make some noise for a while, here is how to make them want to stay forever. Refer to your rental house as "their home."

Give them a project. Tell your tenants you can help them out if they want the new carpet. Tell them you will buy the carpet if they will get it installed.

Instruct your tenants to go "carpet shopping." Give them some places to go. There are carpet remnant stores and outlets in almost every town. Tell the tenants to be reasonable and give them specific guidelines . . . no gold-laced carpet allowed. The tenants go carpet shopping and get a bill from the carpet store. Have the tenants mail or fax the bill to you. You create a check payable to the carpet store.

Even though you are a tightwad, you should not have to replace the pad. Your tenants are going to round up their own installer. Do not worry about the installer. Odds are, your tenants will choose better quality carpet than what you usually install. By the time they move out, it really won't matter how it was installed because you will probably remove it and replace it again.

Now think about this in the big picture. Tenants contacted you with a request. You are a good landlord. You acknowledge their concern, and you give your tenants a project. In their mind, they are going shopping on your dollar to buy carpet they choose for their home. No more phone calls on your part, and I'll bet the carpet is cheaper than your system in the long run. I doubt that the cost of the carpet will be more than the expense of your installer and the carpet.

Using your system, your tenants are reminded they are tenants living in your house. They will be sitting at home waiting for your system to do their thing. Your tenants have time to waste on projects to make them feel good. Give them time-eating projects. Your tenants will win, and you will win.

This is a great program. Think about it from the tenants' perspective:

- You did not challenge their request.
- Carpet-shopping time has just become a priority, and they will place it at the top of their list of things to do.
- Maybe they need transportation to go carpet shopping. They may call family, friends, church people, to take them carpet shopping because their landlord is going to buy them new carpet. . . . Wow, free advertising as well.
- They will spend hours at the carpet store listening to all the bull from the salesperson. We hate it. They love it, along with all the attention.
- Maybe they need to think about it and return for a second trip or opinion or maybe go to three, four, or five carpet stores to find the best deal. Yes, it sounds stupid, but this is a major project to them and they may truly try to find both the best price and quality. (Haven't you seen coworkers who spend 60 hours comparison shopping prices on car tires only to discover their best

deal is $12.25 a tire cheaper at XYZ tire store? It sounds like they worked 60 hours to save $49.00. They worked for about $0.81 an hour.)

- You are instilling your tenants' pride in their home by allowing them to choose the carpet for their home. You will also become a hero and the best landlord in the world.

- Now they must consider a lot of stuff—color, texture, quality, fiber, cost—wow, a lot of stuff they never dreamed of all are important parts of the project to install carpet in their living room. They had no idea how much stuff their landlord had to go through for carpet.

- Moving on, they finally make a decision on a piece of carpet. Now they make the salesperson write up some kind of bill; I recommend that you have your tenant hand-deliver the bill to your office (this is another miniproject). If you do not have an office, have them fax it or mail it.

- Once you receive the bill, make the tenant return to your office (if you have an office) to "pick up the check" made payable to the carpet store (another miniproject).

- With no office, simply mail the check to the tenant or drop it off at their home if your office is on wheels. Nothing better than giving them a check in person for their carpet purchase. Wow, what a landlord!

- Now the tenant needs to make arrangements to get back to the carpet store to purchase the carpet, another project.

- Don't forget about the installer, which is another project and a cost for the tenant. Now they have another project to research and will spend their time shopping for the best deal for a carpet installer.

- Still yet another miniproject involves making arrangements to schedule the installation, moving furniture, and on and on.

- They do not mind all these projects and time-eaters that benefit them. We despise time-eating projects. They love it and will probably seek an atta-boy from you for the results of their efforts while thanking you for all your help.

- You have really turned your house into their home. They will be proud of their new carpet that they picked out as well as all the experiences of their project.

- Question: If you delegate this project to them, how long will this carpet be labeled or referred to as "new"? I'll bet it will be called new for a lot longer than your carpet would be called new. If you used your system and installed your generic run-of-the-mill cheap carpet, it will not last a year being called new. Next year, it will be called "old carpet" because it is over a year old.

- Now your tenant loves their home with their new carpet, and their landlord is the best.

Because we are in so much of a hurry and have no patience, we assume we are normal and everyone should be like us. Wrong. *We are the one-percenters.* We are the weird ones and proud of it. It is what makes us successful.

Use the same methods described here on almost any improvement request by a tenant. Do not use it on repairs involving skilled or licensed trades such as furnaces, plumbing, or electric circuits.

It works great for requests for such things as painting, landscaping, or window air conditioners.

So slow down, be patient, and the next time you receive a request for something, use your creative abilities and turn it into a time-eating enjoyable and challenging project to benefit you. It is a variation of the Tom Sawyer story of whitewashing the fence—he got helpers to *pay him* for the privilege of using his brush to slop the whitewash on the fence. Try it: You might surprise yourself, and your tenants will thank you.

To really nail it down, drop them a note about how good a job they did or simply stop by with a positive attitude to see the result of their efforts, not to inspect it. Let them bump their gums again, and tell them they did great on colors and all. They are decorating their home. Help them feel proud and they will take care of it better and stay forever.

CHAPTER 23

Mike's Move-Out Package Makes You Money

As an aggressive investor, landlord, and property manager, I behaved like a sharp business owner and watched my real estate intensely. The powerful reporting features of my *Investor Books Made EZ* system allowed me to keep my finger on the pulse of my investments as it was happening. This same system also allowed me to keep the big picture focused perfectly.

I began studying the big picture. Where was I making money? Where was I losing money? How could I increase cash flow and profits? How could I reduce expenses?

It didn't take me long to discover tenant turnovers and the move-out process were cleaning my clock. In fact, just like you, I had been shocked at how some of my great tenants crapped on me when returning possession to us. It was mind boggling. Why and how was this happening?

Well, I remembered when I, too, was a tenant. My first apartment was just a few blocks north of Churchill Downs. This is not a good neighborhood, but I didn't know this when I was 18. This first apartment was originally part of a three-bedroom shotgun-style house. The landlord chopped it up into one-bedroom junky apartments, and he paid the utility bills. He owned the house next door and did the same thing. He was so tight, he used one 30-gallon water heater for both houses. That's right, one water heater for all six apartments! It was my first exposure to tightwad, slumlord landlording.

I rented this junky trap for $30 per week including utilities while I worked part-time at Winn-Dixie stocking shelves at night. My furniture consisted of milk crates, bricks, and boards, along with a little black-and-white TV. When I went on full-time, I got my butt out of there fast. I was moving up to a nice apartment with curtains on the windows.

I can remember being so excited about the move that I couldn't wait to get out of the old apartment and give the landlord the key so he could get it ready to rent again. This is what our tenants do to us. They simply don't know any better. We are the investors, and we assume they should know what to do. Have you ever given them instructions?

Because I was getting my clock cleaned with tenant turnovers, I created and developed a system to stop this nightmare. The result is my Move-Out Package. It is a four-page package that we mail to the tenants on receiving notice that they intend to move. You should also use it with tenants who are getting evicted—they're moving, too! The following items are in the package:

- Landlord's acknowledgment and *Receipt of Tenant's Notice to Vacate* (see Form A.26: Receipt of Notice to Vacate, in Section III)
- *Move-Out Instructions* (see Form A.27: Move-Out Instructions for Tenant, in Section III)
  —How to save their security deposit
  —Encourage them to earn a referral fee if their help produces a new tenant.
  —Keeping the place sharp is basic to pursuing a referral fee.
- *Move-out procedures:* How the move-out inspection process works
- *Survey:* This is a thoughtful review of how you, the landlord, operated (see Form A.29: Survey for Tenant to Grade Landlord and Your Property, in Section III).
  —This is a powerful psychological tool. Even if they trash the form, at least they saw it, and they may recall what a great landlord you have been to them.

Do not balk at the idea of a referral fee. Do you want to get the property rented quickly and have your tenants contribute their efforts to accomplishing your objective? A referral fee is an easy price to pay.

After you complete the move-out inspection using your Move-Out Inspection Form, use the included *Summary Report* and *Office Checklist* (see Form A.30: Move-Out Summary and Form A.32: Office Move-Out Checklist, in Section III) to cover bases properly. These work great with Tenant Tracking.

As a last resort, a *Return Possession Notice* (see Form A.33: Return Possession Notice, in Section III) is for use when a tenant wants to return possession on the spot. If you have an office, use this form if they stop by the office unexpectedly to turn in or drop off their keys. Without an office, keep this form in your car or folded in your day planner. Although you have good planning and organizational skills, there are always exceptions to every rule. You may still receive a phone call from a tenant informing you they have already moved out or an eviction-pending tenant may contact you to report they are out (or you may encourage them to move out a little sooner). When these situations arise, use this last form to document properly that they have returned possession to you.

Tips

- Send move-out packages on receiving notice and again seven days prior to move-out date.
- Send move-out packages to tenants with evictions pending. Some tenants with evictions have followed the move-out instructions.

Good Luck.

CHAPTER 24

Landlording on Auto-Pilot Tool Box

Pager: Used for emergency contact for tenants.

Fax machine (copier): You can have a perceived dedicated fax line by getting a distinctive ring service from your phone company. BellSouth calls this "Ringmaster." You get a separate phone number you can use as the fax number. (This feature was originally created to help identify phone calls; for example, your kids could have their own number.) This second number on your phone line has a different ring, usually two short loud rings, a pause, and two short rings. You can even set most fax machines to answer only the two short rings. This feature cost about $5.00 per month when I used it. Keep in mind, it doesn't give you two phone lines, only two numbers on one line.

Many fax machines have a copy feature built into them.

Investor Books Made EZ: Takes care of your bean counter hat needs and concerns. It's an investor-friendly system allowing investors a huge double benefit, As you pay bills and make bank deposits, it does your books using the number one accounting software in the United States, Quickbooks Pro. It is already set up for investors and is the same system I use in my real estate business.

Tenant Tracking: Takes care of your landlording hat. It's your property management system for keeping track of all those who owe you money, along with many landlording concerns such as move-ins, move-outs, rent increases, security deposits, work orders, and much more. It's not limited to just tenants. I use it for my lease/option and rent with option to buy tenants, loan customers, IRAs, and my education company, too. Investors are using Tenant Tracking for boat slips, marinas, trailer parks, Curves, developments, apartment communities, condo associations, and commercial property.

Both of the preceding systems are the only two-part complete system for investors using Quickbooks Pro. Investors are using this system in all 50 states,

Canada, England, Singapore, and Australia. Since investors never read instructions, I've created the Lazy Investor's Fast Start Guide as a bonus allowing investors to get 10 properties and 10 tenants up and running in less than 60 minutes.

This is the system I use to dump over 100 percent of my rents into my bank account every year. Investors from all over America are doing the same. The national average for landlords with 15 or more units is only 85 percent. That is correct. Investors with 15 or more units are getting only about 85 percent of their rents annually. Investors using this system are getting more than 110 percent of their rents! Check it out at www.TenantTracking.com.

It includes investor-friendly manuals allowing you to grow without huge headaches. When you hire office persons, you just hand them the manuals and they're off and running without you babysitting them. One software handles both hats you wear as an investor.

Computer: Would be helpful, is almost essential today.

Web site: In today's market, I highly recommend a web site detailing all your policies, procedures, application process, fees, and how to view vacant units, along with a detailed list of your available and expected-to-be-soon-available units. Include photos, inside and out. Get used to this . . . the market is already there. Home buyers can shop and tour houses for sale online without visiting them. Tenants can do this now, too. You shouldn't get raped on this. Perhaps $20 monthly.

File cabinet (letter size): Use green hanging file folders with a manila, one-third cut file folder for each tenant.

Forms: Don't go overboard here. For example, perhaps the ultimate stupid form for landlords that I've seen is a Bad Check Form. Why in the world would a landlord send a tenant a Bad Check Form if a tenant bounced a check? I'd send them a late notice and cock the trigger to launch the eviction process. Phooey on a bad check letter.

Your forms should be legal in your town. Make sure they are. Take all the ideas you learned from this book and other sources you have discovered and incorporate them into your own forms. Keep them simple—don't overburden yourself with 500 forms. The fewer the better, but you'll find a core group of a couple dozen that you use frequently in your landlording, such as Mike's Move-Out Package. Many forms are seldom used.

Excellent real estate attorney: Get the best. An attorney who is knowledgeable about your landlord/tenant laws and real estate would be ideal. One who is an investor and landlord would be a home run. Avoid family friends and neighbors who offer to help you and do stuff for free. You will get your clock cleaned.

Expert real estate Certified Public Accountant (CPA): My CPA, Mike Grinnan, is a real estate investor and understands investor concerns. He ain't cheap, but he's worth every penny to me.

Credit report resource: National Tenant Network is a great resource for mom-and-pop operations that need to access this information. Call J. R. Hutto in Louisville, Kentucky, at (502) 895-6811 to find out who your local contact would be. If you have a larger operation, you can join a specific group such as TransUnion or Equifax allowing you to pull reports and public records.

Digital camera: Nothing fancy, just an ordinary digital camera. I like the Sony Mavica camera which uses 3.5 floppy disks to capture the photos. Unfortunately, 3.5 floppy disks are almost in history museums next to 8-track tapes. In fact, my newest, recently purchased laptop does not have a 3.5-inch floppy drive. Most cell phones today have digital cameras built in. Figure out how to use it and make it easy for yourself.

Office stuff: Rubber stamps (ORIGINAL, COPY, RECEIVED, PAID) for about two or three bucks apiece; phone message pad with carbonless copies ($5.00). This is an excellent tool to chronologically document your messages from your answering machine. It keeps a record providing you scribble down date and time of the message. Don't use those pink "while you were out" message pads. There's no way to keep a record of your messages.

Answering machine: Get an inexpensive digital answering machine allowing you to retrieve your messages from another phone as well as change the greeting. Your greeting on this machine could include pitching vacant units and stating hours of operation, and should include your web site address for more information and your emergency number (pager).

Yard sign: Some kind of yard sign is almost a must.

Bank account(s): Use dedicated bank account(s) for your real estate activity. Don't lump your personal stuff with your real estate stuff. If your town requires it, you may be required to have a bank account exclusively for tenant security deposits.

Competent insurance agent: Find one who is knowledgeable about investment property. Also, recommend your agent to your tenants for their renter's insurance.

Education: Your education should never stop. It sets you apart from your competition and helps to "Sharpen Your Saw" as Steve Covey says. There are many possibilities, from joining your local investor group or apartment association to attending regional conferences, workshops, and seminars. Also, read to help you stay polished and on top of your business.

Your team: This includes trade-specific vendors and contractors (plumbers, painters, roofers, lawn service, tree service, siding, and so on), and a part-time office person. Build your team of qualified, licensed contractors, which will allow you to handle problems with a fax, e-mail, or phone call. Avoid having your spouse as your part-time office person. If you do this, you probably can't leave town together for an extended vacation.

FORMS AND MORE FORMS

Warning! You Must Read the Rules First!

A ll the forms in this book are secured by copyright (© by Wealth Building 24-7 LLC. All Rights Reserved).

Rule 1: Because you have purchased *Landlording on Auto-Pilot,* you have special exclusive rights. You have the exclusive permission to copy and edit these forms for your personal use and for your own real estate business use. You cannot copy these forms and share them with other investors. You bought this book: You get the exclusive right.

Rule 2: This is very important and is not always highlighted in other publications for landlords. Most states have their own landlord/tenant laws. I'm telling you right now that the forms I use in Louisville, Kentucky, most likely will not work in California and New York; however, the ideas and concepts can probably be worked into forms that follow your local landlord/tenant laws.

I love getting my hands on another sharp investor's lease or rental agreement. I review it in detail. If I find a paragraph or section I really like, I simply take the concept, or sometimes copy the entire section or paragraph, and add it to my rental agreement. I have never taken someone else's lease, changed the name of the landlord, and used it with my tenants. *It is dangerous* to operate in this manner.

It is your responsibility to make sure your forms and content are in compliance with your local landlord/tenant laws.

How Do You Ensure Compliance?

Get your own copy of your local landlord/tenant laws. Odds are, you can get on the first available computer with a printer, go to google.com and enter "[Your State] Landlord/Tenant Law." Google should give you a list of web sites with your answer. Just be supercareful that you get the real McCoy and not a *tenant guide*. Many tenant associations are creating their tenant-friendly version of the landlord/tenant laws. Just make sure you get the government version for your area.

I might seem a bit brutal on these forms; but, just like my parents, who would crack our butt if one of us young kids started to dart out into the street with traffic, I feel a parental obligation to cause you a little pain now to prevent a train wreck down the road.

The following examples show why you should make sure you have the government forms:

Example 1: In my town, landlords are required to disclose the bank name, account number, and address of the bank where their security deposit money is being held. If I used another expert investor's fill-in-the-blank lease, it might not contain this information and I would get clobbered in court for trying to pursue legal action against a tenant.

Example 2: What little bit I know about Pennsylvania's landlord/tenant law involves language in the landlord's lease. It must be simple, and I've heard comments about being "approved by the Pennsylvania Attorney General." I don't know the details of this law, but I promise you that if I operated in Pennsylvania, I sure would make it a priority to understand all this stuff.

Example 3: Almost all states require serving a "Pay or Quit Possession Notice" to the tenant from the landlord before a landlord can file for an eviction in court. The danger for you, the investor, is that the number of days' notice and the language that must be contained in the form, along with how it is delivered to your tenant, vary from state to state. Kentucky has a seven-day letter, Ohio uses a three-day letter, and so on.

Now that you know the hazards, here are the free forms that are available to you.

They are separated into three groups:

1. Application forms are identified as A1, A2, A3, and so on.
2. The New Tenant Package will be identified as NT1, NT2, NT3, and so on.
3. Move-out forms are identified as MO1, MO2, MO3, and so on.

You can go to www.WealthBuilding247.com/LandlordingOnAutoPilotFreeStuff to download your fully customizable Microsoft Word Document for all the forms you want to use for your business.

Application Forms

Key Sign-Out Form: We use this powerful form to save money and make money. Prospects stop by our office, fill out this form, produce a valid photo ID, from which we make an enlarged photocopy. We give a copy of this completed form to the tenant, along with a key for the vacant unit. A $20.00 cash key deposit is required for each unit they want to view.

Rental Application: See Chapter 12 for an in-depth explanation of specific phrases and questions and their purpose.

Deposit to Hold with Application: This form was developed when my market conditions got tougher. If somebody wants to flash cash at you, *grab it*, and get the applicant to sign this form. This is a double benefit for you. They will stop looking at other landlords' vacant units and remain loyal to you *because you have their money.* You must take your vacant unit off the market when an applicant completes this form.

Application Worksheet: This cover sheet goes on top of all the documents involved in processing each application. Its purpose is to give you, the investor, a quick summary highlighting important information in the complete package. I use a paper clip to put my work copy, the original, credit reports, landlord and employment verification, and any other documents involved in their application process. It keeps it all together for you. This is the form I fold in half vertically to document, in chronological order, the activity of each application process, including phone calls.

Deposit to Hold after Approved: We use this form most frequently with out-of-towners. Suppose applicants are approved and are now living in another town. To capture them, you could fax, e-mail, or snail mail this form to them, make some money, and take your vacant unit off the market. This secures your position and sets the stage to complete the rental agreement papers or new tenant package when they get to town.

Employment Verification: This speaks for itself.

Landlord Verification: This speaks for itself.

Qualifying Poster: This is printed on 8.5-inch x 11-inch bright yellow paper and is inserted into a clear acrylic easel that sits on the table where applicants usually fill out their applications.

New Tenant Package Forms

New Tenant Office Checklist: Use this form to make sure you dot all your i's and cross your t's.

Renter's Insurance: The payment plan suggested on this form does not mean we are selling insurance. It is a benefit we offer to all tenants. In this arrangement, the landlord collects and holds the tenants' money for the premium, making sure it gets paid without additional hardship on them. It is similar to a lender's escrow account to hold funds for taxes and insurance for payment at a later date.

Rental Agreement (8 pages): This is not the ultimate best-ever rental agreement, but it should be a valuable resource for you to borrow ideas and concepts and incorporate them into your lease or rental agreement.

Lead-Based Paint Disclosure

Plumbing—Sinks and Drains

Move-In Inspection

Welcome New Residents!

All-Star Program: This is our tenant reward program.

Animal Addendum

Cosigner Agreement

Information Release

Section 8 Additional Provisions

EPA Publication: "Protect Your Family from Lead in Your Home"

Rent Talk Package: These flip charts are used with a 1-inch, 3-ring binder (see Chapter 16).

Move-Out Forms

Mike's Move-Out Package is discussed in depth in Chapter 23.

Move-Out Package Summary Instructions

Head Off Eviction—Cash for Keys

Receipt of Notice to Vacate

Move-Out Instructions for Tenant

Price List and Fees for Tenant

Survey for Tenant to Grade Landlord and Your Property

Move-Out Summary: Fill out this form by yourself, out of sight of tenant, after you complete your move-out inspection. This summary report is entered into Tenant Tracking to create your Move Report and final settlement for this tenant's tenancy.

One Page Move-Out Inspection (Tenant comments go on the back of this page.)

Office Move-Out Checklist

Return Possession Notice: Use this form when weird things happen such as a tenant throwing keys at you in a Burger King parking lot. Its sole purpose is to document that your tenant has vacated the property returning possession to you, the landlord. Odds are, you probably completed a rental agreement or lease previously where you let them have legal possession of 123 Main Street until the expiration date noted on your lease. This notice simply kills the agreement allowing you to rent to another tenant legally without this one having any legal interest in your property.

More benefits for landlords are listed for you on the web site. They include such things as Ernie Riddle's Landlord Lock Service, which makes me money. Resources for yard signs, business cards, credit checks, and more can be found at www.WealthBuilding247.com/LandlordingOnAutoPilotFreeStuff.

Keep on Cranking It 24-7.

DOWNLOADABLE FORM A.1   Application: Key Sign Out*

KEY SIGN OUT FORM
Used for Showing Available Properties

Date: _____   **Home to View:** _____
Time: _____   *(Address of Home to See)*

Key to be returned to: **Vista Properties, Inc.**
4012 Dupont Circle, Suite 203
Louisville, KY 40207

Key will be returned by (Time): _____ **Date:** _____ , **2003**

I hereby acknowledge receipt of a key to view the house located at the above address and agree to return key by the time and date stated above or forfeit my twenty dollar *($20.00)* key deposit.

I understand I have no agreement to rent the house and will not occupy the house. I will only inspect it.

I will securely lock the house and turn off any lights, water, gas, etc. before leaving. I will not allow anyone to smoke in the house, nor use the toilets, and I will be responsible for the actions of others that accompany me to the property.

I will not reproduce the key and I accept sole responsibility for returning the key(s) and I must produce a valid picture ID and allow a copy of my ID to be kept with this form for verification of ID purposes.

In the event property is damaged due to my negligence, I agree to pay the reasonable cost of repairs including labor, material, and reasonable attorney fees.

Select One to receive key to see Vista Home
☐ $20.00 Cash w/ valid photo ID
☐ hold original Valid Photo ID
☐ Credit Card with valid photo ID. Charge my card if key not returned by time above.

___ *Visa*   ___ *MasterCard* ___ *Discover*   ___ *American Express*

Card Number: _____   Exp Date: _____

_____ _____   _____
(Phone)   *(Cell Phone)*   *(PRINT Full Name)*

_____
(Your Home Address Now)

_____   _____
(City, State, Zip Code)   *(Signature)*

Vista Office Initials: _____

KEY RETURNED on Date: _____ **at Time:**_____ **Initials:____**
Comments:

Date: _____   Address Applying for: _____   Last Name:_____

| (VISTA) | $20.00 Per Adult | **RENTAL APPLICATION** | $20.00 Per Adult | (house logo) |

ONLY CLEAN & RESPONSIBLE PEOPLE WHO PAY RENT ON TIME MAY APPLY with valid Picture ID

(502) 896-2595   4012 DUPONT CIRCLE, SUITE 203, LOUISVILLE, KY 40207   HOURS: MON-FRI 9AM-4:00PM   SOMETIMES SAT:10AM-2PM

First Name:		MI:	Last Name:		Jr.,Sr?
SSN:	Date of Birth:	Phone:		Is this your phone?:	
Cell Phone:	Pager:	Alternate Phone:		Whose Phone?:	

List your Addresses for the Previous 5 years

Current Address:	City, State, Zip:	
Owner/Manager:	Phone:	Monthly Rent:
Moved In date:	Why are you moving?	
Previous Address:	City, State, Zip:	
Owner/Manager:	Phone:	Monthly Rent:
Moved In date:	Moved out date:	
Previous Address:	City, State, Zip:	
Owner/Manager:	Phone:	Monthly Rent:
Moved In date:	Moved out date:	

Employment and Income

Current Employer:	Address:		
Position:	Phone:	Hire Date:	Hours worked per week:
Gross Wages: $	(___month ___week ___hour)	What other income & source?:	
2nd Job Employer:	Phone:	Income $	___wk, ___Mon ___Hr
Are You on Section 8?:	If Yes, Have You had your briefing?:	If yes, I have a	BEDROOM Voucher
How long will you live here?: 1 yr ___ 2 yr ___ 3 yr +		Your Attorney's Name:	
Is the total move-in amount available now?:	Have you broken a lease?:	Are You a Convicted Felon?:	
How many Evictions have been filed on you?:	What kind of animals do you have?:		
What may interrupt your income or ability to pay rent?			

If accepted the following persons will be living with me

1.)	4.)
2.)	5.)
3.)	6.)

Credit References

Lender	Purpose of Loan	Balance	Monthly Payment	
1.)				Do you have a Checking Account?:
2.)				Do you have a Savings Account?:
				Do you own Real Estate?:

EMERGENCY CONTACTS including help to pay rent

	NAME	ADDRESS	PHONE	RELATIONSHIP
1.)				
2.)				

LIST Vehicles & Trailers your household will possess: _____

HOW DID YOU FIND THIS HOME: (friend, yard sign, etc.) _____   Your requested move-in date: _____

Do You want Rent with Option to Buy or Rent to Own? _____   How much Cash do You Have: $_____

(continued)

DOWNLOADABLE FORM A.2 (Continued)

Date: _____ Address Applying for: _____ Last Name:_____

Other comments or explanations:

_____
_____
_____
_____
_____
_____
_____
_____

This agreement made this date by and between Vista Properties, Inc., manager for the Owner, hereinafter "Landlord" and the below signed, hereafter "Applicant". The Applicant shall pay to the Landlord nonrefundable fee upon the execution of this agreement in the amount listed on application to cover the administrative costs, expenses, and time of the Landlord to verify information submitted by the Applicant. Applicant authorizes the Landlord, his employees, agents, or representatives to make any and all inquiries necessary to verify the information provided herein, including but not limited to direct contact with Applicant's employer, landlords, credit, neighbors, police, government agencies and any and all other sources of information which the Landlord may deem necessary and appropriate within his sole discretion. The Applicant represents to the Landlord that the application has been completed in full and all the information provided for herein is true, accurate and complete to the best of the Applicant's knowledge and further, agrees that if any such information is not as represented, or if the application is incomplete the Applicant may, at the Landlord's sole discretion, be disqualified. The Applicant provides the information contained on this form. Landlord is not liable to the Applicant, his heirs, executors, administrators, or assigns for any damages of any kind, actual or consequential by reason of the verification by the Landlord of the information provided by the Applicant, and Applicant hereby releases the Landlord, his agent, employees and representatives from any and all actions, causes of action of any kind or nature that may arise by virtue of the execution or implementation of the agreement provided herein. This property requires a **Security Deposit** equivalent to one month's rent plus $50.00 that must by paid in full before any rental agreement is made. Animal deposit(s) are in addition to security deposit. Applicant, once approved, must obtain renter's insurance and Landlord will attempt to contact the Applicant by the phone numbers listed on this application. Applicant has 24 hours from time of approval to fulfill rental agreement by producing all monies required and signing all rental agreement papers. If Applicant fails to perform within 24 hours of Landlord's approval, Applicant may be disqualified and Landlord may rent this home to the next qualified Applicant.

Our required standards for qualifying to rent a home are simple and fair. They are:
- All homes are offered without regard to race, color, religion, national origin, sex, disability or familial status.
- Each adult occupant must submit an application.
- Your gross monthly income must equal approximately three times or more the monthly rent
- A favorable credit history.
- Be employed and be able to furnish acceptable proof of the required income.
- Good references, housekeeping, and property maintenance from your previous Landlords.
- Limit the number occupants to 2 per bedroom.
- Compensating Factors can include additional requirements such as double deposit or rent paid in advance for applicants who fall short of above criteria.

The Applicant authorizes release of all information to Vista Properties, Inc.

APPLICANT: _____   DATE: _____

www.VistaKY.com   *E-mail: WeRentHomes@aol.com*

OFFICE USE ONLY, Do NOT Write Below This Line				
Received By:	App Fee	Viewed Property	Picture ID Copy	Source

DEPOSIT TO HOLD AGREEMENT with Application

Date: _____   Property: _____

County: _____   City, State, Zip: _____

HOLD DEPOSIT: $_____

TERMS
Proposed Rent: $_____   Proposed Security Deposit: $_____

_____ accepts "HOLD DEPOSIT" monies from Applicant(s) as a non-refundable intent to rent fee for the property listed above and funds will be deposited into a deposit account serviced by an agent for Owner. The Intent to Rent Fee removes this property from public offering and holds the property for Applicant(s) pending approval of their application. Applicant must properly complete a rental agreement **before 4pm on** _____, 200__. Time is of the essence.

If Applicant(s) fail to perform by the listed date and time, the Hold Deposit fee will be forfeited to Manager for Owner for lost rents, administrative costs, advertising, and holding costs. All parties understand this document is not a rental agreement and no possession is permitted until an entire rental agreement has been properly completed.

Should Applicant(s) fail to qualify to rent property, Hold Deposit will be returned to the Applicant(s) within 30 Days, except the cost of processing each application. If Applicant wishes to receive funds before the one time monthly disbursement from Manager's Deposit account, applicant will pay an $85.00 service charge to the Property Manager.

Additional Provisions:

_____

_____

_____

Property Manager   **Applicant(s)**

_____

| Signature | Date |
| Signature | Date |

APPLICATION WORK SHEET

Date: _____ **Address:** _____ **Last Name:** _____

Rent: $ _____ Desired Move-In: _____ Animals? _____

Credit   Empirica: _____ Discrepancies? _____

Employment Verification   Hire Date: _____   Employer: Hours / Detail: _____

Income Verification   Rate of Pay _____   Who spoke with _____

GMI= $ _____   **GMI x.30 =** $ _____   **Monthly Installments =** $ _____

CURRENT Landlord/ Mgr:	PREVIOUS Landlord/ Mgr:	2nd PREVIOUS Landlord/ Mgr:
Address:___	Address:___	Address:___
___ Did tenant pay on time?	___ Did tenant pay on time?	___ Did tenant pay on time?
___ Have you received any complaints?	___ Have you received any complaints?	___ Have you received any complaints?
___ Did tenant damage property?	___ Did tenant damage property?	___ Did tenant damage property?
___ Would you rent to tenant again?	___ Would you rent to tenant again?	___ Would you rent to tenant again?
How long at this address? ___ Years NOTES:	How long at this address?: ___ Years NOTES:	How Long at this address?: ___ Years NOTES:

SCORING

Credit History: -3 -2 -1 0 +1 +2 +3   _____

Rental History: -3 -2 -1 0 +1 +2 +3   _____

Income/Employment: -3 -2 -1 0 +1 +2 +3   _____   [ ] BR VOUCHER

Decision Guidelines: Reject = <4   Consider = 4,5,6   Approve = >6   **Total Score:** [ ]

COMMENTS: *(Applicant issues to address / correct)*

_____
_____
_____
_____

_____ **ACCEPTABLE**   _____ **UNACCEPTABLE**   _____ **INCONCLUSIVE**

Date:_____ Time:_____ By:_____

DOWNLOADABLE FORM A.5   Application: Deposit to Hold after Approved*

DEPOSIT TO HOLD AGREEMENT (after approved)

Date: _____   Property: _____

County: _____   City, State, Zip: _____

Amount Collected: $ _____   **Amount Due:** $ _____

TERMS

Proposed Rent: $ _____   Proposed Security Deposit: $_____

_____ accepts the above amount collected monies from prospective tenant(s) as a non-refundable fee to purchase an intent to rent on the property listed above. The Intent to Rent removes this property from public offering and holds the property for prospective tenant(s) to produce "amount due" monies needed to properly complete a rental agreement **before 4pm on** _____**, 200__**. Time is of the essence. If prospective tenant(s) fail to perform by the listed date and time, a fee for lost rents, administrative costs, advertising, and holding costs will be assessed to prospective tenant(s) in an amount equal to amount collected. All parties understand this document is not a rental agreement and no possession is permitted until an entire rental agreement has been properly completed.

Additional Provisions: _____
_____
_____
_____
_____

Property Manager   **Prospective Tenant(s)**

_____

Signature	Date
Signature	Date

We Buy Houses! We Rent Homes!

4012 Dupont Circle, Suite 203, Louisville, Ky. 40207-4810
Office: (502)896-2595   Fax: (502) 896-6688

EMPLOYMENT VERIFICATION of Applicant

Date:_____   Please respond by:_____

TO: _____   RE: _____

_____   _____

The above individual(s) applied for housing. We respectfully request your assistance in completing this form. Thank you for your prompt response in providing the information requested below. If we can assist you in the future on any applicants, please call or fax and we will respond promptly.

_____   _____
(Property Manager)   (Signature of Applicant)

TO BE COMPLETED BY EMPLOYER

Name of Applicant: _____

Position held: _____

Rate of pay: _____

Hire date: _____

COMMENTS: _____
_____
_____
_____
_____
_____

_____   _____   _____   _____
(SIGNATURE)   (TITLE)   (PHONE#)   (DATE)

Thank You!

*We Rent Homes • Apartments • Rent with Option to Buy • EZ Credit
Owner Finance • Property Management • We Buy Loans • Mortgages*

DOWNLOADABLE FORM A.7   Application: Landlord Verification*

We Buy Houses!   We Rent Homes!

4012 Dupont Circle, Suite 203, Louisville, Ky. 40207-4810
Office: (502)896-2595   Fax: (502) 896-6688

LANDLORD VERIFICATION of Applicant

Date:_____   Please respond by:_____

TO: _____   RE: _____

_____   _____

The above individual(s) applied for housing. We respectfully request your assistance in completing this form. Thank you for your prompt response in providing the information requested below. If we can assist you in the future on any applicants, please call or fax and we will respond promptly.

_____   _____
(Property Manager)   (Signature of Applicant)

TO BE COMPLETED BY LANDLORD

Date of residency: From_____ To:_____   MONTHLY RENT: $_____

      1.) ____YES ____NO   Did the tenant pay their rent on time?

      2.) ____YES ____NO   Have You received any complaints?

      3.) ____YES ____NO   Did Tenant damage property during Tenancy?

      4.) ____YES ____NO   **Would you rent to Tenant again?**

COMMENTS:

_____

_____

_____

_____

_____

_____   _____   _____   _____
(SIGNATURE)   (TITLE)   (PHONE#)   (DATE)

Thank You!

**We Rent Homes • Apartments • Rent with Option to Buy • EZ Credit
Owner Finance • Property Management • We Buy Loans • Mortgages**

DOWNLOADABLE FORM A.8   **Application: Qualifying Poster***

We Buy Houses!   *We Rent Homes!*

4012 Dupont Circle, Suite 203, Louisville, Ky. 40207-4810 • PO Box 24181, Louisville, KY 40224-0181
Office: (502)896-2595 • Fax: (502) 896-6688 • www.VistaKy.com • E-mail: WeRentHomes@aol.com

Hello...

We are pleased you are considering making your home with us. We are very proud of our community and believe you will be too. Our standards for qualifying to rent a home are simple and fair. They are:

- Your gross income must equal approximately three times the monthly rent of your home.
- A favorable credit history.
- Be employed or be able to furnish acceptable proof of the required income.
- Good references from previous Landlords.
- Limit occupants to 2 per bedroom.

If you have any questions, please consult with our staff for any clarification or details.

VISTA Properties, Inc. Staff

NOTE: Applicants with less than favorable credit may qualify by doubling the security deposit or paying rent in advance.

*We Rent Homes • Apartments • Rent with Option to Buy • EZ Credit
Owner Finance • Property Management • We Buy Loans • Mortgages*

New Tenant: Tenant Information Sheet

Address: _____ Date: _____

Tenant Name: _____ Phone: _____

SSN: _____ DOB:_____

Monthly Rent: $_____ Security Deposit: $_____

Occupants: _____ DOB: _____

    (Name & Number)

    _____ DOB: _____

    _____ DOB: _____

    _____ DOB: _____

    Moved-In Date: _____ Phone: _____

    Rental Agreement: _____ Expire date: _____

Emergency/Alternate Contact: _____

Remarks: _____

DOWNLOADABLE FORM A.10   New Tenant: Office Checklist*

OFFICE: New Tenant Check List

*Tenant:*_____ *Date:*_____

*Address:*_____

1.) _____ Move In Inspection SIGNED

2.) _____ Trans Union Form

3.) _____ Pamphlet "Protect Your Family…"

4.) _____ Lead based Paint form

5.) _____ Keys _____ # of Keys (**VP-00____**)
Enter KeyCode in RESALE number QB

6.) _____ Utilities, Verify, **note on LG&E log.**

7.) _____ If signed after 20th, next month pay now

8.) _____ Security Deposit money by itself
_____ All other money by itself

9.) _____ Valid Photo ID – copy

10.) _____ Customer Entered in QB properly

11.) ___ Memorize Rent statement chrg in QBPro

12.) _____ Enter new "TO DO" for 13th month RENT

13.) ___ Section 8? ___Yes ___No
___ Memorize " Section 8 Expected paymt..."
___ Create 90 Day TO DO for expire date

14.) _____ Birthday = To Do

15.) _____ Anniversary Date = To Do, (75 days prior)

16.) _____ "Plumbing Drains & Sinks" Form

17.) _____ "Animal" Addendum

18.) _____ Lawn Service terminated

19.) _____ Change out 7 cylinder on front door

20.) _____ Remove Yard Sign   by:_____

21.) _____ Calendar

22.) _____ Folder

23.) _____ Key Tag

24.) _____ Business Card

25.) _____ Renter Insurance MUST Form, $14 month

Section 8 ONLY
                               DATE
Tenant picked up package: _____
Turn in to HAJC worker by: _____
10 Day deadline inspection: _____
          Inspection Date: _____

SECURITY DEPOSIT: $ _____
NOTES:

Rental Agreement sign Date: _____

Rental Agreement start Date: _____

Move In Date: _____

Rental Agreement Expires Date: _____
(Anniversary Date)

Option To Buy: ___YES ___ NO
     Option Price: _____
     Option Fee: _____
     Option Expires: _____

Place in top bucket to be reviewed:

*REVIEWED BY:*_____ *Date;*_____

RENTER's INSURANCE

Address: _____

(Check One)

❏   **I have provided proof of paid policy.**

Insurance Co: _____

Policy Number: _____ **Effective Date:** _____

❏   **I need assistance in obtaining Renter's Insurance and I want my monthly rent increased $15.00 to cover the cost of my Renter's Insurance. When I receive the bill from the insurance company, I will mail the bill to Vista for payment so long as my account is current. I understand I must pay a full year premium at the start of my rental agreement.**

- Renter's Insurance is for *YOUR* protection.

- If you need assistance, a licensed insurance agent will be contacting you within 10 days.

- I acknowledge receiving literature explaining details, services, and benefits of Renter's Insurance.

Tenant:_____   **Date:**_____

Tenant:_____   **Date:**_____

DOWNLOADABLE FORM A.12   New Tenant: Rental Agreement*

Rental Agreement

Property Manager for Owner (Landlord):   **TENANT(s)** *(PRINT FULL REAL NAME)*:

Vista Properties, Inc.

Manager for Owner   **Name:** _____   **SSN:** ___ - ___ - ___

4012 Dupont Circle, Suite 203

Louisville, KY 40207-4810   **Name:** _____   **SSN:** ___ - ___ - ___

Office: (502) 896-2595

RENTED PROPERTY: _____   City: _____   KY   Zip: _____

County: Jefferson _____   Single Family Dwelling

Check One:

☐ *VISTA's* **Standard Package**

☐ *VISTA's* **Custom Package** (any two items, add $25.00 to monthly rent)

☐ *VISTA's* **Deluxe Package** (any four items, add $49.00 to monthly rent)

1.) TERM: Tenant(s) agrees to rent beginning on _____, 200___ and ending on _____, 200___ at 11:59 p.m.. All terms start on the first day of the month and end on the last day of a calendar month. Upon expiration of this Rental Agreement and if Tenant remains in possession of the rented premises with the consent of the Landlord, a new 12 month tenancy shall be created between Landlord and Tenant which shall be subject to all the terms and conditions. Sixty (60) days written notice served by either Landlord or Tenant on the other party is required to terminate this rental agreement.

_____ Standard Package   = $ _____
_____   + $ _____
_____   + $ _____
_____   + $ _____
_____   + $ _____

MONTHLY   SECURITY   ANIIMAL
RENT: $ _____   DEPOSIT: $ _____   DEPOSIT: $ _____

DOWNLOADABLE FORM A.13   New Tenant: Lead-Based Paint Disclosure*

LEAD PAINT POISONING

Children get lead poisoning when they eat bits of paint that contain lead. Older houses often have layers of lead paint on the walls, ceilings, and woodwork. When the paint chips off or when the plaster breaks, there is possible danger for babies and young children. Outdoors, lead paints and primers may have been used in many places, such as walls fences, and porches.

Be sure to tell your family and any guests with small children about the danger of lead poisoning. Your child can be poisoned by eating paint, dirt, or other non-food substances containing lead. Some other items which contain lead include newspaper, pottery, furniture and even common household dust.

Since your home was probably built before 1978 it may have been painted with lead based paint years ago. We wanted to warn you of the possible dangers. Realizing this, and still wanting to rent this property from us, you hereby agree to hold Vista Properties, Inc. and its members, agents, and property owner harmless of any problems which could result from lead based paint, and any costs involved in diagnosis and treatment of the same. This includes all who will be living with you for whom you are responsible and all of your guests.

Tenant:_____   **Date:**_____

Tenant: _____   **Date:**_____

PLUMBING – SINKS & DRAINS

Vista Properties, Inc. is concerned about the health, safety, and welfare of all our residents and those who provide services to our properties.

Do NOT put any kind of chemical treatment into any plumbing fixture – (sinks, toilets, drains).

- Products such as Liquid Fire, Drano, and Liquid Plumber can cause serious physical injury to you and/or our service person.

- These products can cause property damage to plumbing pipes and drains. Some products actually melt pipes.

- If your home is on a septic system, these kind of products can upset the natural processing of waste that occurs in a septic system.

In order to avoid injury to anyone and costly charges to your account, do not put food, grease, etc., or chemical products in waste lines.

Tenant:_____   **Date:**_____

Tenant:_____   **Date:**_____

DOWNLOADABLE FORM A.15 New Tenant: Move In Inspection*

MOVE IN INSPECTION

VISTA

Address: _____ Date: _____

ITEMS	NEW GOOD	OTHER

Living Room
- Walls
- Ceiling
- Floor

Dining Room
- Walls
- Ceiling
- Floor

Kitchen
- Walls
- Ceiling
- Floor
- Cabinets
- Range
- Refrigerator
- Vent Hood

- Dishwasher
- Disposal
- Countertop

Hall
- Walls
- Ceiling
- Floor

Bedroom #1
- Walls
- Ceiling
- Floor

Bedroom #2
- Walls
- Ceiling
- Floor

Bedroom #3
- Walls
- Ceiling
- Floor

Bathroom
- Walls
- Ceiling
- Floor
- Fixtures

Other _____
- Walls
- Ceiling
- Floor

General KEYS Number Received: ___ KEYCODE #: _____
- Floors
- Windows
- Doors
- Light Fixtures
- Yard
- Basement

	Good Clean	Other	Notes
Exterior			
Crawl			
Basement			
Garage			
Attic			
Lawn			
Shed			
Kitchen Cabinets			
Closets			
Vanity			
Medicine Cabinet			
Doors			
Drawers			
Porches			

Utilities:
Water: On:___ Off:___
Electric: On:___ Off:___
Gas: On:___ Off:___

Smoke Alarm

Tenant Comments:

I and/or we accept the aforementioned "Inspection" as a part of the rental agreement with Vista Properties, Inc. including my/our comments noted under "Tenant Comments" and agree that this is an accurate account of the condition of this property and understand that the balance of our security deposit will be forwarded via U.S. Mail within 30 days to the address listed below.

NEW ADDRESS: _____ CITY: _____ ST: _____ ZIP: _____

Landlord: _____ Date: _____ Tenant: _____ Date: _____
Vista Properties, Inc. by: TIME : _____ Tenant: _____ Date: _____

DOWNLOADABLE FORM A.16   New Tenant: Welcome New Residents!*

We Buy Houses! *We Rent Homes!*

4012 Dupont Circle, Suite 203 • Louisville, KY 40207-4810
Office: (502) 896-2595 • Fax: (502) 896-6688 • www.VistaKy.com • E-mail: WeRentHomes@aol.com

Welcome to Vista!   Congratulations!   Vista Properties, Inc. takes pride in offering clean quality homes at an affordable price. We are committed to this goal long-term and want you to know that you are not renting from a "part-time Mom & Pop operation".

Enclosed is your Rental Agreement and other information for your home. On the 20th of each month, you will receive a statement with a pre-addressed return envelope. Please return your payment in the enclosed envelope post marked on or before the 1st of the month. (Remember, your payment received date is recorded as the post mark date stamped on your payment envelope).

Note: Please, Do NOT make payments at office

For fastest processing, Please MAIL all payments to:

**VISTA Properties, Inc.
P.O. Box 24181
Louisville, KY 40224-0181**

We strive to be the best. Please let us know how we are doing by dropping a note with any monthly payment. We value your comments, suggestions, and feedback.

Here are some helpful phone numbers:

Louisville Gas and Electric: 589-1444
Louisville Water Company: 583-6610

Good Luck with your move,

Shirley Hamilton
Office Manager

*We Rent Homes • Apartments • Rent with Option to Buy • EZ Credit
Owner Finance • Property Management • We Buy Loans • Mortgages*

DOWNLOADABLE FORM A.17   New Tenant: All-Star Program*

Earn FREE Rent!
Simple & Easy to become a VISTA ALL-STAR!
Consecutive months with no late payments & no violations!

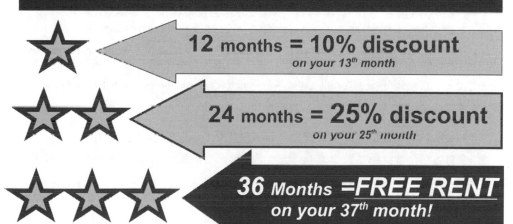

12 months = 10% discount
on your 13th month

24 months = 25% discount
on your 25th month

36 Months =FREE RENT
on your 37th month!

The FREE RENT credit for the 37th month will be credited upon signing a new 36 month rental agreement.
This program does NOT apply to Section 8 Program Participants.

By utilizing Vista's ALL STAR PLAN, you can save actually LOWER your rent even after annual cost of living.

FOR EXAMPLE, using $600 monthly rent,
You receive discounts of $60.00, $154.35, & $635.30 totally almost $850.00 in FREE RENT!
THIS WIPES OUT ALL of the cost of living PLUS $400 !

RENTAL AGREEMENT ADDENDUM

Address: _____ Date: _____

ANIMAL AGREEMENT

_____ has permission to have _____ animal(s) in the rental unit as provided for in the original Rental Agreement and described below:

Animal Type: _____ Sex: _____ Weight: _____ Color: _____

Animal Type: _____ Sex: _____ Weight: _____ Color: _____

Animal Type: _____ Sex: _____ Weight: _____ Color: _____

A $25.00 charge per Animal will be added to the monthly Rent Agreement and the additional Animal charges will be included as part of the monthly rent.

No animal of any kind, not provided for and described on this agreement, shall be allowed without the full written consent of the Landlord. Tenant understands and acknowledges that should any local ordinance or rental agreement violations that can be attributed directly or indirectly to these animal(s) will require the Tenant to immediately remove all animal(s) involved from property within 7 days after receiving written notice from Landlord.

$ _____ has been paid this date as a Animal Deposit for listed Animal(s) as permitted.

This Animal Deposit shall be returned to Tenant utilizing the same procedures noted in the Rental Agreement involving Security Deposits.

Agent, Owner, Landlord, and Tenant further agree that agent and owner will not be liable for any damages or losses to person or property caused by Tenant's Animal(s).

Vista Properties, Inc. by: TENANT: _____
                                                                                          Date

_____   TENANT: _____
                          Date   Date

FORBIDDEN Animals: NOTES:
- Pitbull
- Rottweiler
- German Shepherd
- "Husky" Alaskan Malamute
- Doberman Pincher
- Chow Chow
- Great Dane
- St. Bernard
- Akita
- Wolf Hybrids

(List compiled from Center for Disease Control on dog breeds involved in dog-bite-related fatalities)

 We Rent Homes • Apartments • Rent with Option to Buy • EZ Credit Owner Finance • Property Management • We Buy Loans • Mortgages

COSIGNER AGREEMENT
(Addendum to Rental Agreement)

This agreement is between

_____, Owner,

_____, Resident(s), and

_____, Cosigner.

The above parties entered into this cosigner agreement on _____.

The resident(s) has leased from the owners the premises located at

_____.

The rental agreement, which was entered into on _____ is attached and this cosigner forms a part of that Rental Agreement. The cosigner agrees to be jointly and severally liable along with the Resident(s) for Resident's obligations stipulated in the rental agreement between Resident(s) and Owner. The obligations include but are not limited to unpaid rent, charges, property damage, cleaning and repair costs that exceed the Resident's security deposit.

Under the terms of this agreement, the cosigner has no intention of occupying the dwelling referred to in the Rental Agreement above and has read and understood the Rental Agreement referred to above, promise to guarantee the Resident's compliance with the financial obligations of this Agreement. The cosigner understands that he or she may be required to pay for rent, charges, cleaning and repair costs for damages in such amounts as are incurred by the Residents under the terms of this Agreement if, and only if, the Residents fail to pay.

Owner will attempt (but is not required) to notify cosigner of any financial obligation that the resident fails to pay and give the cosigner an opportunity to pay the financial obligation. However, if cosigner does not cover resident's obligation within specified period of time on notification, and the obligation remains unpaid, the owner may pursue legal options to obtain a judgment against both the resident(s) and the cosigner. In addition, the Owner may pursue collection procedures and recover debt from both parties as well as report the debt of both the resident(s) and cosigner to all three credit bureaus.

If Owner, Resident and Cosigner are involved in legal proceedings, the prevailing party shall recover reasonable attorney fees, court costs and reasonable costs necessary to collect and report a judgment.

Cosigner _____ Date _____

Resident(s) _____ Date _____

Owner _____ Date _____

Authorization to Release Information

I/We hereby authorize you to release _____ any
and all information that they may require for the purpose of a credit transaction
or loan transfer. You may reproduce this document to acquire reference from
more than one source.

Thank You.

_____   _____

Signature   Soc. Sec. #   Date

_____   _____

Signature   Soc. Sec. #   Date

DOWNLOADABLE FORM A.21   New Tenant: Information Disclosure*

9075 Federal Register / Vol. 61, No. 45 / Wednesday, March 6, 1996 / Rules and Regulations (Sample Disclosure Format for Target Housing Rentals and Leases)

Disclosure of Information on Lead-Based Paint and/or Lead-Based Paint Hazards

Lead Warning Statement

Housing built before 1978 may contain lead-based paint. Lead from paint, paint chips, and dust can pose health hazards if not managed properly. Lead exposure is especially harmful to young children and pregnant women. Before renting pre-1978 housing, lessors must disclose the presence of known lead-based paint and/or lead-based paint hazards in the dwelling. Lessees must also receive a federally approved pamphlet on lead poisoning prevention.

Lessor's Disclosure

(a) Presence of lead-based paint and/or lead-based paint hazards (Check (i) or (ii) below):

(i)—— Known lead-based paint and/or lead-based paint hazards are present in the housing (explain).

_____

(ii)——Lessor has no knowledge of lead-based paint and/or lead-based paint hazards in the housing.

(b) Records and reports available to the lessor (Check (i) or (ii) below):

(i)—— Lessor has provided the lessee with all available records and reports pertaining to lead-based paint and/or lead-based paint hazards in the housing (list documents below).

_____

(ii)——Lessor has no reports or records pertaining to lead-based paint and/or lead-based paint hazards in the housing.

(continued)

Lessee's Acknowledgment (initial)

(c)——Lessee has received copies of all information listed above.

(d)——Lessee has received the pamphlet Protect Your Family from Lead in Your Home.

Agent's Acknowledgment (initial)

(e)—— Agent has informed the lessor of the lessor's obligations under 42 U.S.C.

4852d and is aware of his/her responsibility to ensure compliance.

Certification of Accuracy

The following parties have reviewed the information above and certify, to the best of their

knowledge, that the information they have provided is true and accurate.

_____ _____ _____ _____

Lessor Date Lessor Date

_____ _____ _____ _____

Lessee Date Lessee Date

_____ _____ _____ _____

Agent Date Agent Date

(Sample Disclosure Format for Target Housing Sales)

Disclosure of Information on Lead-Based Paint and/or Lead-Based Paint Hazards

Lead Warning Statement

Every purchaser of any interest in residential real property on which a residential dwelling

was built prior to 1978 is notified that such property may present exposure to lead from

lead-based paint that may place young children at risk of developing lead poisoning. Lead

poisoning in young children may produce permanent neurological damage, including learning disabilities, reduced intelligence quotient, behavioral problems, and impaired memory. Lead poisoning also poses a particular risk to pregnant women. The seller of any interest in residential real property is required to provide the buyer with any information on lead-based paint hazards from risk assessments or inspections in the seller's possession and notify the buyer of any known lead-based paint hazards. A risk assessment or inspection for possible lead-based paint hazards is recommended prior to purchase.

Seller's Disclosure

(a) Presence of lead-based paint and/or lead-based paint hazards (check (i) or (ii) below):

(i)—— Known lead-based paint and/or lead-based paint hazards are present in the housing (explain).

_____

(ii)——Seller has no knowledge of lead-based paint and/or lead-based paint hazards in the housing.

(b) Records and reports available to the seller (check (i) or (ii) below):

(i)——Seller has provided the purchaser with all available records and reports pertaining to lead-based paint and/or lead-based paint hazards in the housing (list documents below).

_____

(ii)—— Seller has no reports or records pertaining to lead-based paint and/or lead-based paint hazards in the housing.

Purchaser's Acknowledgment (initial)

(c)——Purchaser has received copies of all information listed above.

(d)——Purchaser has received the pamphlet Protect Your Family from Lead in Your Home.

(e)——Purchaser has (check (i) or (ii) below):

(continued)

(i)—— received a 10-day opportunity (or mutually agreed upon period) to conduct a risk assessment or in-spection for the presence of lead-based paint and/or lead-based paint hazards; or

(ii)—— waived the opportunity to conduct a risk assessment or inspection for the presence of lead-based paint and/or lead-based paint hazards.

Agent's Acknowledgment (initial)

(f)——Agent has informed the seller of the seller's obligations under 42 U.S.C. 4852d and is aware of his/her responsibility to ensure compliance.

Certification of Accuracy

The following parties have reviewed the information above and certify, to the best of their knowledge, that the information they have provided is true and accurate.

_____ _____ _____ _____

Seller Date Seller Date

_____ _____ _____ _____

Purchaser Date Purchaser Date

_____ _____ _____ _____

Agent Date Agent Date

DOWNLOADABLE FORM A.22   New Tenant: Landlord's Additional Provisions to Rental Agreement—Section 8 Housing

Landlord's Additional Provisions to Rental Agreement with Louisville Metro Housing Section 8 Program

Tenant: _____   Address: _____

Owner: #   Date: _____

1) Tenant is responsible to test smoke alarm(s) monthly and replace batteries as needed.
2) Rent: Tenant portion of rent is due on or before the 1st of each month or
3) Late Charge: 10% late charge is added on the 2nd & $5.00 per day daily late charge thereafter.
4) Payment received date will be recorded as the date post-marked on the envelope the payment is received via First Class Mail.
5) Tenant is responsible for all occupants and guests and will comply with and not violate the City of Louisville's and/or Jefferson County's Public Nuisance Ordinance.
6) Missed appointments on scheduled service calls will cost Tenant $30.00
7) Tenant acknowledges receipt of EPA publication "EPA747-K-94-001"(May 1995) "Protect Your Family From Lead In Your Home."
8) Tenant must submit their Section 8 rent package to their worker on or before _____ or Landlord may cancel and terminate the pending rental agreement with Section 8 and the prospective applicant/tenant. For example, if Tenant fails to deliver papers to their worker by the date listed here, Landlord may rent this unit to the next qualified applicant.
9) Although not a Tenant responsibility, Section 8 scheduled Inspection must occur within 10 days of worker receiving Tenant package or Landlord may cancel this rental agreement and rent this unit to the next qualified applicant.
10) Annual renewal agreements with Section 8 will be for an additional 12 month term and will not be deemed a month to month agreement for tenancy.
11) No criminal activity is allowed.
12) Fill out Form Fee: $15.00 fee paid in advance required with any form to be filled out by Landlord for Tenant.
13) Keys and Lock Out: If Tenant becomes locked out of home:
    • During office hours:
        1.) Tenant may purchase another key at office for $10.00.
        2.) A service person, if available, may unlock door for current rate listed in office.
    • $60.00 After office hours charge to Tenant to solve problem.
14) Single Family Homes Only:
    a.) Tenant responsible for all lawn care and maintenance.
    b.) Tenant responsibility to change furnace filters monthly and Tenant will turn off air conditioning in the home while cutting or trimming grass around the outside air unit. If Tenant requests service for malfunctioning HVAC and service person determines failure due to Tenant's failure to change air filter or grass clippings in coil/fins, Tenant will pay for service call.
    c.) Landlord may place sign in yard.
    d.) Extermination Services-this is a Tenant responsible item as per local ordinance.
    e.) Garage(s), if any, are not included in rental agreement.
15) Apartments Only:
    a.) No loitering, drinking, eating, smoking, playing music, trash, litter, debris, or personal property is allowed in hallways or on porches
    b.) Apartment doors will not be left open to "hear music" outside and any device that makes noise shall not be placed projecting sounds from apartment.

Tenant Signature _____ Date: _____

Landlord Signature _____ Date: _____

(Please sign and return copy to Owner/Landlord with copies of HAJC rental agreement)
This form approved by Rudy Heimann, HAJC on April 25, 2001 at 12:05 pm

Copyright © 2006 by WealthBuilding 24-7 LLC. ***To customize this document, download the Landlord's Additional Provisions to Rental Agreement—Section 8 Housing** form to your hard drive from http://www.mikebutler.com/landlordingonautopilotforms.htm.* The document can then be opened, edited, and printed using Microsoft Word or another popular word processing application.

DOWNLOADABLE FORM A.23   New Tenant: EPA Publication—
"Protect Your Family from Lead in Your Home"

The full text of this 17-page brochure can be downloaded from www.epa.gov/lead/pubs/leadpdfe.pdf.

DOWNLOADABLE FORM A.24 Move Out: Package Summary Instructions*

"MOVE OUT PACKAGE"
By Mike Butler

Great Tool with TENANT TRACKING

Knowledge is Powerful
Your Education Should Never Stop

Congratulations! You have a powerful package to reduce your headaches of Tenant Turnover. One of your most discouraging moments of landlording is learning of another expected vacancy.

This package has been prepared after years of experience and hundreds of move outs. Haven't you've learned even your good tenants have disappointed YOU by the condition they return the property. Landlords are in disbelief and cannot understand why good tenants do this to them.

As a rule of thumb, most tenants think of landlords as people with money. Even excellent tenants get tunnel vision involving their move out process. They are focused on where they are going and honestly believe the landlord is focused on "getting the key" quickly to so they can "get the property ready to rent" again. I hope you do not agree.

After realizing this the hard way, I developed this "Move Out Package". Many powerful features and tools have been built in to this package. The forms on this CD are Microsoft Word documents allowing you to edit and customize them to your needs.

After you learn a Tenant is moving (evictions also- they're moving too), send a "Move Out Package" containing:
1.) Landlord's acknowledgement and **Receipt of Tenant's Notice to Vacate**
2.) **Move Out Instructions**
      i. How to save their Security Deposit
      ii. Encourage to earn a referral fee if their help produces a new Tenant
      iii. Keep the place sharp is basic to pursuing a referral fee
3.) **Move Out Procedures** – How the Move Out Inspection process works
4.) **SURVEY** – thoughtful review of how YOU, the Landlord operated.
      i. (very powerful psychological tool, even if they trash the form, at least they saw it, and they will hopefully recall how great a landlord you have been to them.)
Do not balk at the idea of a referral fee. Do you want to get the property rented quickly and have your Tenant contribute their efforts to accomplishing your objective? A referral fee is an easy price to pay.

After You complete the move out inspection using YOUR Move-Out Inspection Form, use the included **Summary Report** and **Office Checklist** to cover bases properly. These work great with Tenant Tracking.

As a last resort, included is a **Return Possession without Inspection Form** to use when a Tenant wishes to return possession on the spot. If you have an office, use this form if they stop by the office unexpectedly to "turn in" or "drop off" their keys. Without an office, keep this form in your car or folded in your day planner. Although you have good planning and organizational skills, there are always exceptions to every rule. You will still receive a phone call from a Tenant informing you they have already moved-out or the Tenant with an eviction pending with no hope. The eviction pending Tenant may contact you to report they are out or you may encourage them to move out a little sooner. When these situations arise, use this last form to document properly that they have returned possession to you.
TIPS:
• SEND MOVE OUT PACKAGES upon receiving notice **and again 7 days prior to Move out date**
• SEND TO YOUR TENANTS WITH EVICTION PENDING – they are going to move too!!
Tenants with evictions have followed the move out instructions!
Good Luck, Mike Butler

DOWNLOADABLE FORM A.25   Move Out: Head Off Eviction—Cash for Keys*

 VISTA **We Buy Houses!** *We Rent Homes!*

4012 Dupont Circle, Suite 203, Louisville, Ky. 40207-4810 • PO Box 24181, Louisville, KY 40224-0181
Office: (502) 896-2595 • Fax: (502) 896-6688 • www.VistaKy.com • E-mail: WeRentHomes@aol.com

CA$H For You

TO:

                                              DATE: _____

_____

_____

_____

_____

Re: Tenancy at _____

This letter is can put CASH in Your Pocket.

It is unfortunate that your account is in serious delinquent status; however, we can still help you with these circumstances. You know this can not continue, we must make our house payments and we get no mercy from the banks.

If we continue with the eviction action, your credit will be ruined and the attorneys get paid. Attorneys make a lot of money.

YOU CAN CHOOSE to save your credit, and **You can get the attorney's money!**

HERE IS YOUR OFFER: Follow the enclosed instructions with our move out package enclosed, and schedule your move out inspection properly and we will give you a month's rent to help with your moving expenses into a new home.

PLEASE DO NOT PLAY OSTRICH – **TIME IS CRITICAL**. Each Day gets uglier! You need the cash now more than the attorneys and we need to get the house rented. We'd rather you get the money than them and save your credit, plus we will give you a good reference if needed to find a new place!

CALL SHIRLEY NOW TO Take Advantage of this Offer.

If you are completely out of your home and have it in "broom clean" condition following the move out instructions, **VISTA WILL PAY YOU A MONTH's RENT CASH**
if you are out by: _____.

Help us to Help You and we can part on good terms. I am looking forward to your call.

Shirley
Property Manager

 We Rent Homes • *Apartments* • *Rent with Option to Buy* • *EZ Credit*
Owner Finance • *Property Management* • *We Buy Loans* • *Mortgages*

DOWNLOADABLE FORM A.26   Move Out: Receipt of Notice to Vacate*

 We Buy Houses! *We Rent Homes!*

4012 Dupont Circle, Suite 203, Louisville, Ky. 40207-4810 • PO Box 24181, Louisville, KY 40224-0181
Office: (502)896-2595 • Fax: (502) 896-6688 • www.VistaKy.com • E-mail: WeRentHomes@aol.com

RECEIPT OF NOTICE TO VACATE

TO:

DATE:

_____

_____

_____

_____

Re: Tenancy at _____

This letter is confirmation that we received notice of your intent to vacate the home you are now renting from Vista Properties, Inc. **before** _____, **20**____.

SECURITY DEPOSIT: In order to prevent any misunderstanding regarding your refund, move out instructions and procedures are enclosed.

MOVE OUT INSPECTION: Please call the office at least *3-5 days in advance* of the exact date and time you will be completely moved out in order to schedule your Move Out Inspection.

UTILITIES: Please make arrangements to transfer the billing of utilities to the first business day *after* your Move Out Inspection has occurred.

It is very important to keep your home looking its best as prospective Tenants may be riding by your home and YOU can earn referral $$$ by helping us find a great Tenant like yourself to rent your home. Be sure to tell friends at work, church, and any clubs or associations. We may also place a Yard Sign to help you earn referral fee.

IMPORTANT: We will NOT send people by to see the inside of your home. We will inform prospective Tenants that your home is scheduled to be available by the date you have listed above. We inform people of the address to allow them to ride by. Again, we will NOT send people over to knock on your door and see the inside of your home without your permission.

THANKS & GOOD LUCK WITH YOUR MOVE!

Shirley
Property Manager

I know things are getting ready to get busy; but, if you get a chance, could you please fill out the enclosed survey and return promptly as we value your comments & suggestions.

 We Rent Homes • Apartments • Rent with Option to Buy • EZ Credit Owner Finance • Property Management • We Buy Loans • Mortgages

DOWNLOADABLE FORM A.27   Move Out: Instructions for Tenant*

We Buy Houses!   *We Rent Homes!*

4012 Dupont Circle, Suite 203, Louisville, Ky. 40207-4810 • PO Box 24181, Louisville, KY 40224-0181
Office: (502)896-2595 • Fax: (502) 896-6688 • www.VistaKy.com • E-mail: WeRentHomes@aol.com

MOVE OUT
INSTRUCTIONS & PROCEDURES

1. ___ **Please phone 3 to 5 days in advance to schedule your move-out inspection.**
2. ___ All floors swept, washed, and waxed.
3. ___ All walls & ceilings dusted down & all dirt, smudges, & grease washed off.
4. ___ Wash down all baseboards, woodwork, and windowsills.
5. ___ Clean and wash all light fixtures.
6. ___ Thoroughly clean all bathroom fixtures - toilet (s), bathtub (s), showers, sinks, and cabinets.
7. ___ Clean & wash inside & outside of kitchen, removing all dirt & grease including kitchen sink & fixtures
8. ___ **Keep all utilities on** until day after your move-out inspection is complete.
9. ___ Clean behind & between stove and refrigerator area.
10. ___ Clean storage area.
11. ___ Sweep & wash hallway floors and dust hallway walls.
12. ___ Vacuum & clean carpets.
13. ___ Clean closets, shelves, & rods wiped down.
14. ___ Clean all windows, storms, screens, and return them to their proper place.
15. ___ Remove all items from attic, crawlspace, basement, yard, shed, etc.
16. ___ Lawn, driveway, garage, outbuildings, to be free of all trash, rubbish, and loose personal property
17. ___ Lawn trimmed and cut properly, including removal of leaves.
18. ___ All trash and garbage to be removed from property. DO NOT PILE up garbage at the curb.
19. ___ Remove all garbage from property before your inspection.
20. ___ Do not remove phone jacks, picture hooks, or curtain rods and brackets.
21. ___ All keys are to be returned as instructed.
22. ___LIGHT BULBS - **ALL** light fixtures are to have working light bulbs in ALL bulb sockets.
23. ___ Smoke alarm(s) will be in working order with good battery.
24. ___ **Please phone 3 to 5 days in advance to schedule your move-out inspection.**

Any repainting, repairs cleaning, trash removal, and any other expenses associated with returning the condition of your home to your move-in condition can be deducted from your security deposit. Your security deposit will be mailed to the forwarding address you provide within 30 days after your Move-out inspection has been completed. Attached is a list of fees and charges for your information.

We only expect you to return your home in the same condition as when you moved in.
If you have any questions, please call.   GOOD LUCK with your move!

Thank You,

Shirley

We Rent Homes • Apartments • Rent with Option to Buy • EZ Credit
Owner Finance • Property Management • We Buy Loans • Mortgages

DOWNLOADABLE FORM A.28   Move Out: Price List and Fees for Tenant*

We Buy Houses!   We Rent Homes!

4012 Dupont Circle, Suite 203, Louisville, Ky. 40207-4810   •   PO Box 24181, Louisville, KY 40224-0181
Office: (502)896-2595   •   Fax: (502) 896-6688   •   www.VistaKy.com   •   E-mail: WeRentHomes@aol.com

Move Out Fees

AIR FILTER dirty or missing air filter	$10.00 each
ANTENNAE – roof antennae unauthorized, removal and sealing roof	$75.00 each
AUTOmobile, vehicle, trailer left on premises – removal charge	$200.00 each
CARPET – Replacement	$20.00 yd. (9 sq ft)
CARPET Cleaning	$25.00 per room
CEILING FAN – replacement	$110.00
CLEANING – if needed before ready to rent to new Tenant.	$24.00 man hour
COVER PLATES - electric switch and receptacle cover plates	$2.00 each
DOOR – Exterior	$150.00 & up
DOOR – Interior	$95.00 & up
DOOR knobs – interior	$15.00 each
ELECTRIC Outlets – replacement	$20.00 each
FLOOR TILE – vinyl 12" x 12"	$2.00 each tile
KEYS – not turned in	$10.00 each
LAWN SERVICE -- Lawn needs cut and trimmed	$50 & up
LG&E - (gas and electric service disconnected)	$75.00
LIGHT BULBS -- Burned out, missing.	$6.00 each bulb
LIGHT Fixtures	$25.00 & up
LOCK - deadbolt lockset	$30.00 each
LOCK - knob locksets	$30.00 each
MINI Blinds -- damaged or missing	$25.00 each
NAIL HOLES larger than 1/8"	$5.00 each
NAIL HOLES larger than 1"	$20.00 each
PAINTING – interior	$150.00 average room
RANGE – replacement	$300.00 & up
REFRIGERATOR – replacement	$475.00 & up
REPAIRS by licensed trades, electrician, plumbers, roofers, etc	As charged to Landlord
REPAIRS by nonlicensed trades	$30.00 hr + material
SHOWER HEAD	$25.00
SHOWER ROD	$25.00
SMOKE ALARMS – 10yr non-removable batteries	$45.00 each
STORM DOOR – pneumatic closure	$20.00
STORM DOOR – replacement	$80.00 & up
STORM DOOR – stop chain	$10.00
THERMOSTAT – replacement	$50.00
TOWEL BARS	$15.00 each
TRASH -- Debris removal interior or exterior	$200 each load
WATER - utility water service disconnected	$75.00
WINDOW GLASS – Cracked or Broken Glass	$25.00 each
WINDOW replacement	$50.00 and up
WINDOW SCREENS	$25.00 each

DEDUCTIONS are made from the security deposits only for just causes. Such charges include, but are not limited to, any replacement of damaged or missing fixtures, appliance parts or other items furnished to Tenants. Labor charges include installation, cleaning, patching, sanding, etc., including the cost of cleansers. If you do not clean or repair the damaged or soiled items prior to moving out, charges will be deducted from your security deposit based on the above schedule. Items not on the list will be charged on a "cost plus labor " basis.

We only expect you to return your home in the same condition as when you moved in.

If you have any questions, please call.   GOOD LUCK with your move!   Thank You,

Shirley

 **We Rent Homes • Apartments • Rent with Option to Buy • EZ Credit
Owner Finance • Property Management • We Buy Loans • Mortgages**

**DOWNLOADABLE FORM A.29   Move Out: Survey for Tenant
to Grade Landlord and Your Property***

 VISTA PROPERTIES, INC

We Buy Houses!   We Rent Homes! REALTOR

4012 Dupont Circle, Suite 203, Louisville, Ky. 40207-4810 • PO Box 24181, Louisville, KY 40224-0181
Office: (502)896-2595 • Fax: (502) 896-6688 • www.VistaKy.com • E-mail: WeRentHomes@aol.com

Your Address: _____   Today's Date: _____

Your Rating of VISTA

Poor	Below Average	Average	Above Average	Excellent

Survey

What do you like *most* about your home?	
What do you like *least* about your home?	
What do you like *most* about Vista?	
What do you like *least* about VISTA?	
Would you refer a good person like yourself to VISTA?	
Would you consider rent increases for improvements to your home?	
What improvement would you like *most* for your home?	
What improvement do you feel is needed most on your home?	

Please list YOUR comments and suggestions about VISTA:

_____

_____

_____

_____

_____

Please return in the enclosed envelope.....Thank you

 NARPM   **We Rent Homes • Apartments • Rent with Option to Buy • EZ Credit
Owner Finance • Property Management • We Buy Loans • Mortgages**

DOWNLOADABLE FORM A.30   Move Out: Summary*

Move Out Summary Address: _____

Qty	Item Description	Remarks
Ea	AIR Filter, dirty or missing	
Ea	ANTENNAE – roof antennae unauthorized, removal, sealing roof	
Ea	AUTOmobile(s), Trailer(s), Vehicles left on property	
Yd	CARPET – Replacement	
Room	CARPET Cleaning	
Ea	CEILING FAN – replacement	
Hr	CLEANING – if needed before ready to rent to new Tenant.	
Ea	COVER PLATES - electric switch and receptacle cover plates	
Ea	DOOR – Exterior	
Ea	DOOR – Interior	
Ea	DOOR knobs – interior	
Ea	ELECTRIC Outlets – replacement	
Ea	FLOOR TILE – vinyl 12" x 12"	
Ea	KEYS – not turned in	
Ea	LAWN SERVICE -- Lawn needs cut and trimmed	
Ea	LG&E - (gas and electric service disconnected)	
Ea	LIGHT BULBS -- Burned out, missing.	
Ea	LIGHT Fixtures	
Ea	LOCK - deadbolt lockset	
Ea	LOCK - knob locksets	
Ea	MINI BLINDS, damaged, missing, needing replacement	
Ea	NAIL HOLES larger than 1/8"	
Ea	NAIL HOLES larger than 1"	
Rm	PAINTING – interior	
Ea	RANGE – replacement	
Ea	REFRIGERATOR – replacement	
Hr	REPAIRS by licensed trades, electrician, plumbers, roofers, etc	
Hr	REPAIRS by nonlicensed trades	
Ea	SHOWER HEAD	
Ea	SHOWER ROD	
Ea	SMOKE ALARMS 10yr non removable batteries	
Ea	STORM DOOR – pnuematic closure	
Ea	STORM DOOR – replacement	
Ea	STORM DOOR – stop chain	
Ea	THERMOSTAT – replacement	
Ea	TOWEL BARS	
Load	TRASH -- Debris removal interior or exterior	
Ea	WATER - utility water service disconnected	
Ea	WINDOW GLASS – Cracked or Broken Glass	
Ea	WINDOW replacement	
Ea	WINDOW SCREENS	
	OTHER	

BY: _____   Date: _____

Lock Cylinder Changed from _____ to _____   Phoned to Office time: _____

*We Rent Homes • Apartments • Rent with Option to Buy • EZ Credit
Owner Finance • Property Management • We Buy Loans • Mortgages*

MOVE OUT INSPECTION

Address: _____   Date: _____

ITEMS	NEW	GOOD	OTHER

Living Room
- Walls
- Ceiling
- Floor

Dining Room
- Walls
- Ceiling
- Floor

Kitchen
- Walls
- Ceiling
- Floor
- Cabinets
- Range
- Refrigerator
- Vent Hood
- Dishwasher
- Disposal
- Countertop

Hall
- Walls
- Ceiling
- Floor

Bedroom #1
- Walls
- Ceiling
- Floor

Bedroom #2
- Walls
- Ceiling
- Floor

Bedroom #3
- Walls
- Ceiling
- Floor

Bathroom
- Walls
- Ceiling
- Floor
- Fixtures

Other_____
- Walls
- Ceiling
- Floor

General KEYS Number Received: ___ KEYCODE #: _____
- Floors
- Windows
- Doors
- Light Fixtures
- Yard
- Basement
- Garage

	Good Clean	Other	Notes
Exterior			
Crawl			
Basement			
Garage			
Attic			
Lawn			
Shed			
Kitchen Cabinets			
Closets			
Vanity			
Medicine Cabinet			
Doors			
Drawers			
Porches			

Utilities:
Water: On:___ Off:___
Electric: On:___ Off:___
Gas: On:___ Off:___

Smoke Alarm

Tenant Comments:

I and/or we accept the aforementioned "Inspection" as a part of the rental agreement with Vista Properties, Inc. including my/our comments noted under "Tenant Comments" and agree that this is an accurate account of the condition of this property and understand that the balance of our security deposit will be forwarded via U.S. Mail within 30 days to the address listed below.

NEW ADDRESS: _____ CITY: ____ ST: ____ ZIP: _____

Landlord: _____ Date: _____   Tenant:_____ Date:_____
Vista Properties, Inc. by:
TIME :_____   Tenant:_____ Date:_____

Office Only – Cylinder Changed ____ Phoned: _____ Summary: _____

Copyright © 2006 by WealthBuilding 24-7 LLC. *To customize this document, download the One-Page Move Out Inspection form to your hard drive from http://www.mikebutler.com/landlordingonautopilotforms.htm.* The document can then be opened, edited, and printed using Microsoft Word or another popular word processing application.

DOWNLOADABLE FORM A.32   Move Out: Office Move-Out Checklist*

OFFICE: Move Out Checklist

*Tenant:*_____ *Date:*_____

*Address:*_____

1.) _____ Move Out Inspection

2.) _____ Move Out Report

3.) _____ Security Deposit Report

4.) _____ Trans Union Form

5.) _____ QUICKBOOKS STUFF

_____ New Address
_____ New Phone
_____ Delete Memorized Stmt Chrgs
_____ Change Customer Type

6.) _____ Keys _____ # of Keys (**VP-00**____)

7.) _____ 7 cylinder on front door

8.) _____ Yard Sign   by:_____

9.) _____ Utilities, if empty

10.) _____ Lawn Service if empty

11.) _____ Pull file to Previous Tenant by Name

Place in bucket to be reviewed:

NOTES:

*REVIEWED BY:*_____ *Date;*_____

DOWNLOADABLE FORM A.33   Move Out: Return Possession Notice*

We Buy Houses!   *We Rent Homes!*

4012 Dupont Circle, Suite 203, Louisville, Ky. 40207-4810 • PO Box 24181, Louisville, KY 40224-0181
Office: (502) 896-2595 • Fax: (502) 896-6688 • www.VistaKy.com • E-mail: WeRentHomes@aol.com

Date: _____

Name: _____

Address of Property: _____

City, St., Zip: _____

Re: Possession of Property listed above

The undersigned has vacated the above listed property as an occupant and has

returned possession and keys to the Owner / Agent / Landlord as of the date and time

listed below with my signature.

Occupant: _____   Date: _____
              (Signature)

Location of this Transaction: _____

Time: _____   By: _____

We Rent Homes • Apartments • Rent with Option to Buy • EZ Credit
Owner Finance • Property Management • We Buy Loans • Mortgages